T0332129

Save Yourself If You Can

THE GERMAN LIST

THOMAS BERNHARD

Save Yourself If You Can

Six Plays

TRANSLATED BY
DOUGLAS ROBERTSON

Seagull
BOOKS

LONDON NEW YORK CALCUTTA

GOETHE INSTITUT

This publication has been supported by
a grant from the Goethe-Institut India.

Seagull Books, 2023

Originally published in German as:

Der Ignorant und der Wahnsinnige
© Suhrkamp Verlag Frankfurt am Main 1972

Die Berühmten
© Suhrkamp Verlag Frankfurt am Main 1976

Immanuel Kant
© Suhrkamp Verlag Frankfurt am Main 1978

Am Ziel
© Suhrkamp Verlag Frankfurt am Main 1981

Einfach kompliziert
© Suhrkamp Verlag Frankfurt am Main 1986

Elisabeth II
© Suhrkamp Verlag Frankfurt am Main 1987

All rights reserved by and controlled through Suhrkamp Verlag Berlin

First published in English translation by Seagull Books, 2023
English translation © Douglas Robertson, 2023

ISBN   978 1 80309 258 4

British Library Cataloguing-in-Publication Data
A catalogue record for this book is available from the British Library

Typeset by Seagull Books, Calcutta, India
Printed and bound by Hyam Enterprises, Calcutta, India

CONTENTS

THE IGNORAMUS
AND THE MADMAN

The fairy tale is a thoroughly musical genre.
—Novalis

Dramatis Personae

The QUEEN OF THE NIGHT

The Queen of the Night's FATHER

The DOCTOR

MRS VARGO

WINTER, the waiter

AT THE OPERA HOUSE

The QUEEN OF THE NIGHT'*s dressing room*
A dressing table
Two unupholstered chairs, one on each side of the table
The FATHER *is sitting in the right chair, the* DOCTOR *in the left one*
A clothes rack

DOCTOR (*holding several newspapers*). Listen
  to what's been written about the premiere
  we're dealing with
  an immortal work
  a genius et cetera

  (FATHER, *who is almost blind, wearing blindness armbands and holding*
  a white cane, takes a sip from a bottle of spirits)

Your daughter's voice
supremely perfect on the one hand
immaculate on the other
and her technique
every other word is the word authentic
every third word the word celebrated
Here
the word coloratura-machine

  (*Tosses a newspaper onto the dressing table*)

There
the word phenomenal
the phrase first-class intonation

  (*Tosses a newspaper onto the dressing table*)

the phrase vocal substance occurs twelve times
the word stupendous nineteen times
an excellent role
What we hear
do you hear me
is nothing but artsy twittering
what we see
a puppet show

(FATHER *takes a sip from his bottle*)

May I draw your attention to the fact
that you have been drinking nonstop
since eleven o'clock this morning
Naturally you have reasons for doing so
naturally
on the one hand listen to this
symptoms of fatigue in the Revenge Aria
not a single symptom of fatigue in the Revenge Aria
on the other hand
one must first of all
consult the bloodwork
but until
I have the results of all the tests my dear sir
the applause
is said to be like a hurricane
on the one hand
and appreciative on the other
overwhelming listen to this
they write of compelling
or
of stimulating penetration in the Revenge Aria
if as I said
the red corpuscles are diminishing at a most terrifying rate
while on the other hand the white ones are
increasing at a most terrifying rate
on the one hand the science of medicine has made
enormous strides

on the other hand for the past five hundred years it has been
standing still
we aren't talking about a science
when we talk about medicine my dear sir
listen to this
what a staccato

FATHER. What a staccato

DOCTOR (*discards the newspapers*). Always the same rubbish
a man like me is invariably disgusted by
the cornucopia of sentiment offered up daily by the arts columnists

(*Rises and paces up and down*)

Listen up my dear sir
one cautiously pushes the hemispheres
apart
back
do you understand
so that the so-called girder the corpus callosum
is exposed to view
next one pulls with one's left hand mark my words
at the upper
exterior of the left hemisphere
and cuts
with the point of the cerebral scalpel

FATHER. With the point of the cerebral scalpel

DOCTOR. into
the upper part of the corpus callosum
the word precision isn't just a word
my dear sir
and thereby discloses
with the greatest expediency
the lateral ventricle's cella media
of which I have already spoken
one takes note of the contents
normally cerebrospinal fluid

occasionally also my dear sir
blood
owing to the hemorrhaging of the ventricle

FATHER. Owing to the hemorrhaging of the ventricle

DOCTOR. The hemisphere is raised
and reveals the posterior and anterior horns
the same as on the other side
look here
then with the thumb and index finger of the left hand
one uses the cerebral scalpel to cut downward
carefully
very carefully my dear sir
all the way to the so-called foramina of Monro
slices through the corpus callosum and the fornix
and peels them back

(FATHER *puts both hands on his knees, bringing his armbands into the foreground*)

Next one dips the scalpel
in water
because a dry scalpel
has the unfortunate tendency
to result in a poor view
of the areas that have been cut
this must be done as often as possible
during the dissection of the brain
next one cuts at a forty-five-degree angle
through the basal ganglia
taking care all the while
to avoid damaging the so-called cerebellar
hemisphere

(FATHER *takes a sip from his bottle*)

The difficult question to be answered
is whether to recommend an institution
or not
on the one hand in institutions there have been

extraordinary successes to be sure
but also a complete lack of success
on the other
Listen up
vis-à-vis cases of edema of marbleizing
of the basal ganglia
my dear sir
one's attentiveness is naturally always highly acute
one's attentiveness
as well as one's resoluteness
as well as one's inconsiderateness
all three of these are incessantly indispensable
so as I said
one sees sections of bright tissue bordered with faded tissue
alternating with reddish sections
regarding bleeding points the latter
may be occasioned by the scission of the vessels
but the blood can easily be wiped away with the scalpel
in cases of congestion
one sees a reddish-gray cortex
and numerous bleeding points in the white matter
in cases of edema
the bleeding points naturally
deliquesce
or disappear

FATHER. The bleeding points disappear

DOCTOR. But in cases of encephalitis the blood is
postmortem
utterly postmortem
it has escaped from the vessels
and cannot be wiped away

(FATHER *takes a sip from his bottle*)

the realization my dear sir
that your daughter's influence on you
is effectively null

on the other hand you haven't the slightest influence
on your daughter
everything develops in this fashion
as we see
I find spirits repulsive
my dear sir
but I have never seen you without a bottle
not once in the entire three years
in which I have known you
this much I know
you have been drinking for a full decade straight
and indeed from the moment your daughter
made her first public appearance
You must admit
it's a colossal development
an utterly astonishing development
when one reflects that your daughter's voice originally
did not justify the faintest trace of hope
without a doubt your daughter's voice
is the work of the extraordinary Mr Keldorfer
of course it's all a matter of
the raw material falling
into the right hands at the right time
of its submitting to the right method
at the right moment
not everybody has such improbable good fortune
all those splendid voices
my dear sir
that have fallen into the wrong hands
it's insane
how hundreds of sophisticated singing teachers
especially in our academies my dear sir
ruin thousands of lovely voices
these people unscrupulously exploit voices
quite shamelessly squeeze out
the livelihoods of thousands of talents down to the last penny

the academies are inhabited by academic exploiters
for the most part they are riddled with charlatanry
one singing teacher in two is a charlatan
my dear sir
or let us say that on the whole singing teachers
or vocal pedagogues as they call themselves
are charlatans

(*Sits down*)

now one cuts through the corpus callosum
and peels it to the left side mark my words
so that the glandula pinealis
behind the commissura habenularum
is exposed to view

(FATHER *slips the armbands off his arms and sticks them in his pocket*)

When we are performing a dissection of the cerebellum
one lifts the cerebellum
cautiously
thrusts one's left hand mark my words
under the cerebellar hemisphere
and tips it slightly

(*Rises and paces up and down*)

so as not to damage either the so-called rhomboid fossa
or the lamina quadrigemina
during the subsequent scission of the vermis
one holds the scalpel
as if it were a fiddle bow

(*Mimes the grip*)

FATHER. As if it were a fiddle bow

DOCTOR. Moistens it
and proceeds along the median sagittal plane
until one is gazing into the fastigium
as if into a gaping hole

FATHER. As if into a gaping hole

DOCTOR. Next one rotates the scalpel
 and elongates the incision
 both in front
 and behind
 next one meticulously inspects
 the rhomboid fossa
 My dear sir
 at this moment one must above all else
 be attentive to changes in the so-called ependyma

(*Sits down*)

 one may already have noticed these in the lateral ventricle
 but empirically speaking changes in the ependyma are
 more pronounced
 here
 in the rhomboid fossa

(FATHER *takes a sip from his bottle*)

 And hence easier to diagnose
 your mode of living my dear sir
 is infectious
 two hours of sleep the night before
 and inordinately busy
 throughout the day
 when one is laboring on a so-called scientific work as I am
 one cannot allow oneself to indulge in such excesses
 on the other hand the idea of letting oneself go exerts
 an incredible fascination
 naturally your insomnia is bound up with
 your mental condition
 and your mental condition
 is the consequence of this decades-old unnatural relationship
 between you and your daughter
 when two completely different characters
 who also happen to be father and daughter
 are together uninterruptedly
 whereas each of the two ought to exist entirely

on their own
when I think that while your daughter is sleeping my dear sir
but of course I am actually only thinking
while your daughter's voice is sleeping
her voice
incessantly my dear sir only her voice
while your daughter's voice is sleeping
you are sitting around in taverns
on the other hand you have such an excellent constitution
the very sort of constitution I lack

FATHER. You lack it

DOCTOR. In the ependyma at the opening of the ventricle
regarding ependymitis granularis
the fine granulation of the ependyma
small button-shaped
semolina-like lumps

FATHER. Fine semolina-like lumps

DOCTOR (*as he rises from his chair*). One makes a cut of the largest
circumference
into and along the edge of the cerebellar hemisphere
where a white medullary ray extends extremely far
all the way to the
surface
and inspects the cerebellar matter
above all my dear sir
the nucleus dentatus cerebelli
one makes the same cut on the other side
Next one folds up the brain
and rotates it
so that its base and the medulla oblongata
are turned towards the dissector
next one goes below the cerebellum
which one props
up
and slices through the peduncle of the brain

(*Sits down and looks at his watch*)

it is striking
that your daughter arrives at an ever-later time
with every performance
but the utmost concentration inheres
in celerity
and consequently in spontaneity
this is not the first time
listen the orchestra is already in the pit
and there's no sign of your daughter
no sign of
Mrs Vargo
The whole time I listen out
but I hear no footsteps
then
suddenly
I hear the footsteps
and then everything happens with uncanny rapidity
taking a walk before the performance
a walk into the park
a furiously fast walk
along its flower-bordered paths my dear sir
which has become a ritual for her of late

(FATHER *takes a sip from his bottle*)

The dissector always moves along the right side of the corpse
the head of the corpse must be supported by a wooden block
so that the skin of the throat is stretched taut
the skin of the upper throat area
my dear sir
must not be damaged
because the corpse must be kept presentable
for lying in state

FATHER. An inconsiderate child
an inconsiderate child
Haven't you got at least a tiny bit of influence

on my daughter
can't you influence her
in such a way that

DOCTOR. One must come to terms with the fact
that an artistic creature
renders itself completely self-sufficient
it is generally no longer capable of coexisting
with others
with members of its own family especially
but with everybody else as well
at a certain point in time
my dear sir
such a completely artistic creature
a human being that has been transformed into a completely artistic
    creature
which in fact is no longer a human being at all
generally stops being able
to see
anything outside itself
there is no longer anything
but me
such a creature says to itself
then
when it completely isolates itself
and has isolated itself
cut itself off
when it exists permanently for its own sake
one need no longer be afraid
my dear sir
one's fear is completely superfluous
You'll see she will walk in here at just
the right moment
and she will make her entrance at just the right moment
just
when you can no longer put up with it
and have racked your brains to pieces

so-called ordinary human beings
are always afraid of creatures
my dear sir
and human beings and creatures are two distinct types of entity
and with regard to an artistic creature in particular

FATHER. It serves her father right
her father who never sets
eyes
on what he's earned

DOCTOR. The possession of such a creature
is a moot point
but the naivety of the crowd
is appalling
the crowd that disowns
the most artificial of all mechanisms

(FATHER *takes a sip from his bottle*)

Life or existence
these are by no means existential questions
my dear sir
but wielding nothing but a good attitude
is also ineffectual
life is a torture session
anyone who does not comprehend this
and platitudes
make nothing better
and especially not the cause of the pain
has comprehended nothing
on the other hand it is precisely in frightening situations
that we come to our senses

(*Rises*)

the cartilage scalpel is held in one's fist
one takes the cartilage scalpel
into one's fist
and now executes the principal incision
from the prominentia laryngea

to the symphysis
look here
as the incision passes through the omphalic area mark my words
one veers slightly to the left
my dear sir

(FATHER *turns on the loudspeaker. The din from the orchestra pit and the audience grows steadily louder from this point on*)

In the region of the sternum one presses forward with the incision
all the way to the periosteum
then one makes the cross section
and cuts through skin
subcutaneous cellular tissue et cetera
the anterior abdominal muscles along with the fascia
and presses forward cautiously to the peritoneum parietale
so as not to damage the latter and the intestines beneath it
normally
one sees clear serous fluid my dear sir
in pathological conditions my dear sir
the bulk of the fluid can infiltrate
the abdominal cavity
Ascites

FATHER. Ascites

DOCTOR. Which allows one to infer cirrhosis of the liver
cardiac congestion et cetera
or thrombosis of the portal vein
in the various forms of peritonitis
a purulent
fibrous exudate may be present
Hemoperitoneum
Choloperitoneum et cetera

FATHER. Hemoperitoneum
Choloperitoneum

DOCTOR. One inspects the omentum majus
draws the latter away from the taenia omentalis

of the colon traversum
which is shaped like an apron mark my words
down into the lesser pelvis
in inflammatory processes
in the abdominal cavity my dear sir
there may even be adhesions of the omentum
the omentum is warped in this direction
a completely warped omentum
from which one may deduce the process of the outcome
one simply peels the omentum upwards
and contemplates the situs of the abdominal organs
observes whether the lower liver extends far down

(*To* FATHER *while palpating his abdomen*)

you see
down to here
to this spot
whether the intestinal loops are swollen to the bursting point
the lower stomach extends far down

(*Poking at his stomach*)

Gastroptosis naturally
and whether the spleen is enlarged

(*Looks at his watch*)

Lately she has been walking with gusto in the park
on the spur of the moment in the park
amid the twittering of the birds
do you understand

FATHER. Or she locks herself in her room

DOCTOR. You yourself say
   this is a most peculiar ritual

FATHER. In which she never used to lock herself

DOCTOR. In her room

FATHER. To the best of my knowledge

DOCTOR. With the curtains drawn
But not as she herself admits
in order to study her part
quite to the contrary by means of
the most varied self-devised stratagems
she distracts herself from her vocal part
pacing up and down
dictating into a tape recorder
she attends
to her correspondence
or she memorizes a passage from a play
she recites entire speeches from *Lear*
or more recently as I know for a fact
from Tasso
or she sits at the window and rests the palms of her hands
on the windowsill
with her eyes closed
my observations
my dear sir
naturally lead to apprehensions

FATHER. To apprehensions
to apprehensions

DOCTOR. Indeed to apprehensions
The fact is that your daughter has lately
undergone a most alarming change
she is no longer the same
what we now behold
is something entirely different
it is the antithesis of what
we beheld a year ago
but because we are dealing with an artistic creature
it is also the same
do you understand
on the one hand she is the same
on the other hand she isn't
this is the greatest difficulty confronted

by the people around her
the fact that they are dealing first and foremost with a voice
and indeed a quite specific voice
that is one of the most celebrated
and in fact mark my words one of the most beautiful voices in existence
but that they are not dealing with a human being
this is naturally impossible for a father to comprehend

(FATHER *takes a sip from his bottle.* DOCTOR *sits down*)

An even greater
an even much greater degree of watchfulness my dear sir
and wariness too
is now advisable
because we are dealing with a perfect creature
housed in an undoubtedly headless subjectivity

(FATHER *slips his armbands back on with lightning speed. Enter* MRS
VARGO *with the crown. She hangs it on the clothes rack, briefly lingers,
looks at* FATHER *and then at* DOCTOR *with a reproachful, scrutinizing
eye, and then exits*)

Naturally I ask myself
what kind of individual am I faced with
when I see this person
an excellent person undoubtedly
undoubtedly excellent
Mrs Vargo is undoubtedly a thoroughly excellent person
Look here my dear sir
you can set your mind at rest
Mrs Vargo has made her entrance
and it will not be long before your daughter arrives
this means that your daughter is already in the house
I realize that you regard the fact
that the crown is now hanging on the clothes rack
as a favorable omen
if we lacked the capacity to distract ourselves
my dear sir
we would have to admit

that we pretty much no longer existed
existence mark my words is invariably
distraction from existence
we exist because
we distract ourselves from our existence
at first you kept your bottle hidden
then you tried to keep
your bottle hidden
then years ago you stopped making the attempt
you drink quite brazenly
and without the slightest scruples my dear sir
and what's more in your daughter's dressing room
you drink straight from the bottle
and you are perfectly aware
that you are perpetually intoxicated
but this fact fully redounds to the benefit
of this conversational mechanism
one can unhesitatingly
subordinate a person like you to a science
granted
you have all the merits of an object that is uncommonly useful
to someone in my position
which is in point of fact an excellent thing
if you loathe a person
like Mrs Vargo
you gain nothing by it
these people are constantly observing
and they make their observation into a pathological condition
from which they can no longer divorce themselves
because they are not masters of their own heads
here results can only be achieved
through surprise effects
by which however I do not mean an external surprise
I am once again thinking about the head
but all these people take such great pains on its behalf
and how emphatically they also always demonstrate that
they aren't even wearing a head

hence naturally and in general they
lack all power of judgment
You are walking
sometimes logically sometimes not
as long as you are walking
through a completely headless society
and carrying history in its entirety on your back
for your entire life you have been literally
dragging history behind you
and seeing not a single head owing to the sheer abundance of heads
and therefore incessantly worrying about being
suddenly stricken by a blood clot
if my dear sir you picture to yourself all the other heads
as a viscous stinking
or completely odorless mass
as a hydrocephalic mirror
so to speak
out of which your own head protrudes
and all the while this head is on the verge of vomiting
hence it can only ever invoke lunacy
and never prosperity
my dear sir
Is such a head amid an abundance of heads
not a pitiable state of affairs
each and every day the question is
by means of what trick
what new trick each and every day
am I to make it through the day
this is disgraceful and undoubtedly sickening

(*Rises and paces up and down*)

Your daughter is extremely unstable
undoubtedly also extremely subtle
in her development
terrifyingly so for the people around her
everything about her is different now
If only it were so simple

as recommending an institution
but there is no institution
that is recommendable
people are stuck into a course of treatment
for the purpose of withdrawing them from a feeling of nausea
they submit to a course of so-called withdrawal treatment
but nothing can be withdrawn
from a human being
and certainly not a fatal natural talent
If a person drinks
one must let him drink
watch how he drinks
and where his drinking takes him
if he goes mad
there is nothing we can do about it
if only it were so simple
if we stick a drinker
a madman
a lunatic
my dear sir
into an institution
that is a felony
we are actually ashamed
before the bench of the supreme court of nature
which shows itself to us at the apex of despair
believe me
your daughter means well
when she says
check back into an institution
submit to a course of withdrawal treatment
but she is hardly competent

(FATHER *turns on the loudspeaker*)

The musicians
I can clearly hear them
they're already in the pit

FATHER. One's own child
    is always the most inconsiderate child of all

DOCTOR. One's entire life
    is the most inconsiderate thing of all
    my dear sir
    and a unique instance of humiliation

    (FATHER *turns the loudspeaker on again*)

    But you will see
    when the Three Ladies enter
    and the serpent is slain
    your daughter
    already dressed
    for her entrance
    the most reliable things in this house
    are undoubtedly the stage managers
    I have always been in the habit of saying
    here though chaos may defy
    on the stage managers you may rely
    set your mind at rest
    remember the cool-headedness
    and the sagaciousness of a person
    like Mrs Vargo
    and keep in mind
    your daughter's zealous professionalism
    she would never allow herself
    to arrive too late
    later and later to be sure
    but never too late
    walking through the door at the last minute
    gives one an enormous advantage
    no matter what the situation is
    a common tactic at conferences
    the best tactic
    a couple of coloraturas in the stairwell
    a couple of footsteps

and your daughter will be here
and you will no longer need to be in the anxious state
in which you always find yourself at moments like these
it is always the same
Mrs Vargo hangs the crown on the clothes rack
and your nerves my dear sir
are stretched to the breaking point
taken as a whole
art and everything having to do with it
is a colossal nervous tension

(FATHER *turns the loudspeaker on again*)

When she loathes the conductor
as she does this one
her singing is at its most reliable
and its best
and she loathes nobody with more loathing
than the man
who will be conducting today's performance
this man should have become a butcher
not a conductor
my dear sir
when you hear him you're always hearing
a butcher
your daughter is probably
downstairs at the canteen
and drinking a cup of hot tea
but I'm sure she's already in the house
that trip last year
to the Teatro Fenice
during that performance of Falstaff my dear sir
it happened then
her transformation dates from that point
because she happened to want to see
the most beautiful theater in the world
and also to hear a certain to my mind quite mediocre colleague sing
one must simply

take everything into account as a possible cause
anything can be a cause
quite possibly it was a terminal illness
my dear sir
that she caught at the Teatro Fenice
but I am convinced
that this illness
will not
or at least not in the next five or even ten years
have any effect on her voice
this most beautiful of all talents my dear sir
will continue to develop for another five or even ten years
if it suddenly breaks down afterwards
that won't make a bit of difference my dear sir
undoubtedly it is
like when a machine is thrown out of gear

(*Sits down*)

the day before yesterday she had an argument
with her coach
these arguments are injuring
her voice

(FATHER *takes a sip from his bottle*)

We have
and this is horrifying my dear sir
invariably only effects before us
the causes we do not see
owing to the sheer abundance of effects
we fail to see any causes
Moreover the essence of Rokitansky's method
is the preservation to the utmost extent possible of the normal
    physiological integrity
of the individual organs
because thanks to crude scissions
interconnections that are normally present
and often important anatomical discoveries

vanish
on the other hand
either we eviscerate all the internal organs
and perform our dissections on a table

(*Rises*)

or we opt for Virchow's
renunciation of organic integrity
amputate
eliminate et cetera
my dear sir
for the prevention of infection
the wearing of rubber gloves
is useful
but on account of the impairment of the sense of touch
one refrains from this practice
we distinguish between
general
and detailed description
the proliferation of external changes
for example
is recorded with great exactitude
during forensic postmortem or in the case of an unidentified person
who has been found dead
for instance
an exact description of tattoos of scars
of the teeth
including all their fillings
may be required
we then distinguish
first and foremost
between male and female corpses
something of great importance
is the ascertainment of the corpse's weight
this can under normal circumstances
play an important role
for example an unusually thin corpse

a sure sign
of an illness caused by a poorly ingested diet
owing for example to the constriction of the esophagus by
a malignant tumor
my dear sir
and the consequent impedance of swallowing
the simplest method
is to weigh the corpse

FATHER. To weigh the corpse

DOCTOR. Otherwise the weight is estimated
and one states
whether the corpse is cachexic
or corpulent
a Falstaff type
a jodhpurs type et cetera
the ascertainment of the length of the body is important
because it allows one to infer abnormalities in the condition
of the body
the length of the body is quite basically measured
relative to the median bodily length of the population
in our part of the world one meter sixty-five centimeters
is the median bodily length
originating from this median are certain extremes
if an individual is longer than one meter and eighty centimeters my
        dear sir
this is termed macrosomia
whereas a bodily length in excess of two meters
is termed gigantism

(*Paces up and down*)

regarding an individual under one meter twenty centimeters
one speaks of dwarfism
but along with the length of the body
its proportions must also be considered
especially the proportions of the skeletal frame
which is the principal determinant of the length of the body

in many very tall individuals the body length is not evenly distributed
for example very long legs
Lower-body length
my dear sir
is the distance from the symphysis to the planta pedis
upper-body length
the distance from the vertex
to the upper edge of the symphysis
this alone is often the actual cause
of the so-called underlying disease
my dear sir
without a doubt what was once your daughter's greatest source of
    delight
has now become a habit for her
namely the fact that for years
she has been coming and going to and from opera houses
and singing her celebrated coloraturas
by the way
and perhaps you don't know this
some twenty years ago my dear sir
I myself used to dabble at singing in a not-unpleasant bass voice
and at private performances
notably at the house of a very distinguished head of a shipping
    company here in this town
alongside simple loveable people
who took all that stuff very seriously
I have sung as the Speaker and Sarastro
and there is not a church in this town
in which I didn't let my bass be heard
at least every other Sunday
it is empirically certain that music
is an art for which physicians have a particular soft spot
and one out of every two doctors plays a violin or a piano
in the evenings
and if you take a look around the dwellings of doctors
you will discover whole galleries of piano arrangements

of every conceivable opera
and as you know the best musicians
hail from long-established medical families
whenever a virtuoso appears on the scene
you can safely say
he comes from a medical family
or that he is one of these butchers' children
who matriculate at our conservatories
or academies

(FATHER *turns on the loudspeaker, applause from the audience is followed by the beginning of the overture to the opera*)

The overture
I can clearly hear it
the overture

FATHER. The overture

MRS VARGO. The overture

FATHER. These never-ending
complications
involving my daughter

DOCTOR. Macrosomia in excess of the normal limits
is a feature of many disorders
of the genital glands
eunuchoid macrosomia
is characterized by an excessive lower-body length
many individuals when sitting
appear to be normal my dear sir
but when standing they are
too short
You yourself are a perfect example of this
You have excessively short extremities
but your torso is normal
This is a signal feature
of chondrodystrophic dwarfism

(*Footsteps*)

FATHER *methodically slips the armbands onto his arms*

Enter MRS VARGO *from stage right, followed by* QUEEN

DOCTOR, *having leapt to his feet, kisses* QUEEN's *hand while* FATHER *remains apathetically seated*

QUEEN *walks up to* FATHER *and kisses him on the forehead*

FATHER. Late my child
  late my child
  this is inconsiderate
  How patient I have been
  but this father has earned himself
  an inconsiderate daughter
  All the world marvels at you
  but I am ashamed of you
  I am mortified by my daughter's
  schizophrenia

DOCTOR (*to* QUEEN). Your father has been at the opera house for two
    hours already
  You are aware of his nervousness
  he is impossible to calm down
  so I have been telling him about my professional activities
  I marvel at your father's attentiveness

  (QUEEN *kisses her* FATHER *on the forehead once again, then exits stage
  right with* MRS VARGO)

  You see
  she's here
  and it's also the last minute

FATHER. Always at the last minute
  it's inconsiderate
  the overture

  (*Takes a sip from his bottle*)

  it's always the same

DOCTOR. You're not thinking carefully
  You always forget

Mrs Vargo's dexterity
it all gets done very quickly
a brief routine procedure involving the costumes

FATHER. It's inconsiderate
in the first place
to send one's daughter off to study
in extremely difficult circumstances
then to be a witness of her inconsiderateness
in extremely terrible circumstances

DOCTOR. You mustn't say that
my dear sir
Your daughter is extremely disciplined
If only you knew
what incredible sloppiness holds sway
in this house
and not only in this house
it's a wonder
that your daughter
can make it onstage at all
in these extremely terrible circumstances
in this madhouse
and that she has managed to forge ahead
to do so she has had to go abroad
now that she is famous
she can
hold her own
here
if she hadn't gone away
today she wouldn't be
what she is today
had she stayed here
her colleagues would have walked all over her
she would have become embroiled in intrigues
she would have given up a long time ago
at best she would be
nothing but an operetta

or she would have been degraded to the position of the general
     manager's mistress
by being more inconsiderate to herself than to anyone else
she has become the most famous of all female coloratura singers
who appears onstage today
just think of how much it has cost her
to overcome the unbelievable nervousness
that as recently as five or six years ago
still used to prevent her from practicing the artistry
she had long since attained by then
naturally the people in her orbit
suffer as a result of it
as a result of what
she is today
but you must admit my dear sir
that the people in her orbit
have made her what she is
the people in her orbit could not ask for anything more
You have a daughter
who sings the most celebrated coloraturas in the world
if this isn't enough for you
you have no choice but to give up all hope
logically speaking you have no choice but to kill yourself
What is happening
here in closest proximity
to your daughter
is undoubtedly
austere and artificial my dear sir
but the people in her orbit will undoubtedly have to put up with it
we are dealing here with an astonishing form
of theater
with a theatrical iciness my dear sir
not with some rudimentary entertainment spectacle
it is quite clear
that everyone in the orbit of such a phenomenon
especially when this phenomenon is a coloratura soprano

as celebrated as your daughter
is condemned
to motionlessness
and to meaninglessness
Naturally one cannot but recoil in terror
from its notionlessness
The fact of the matter is
that your daughter has changed
Her manner of speaking
is different
Her movements
are different
but this is of no concern
to medical science
just as everything human
is of no concern whatsoever to medical science
do you understand
it is a delusion to suppose otherwise my dear sir
because medical science is absolutely incapable of taking a concern in
    anything human
nobody comprehends this
and so medical science my dear sir naturally
meets with complete rejection
medical science takes pretty much no interest whatsoever in human-
    kind
it is a science
of the organs
not a science
of human beings
the interesting thing is their tissue my dear sir
not what lies beneath it
or behind it
or anywhere else
the tools of the medical trade are utterly unphilosophical tools
Admittedly your daughter's voice
has not changed

in any case the public hasn't taken notice
of such a change
the public
always thinks a certain point of time has just been reached
when it has long since passed
the public has absolutely no ear
for changes
but I am sure that you can see as well as I do
that nature has trapped your daughter in a process
that has changed her root and branch
root and branch
Your mistake is
to regard whatever you are thinking about
as always the same thing
that is without a doubt your most basic delusion

FATHER. When I tell her
that I have walked around
for three hours without armbands
she doesn't believe me

DOCTOR. Between you my dear sir
and your daughter
there is nothing but distrust
the cause of every conceivable illness
my dear sir

FATHER. That I have walked
without armbands
through all these streets
and past hundreds and thousands of people
admittedly I am well acquainted with these streets
as a child I walked along all these streets
although they are all completely different today

DOCTOR. The pattern of the streets is the same

FATHER. Yes
the pattern is the same

DOCTOR. Streets that one has walked along as a child
that one often walked along in childhood my dear sir
or really any streets
that one has walked along with any frequency
my dear sir
are streets that one can even walk blind
If you blindfold me
I can find my way from any part of town
to my paternal home my dear sir
that presents me with no difficulties whatsoever

FATHER. Naturally she doesn't believe
what I tell her
she has never yet believed me
Her mother and her
my daughter
my dear doctor
were never anything but a conspiracy against me
a victory over the two of them
was unthinkable
hence from the beginning
I was weakened
after the death of my wife
her mother
I thought there would be
an improvement of this situation
but this situation didn't improve
to the contrary
this situation only began to get worse
she thinks
if she kisses me on the forehead
she's doing enough
all her actions
are directed against me
her father is atoning
for the inanities
the inaccuracies

  the enormities
  of her mother

DOCTOR. A man who feels the passage of time
  as keenly as you do my dear sir
  and takes everything so seriously
  naturally suffers
  with every breath he takes
  this is a natural talent
  thanks to which your natural constitution
  is an unbearable one
  undoubtedly people like you
  should be pitied

FATHER. My reward
  is always
  contempt
  There is a reason
  that I drink
  all day
  and half the night
  as you know

DOCTOR. In the end one must
  surrender control
  everything that is in reality
  a tragedy
  is a comedy
  in the external world's eyes
  my dear sir

FATHER. Two bottles
  a day

DOCTOR. If you were deprived of
  your two bottles
  you would fall to pieces in a most pitiful fashion

FATHER. It has become habitual for me

DOCTOR. One flees
    into senseless activity
    whether
    one from a certain point onwards
    drinks ever-increasing amounts
    or paces to and fro
    or spends all one's time unfolding maps
    reading
    one's own palms
    my dear sir
    or writing letters
    or frantically perusing books
    or every time one wakes up
    one takes a pill
    in order to fall back asleep
    and one carries on like this for years
    for decades my dear sir
    for often enough
    a person's craziest conditions
    last
    an eternity
    one minute we believe
    in literature
    the next we believe
    in music
    the next we believe
    in human beings
    but there is no remedy

FATHER. Because that's meaningless
    for the longest time I have been drinking
    nothing but the cheapest spirits available
    I couldn't care less about
    what is in the bottles

DOCTOR. On the other hand alcoholism is
    an artistic medium

Enter QUEEN *with* MRS VARGO. QUEEN *is already in costume but not yet wearing any make-up or the crown, which* MRS VARGO *starts arranging on the clothes rack*

DOCTOR (*to* FATHER). Between two movements your daughter
    is forcing on herself
    a moment of reflection
    this is a highly remarkable novelty
    my dear sir
    that I for one find incredibly fascinating

QUEEN *seats herself at the dressing table.* MRS VARGO *hastily does* QUEEN'*s make-up*

QUEEN (*to* MRS VARGO). Make sure the crown
    doesn't wobble on my head
    The complaints
    you suffer from
    are nothing but figments of your imagination
    You are the healthiest person in the world
    to be sure

    (*Half-sings a coloratura*)

    to be sure you are ashamed
    of being healthy
    You see it as a disgrace

    (*Half-sings a coloratura*)

DOCTOR (*to* FATHER). Then
    when one spends longish intervals with her
    she is silent
    it is quite striking
    Her favorite word is the word air
    very often she uses the phrase change of scene
    also the word autocratic
    and the words situation and condition crop up at every turn
    in whatever she says
    moreover she seems to have stopped
    placing all her trust in the German language

she is constantly using numerous
English and French words
today she will sing the Queen of the Night
for the two hundred twenty-second time

QUEEN. I have reserved a table
at the Three Hussars

MRS VARGO. Your costume has been brushed
your crown has been polished
the assistant director apologizes
for his impertinent manner of speaking
I have canceled
the reception at the music lovers' club

QUEEN. Cancel
cancel
we must cancel everything
from now on cancel everything
do you understand
we will cancel everything from now on
won't we Doctor
henceforth we will cancel everything
we used to show up everywhere
now we will cancel everything
we won't go anywhere ever again
we have already seen everything
heard everything
everything in the world is
familiar ground to us
we are well acquainted with the world
we no longer need anything
anything
anything

(*Half-sings a coloratura*)

We have already heard everything
we have already seen everything

(*Half-sings a coloratura*)

(*To* FATHER) haven't we
we are well acquainted with everything
everything is well known to us
We are acquainted with every opera
every play
we have read everything
and we are well acquainted with the most beautiful places in the world
and secretly we loathe the public
don't we
our tormentors

(*Half-sings a coloratura*)

we make our entrances
and abhor
what we know well

DOCTOR. It's inherent in the nature of the thing

QUEEN. Right you are Doctor
it's always inherent
in the nature of the thing

(FATHER *takes a sip from his bottle*)

As long as I produce coloraturas
I make my entrances

(*Half-sings a coloratura*)

DOCTOR. Undoubtedly the most celebrated of all coloraturas

(QUEEN *half-sings a coloratura*)

Your father went
on a three-hour walk
through the town
and just imagine this
he wasn't wearing his armbands

(QUEEN *half-sings a coloratura*)

QUEEN. Don't believe a word of it
everything he says is a lie
a blind man

without armbands
can hardly get very far
people knock him down
they trample him

(*To* FATHER) Liar

(*Half-sings a coloratura*)

DOCTOR. Your father is absolutely credible

QUEEN. Credible

(*Half-sings a coloratura*)

credible
I'm well aware of that

DOCTOR. I hear
you won't be going
with me to Paris

QUEEN (*half-sings a coloratura*). I am exhausted
no really
I am exhausted
my father is an alcoholic
and I am exhausted

DOCTOR. A trip to Paris
with absolutely no strings attached
just imagine it
on such a trip
you will regenerate yourself completely

QUEEN (*glancing at* FATHER). What about him

DOCTOR. In my opinion

QUEEN. I can't possibly leave him by himself
You yourself can plainly see
that he can't be made
to listen to reason
he refuses to listen
to anything anyone
tells him

    now there are two bottles
    six months from now
    there will be three
    I don't need to take any trip
    Doctor
    quite the opposite Doctor

FATHER. One of these days I'll wait in vain

QUEEN. These constant asseverations
    are naturally
    getting old

    (*Half-sings a coloratura*)

    getting old
    nothing else

    (*To* MRS VARGO) more rouge on my cheeks more rouge
    on second thought
    no
    make my cheeks white
    all white
    make them white white

MRS VARGO. White always looks good

DOCTOR. Naturally

QUEEN. Naturally white
    white naturally
    the Queen of the Night
    looks good in white
    thick white
    (*To* MRS VARGO) you're right about that
    really thick white
    you're being awfully quiet Doctor

DOCTOR. I was doing a run-through of an autopsy

QUEEN. Do sit down

DOCTOR. I was on the point of presenting
    Sigaud's classifications you know

the typus respiratorius

(QUEEN *half-sings a coloratura*)

the typus digestorius
the typus muscularis
the typus cerebralis

FATHER. The typus cerebralis
the typus muscularis
the typus digesorius

DOCTOR. Digestorius
my dear sir
digestorius

FATHER. Digestorius

DOCTOR (*to* QUEEN). Your father
takes an interest in my work
he is the most attentive listener
imaginable

(FATHER *takes a sip from his bottle*)

This afternoon
during his walk
he peremptorily insisted
on having the dissection of the brain
explained to him
but I was pressed
for time
I had things to do at the Institute
but I promised
to give a lecture
here
in the dressing room
before the performance
and since we were kept
waiting so long
I had the opportunity
to propound

several details
that I had not
propounded before
In the canteen
where we bought his bottles
your father acknowledged
his deep affection
so as to avoid having to say the word love
for you
he is dependent
to the very core of his being
on his daughter

MRS VARGO. Shall I put the crown on you

QUEEN. Not now
   not yet

MRS VARGO. Or the belt

QUEEN. Yes get the belt

MRS VARGO *goes to the cabinet and produces from it a broad spangled belt with a doubly broad spangled sash and hangs it on the clothes rack*

DOCTOR. And so I said
   the word peritonitis
   to your father several times
   because on account of a sudden
   confused altercation
   outside the dressing room
   the quarrelers were probably musicians
   musicians in the orchestra
   he could not understand what I was saying
   in another system of classification
   I said
   we distinguish between
   the pyknic type
   the leptosome type
   the athletic type

in the pyknic type one sees
a highly developed abdomen
a compact thorax
adipose deposits et cetera

(*The* QUEEN *half-sings a coloratura*)

An extreme form of the leptosome type is

QUEEN (*in unison with him*). The typus asthenicus

QUEEN (*sola*). Also known as the habitus phthisicus

DOCTOR. Correct
the subcutaneous fat
next to the abdominal area
but also in the area of the extremities

(*The* QUEEN *half-sings a coloratura*)

must be inspected
when people have especially thick layers of subcutaneous fat
we conjecture

The QUEEN *half-sings a coloratura.*

DOCTOR *and* QUEEN. That they had a disorder of the endocrine glands

QUEEN (*sola*). Of the pituitary gland for example

DOCTOR. Dystrophia adiposogenitalis et cetera

QUEEN (*half-sings a coloratura. To* FATHER). This drinking
and this traveling around
this incessant
two-sided togetherness
has got to end sometime

(*Half-sings a coloratura*)

(*To* DOCTOR) My father
has gone completely to rack and ruin

(*Half-sings a coloratura*)

because I caved in

(*Half-sings a coloratura*)

because I went soft
and although I knew full well what it would lead to
I kept taking him along
on my trips
to America
and to Australia
my biggest mistake
was to take him with me to Scandinavia

(*Half-sings a coloratura*)

it was there that he picked up the habit
of drinking spirits
not a day has passed since
without this incessant drinking
straight from the bottle

(*Half-sings a coloratura*)

DOCTOR. Usually there's no
    point
    in taking an alcoholic's
    bottle away from him
    in depriving him of the possibility
    of drinking
    a drinker
    can't be helped

QUEEN (*half-sings a coloratura*, *To* MRS VARGO). If only you'd pin up
    my hair
    every time even under
    the crown I think
    that I'm losing my hair
    a horrible feeling
    a truly
    horrible feeling

    (*Half-sings a coloratura*)

DOCTOR. If for at least a few weeks
    your father

were to go to the mountains
where you have after all got
that lovely house that's totally isolated
and far off the beaten track
in the fine mountain air

(QUEEN *half-sings a coloratura*)

If your father were to pass his time there
doing simple work
ordinary chores for example
like chopping wood
or picking berries
nothing intellectual
in any case
if he were allowed to occupy himself
with books or even with philosophy
his condition would undoubtedly
deteriorate
walking about in fresh air
adhering punctiliously
to a regular meal schedule
and naturally in full consciousness of the fact
that you were constantly thinking about him
wherever you were
be it at the most distant of distances

QUEEN (*to* MRS VARGO). If any flowers come
send them immediately
to the old people's home
If anybody asks about me
give them no information

(*Half-sings a coloratura*)

If there are any invitations
decline them
if any letters are delivered
file them
but don't pester me with them
I won't be signing any more autographs

I find nothing more loathsome
Moreover

(*Half-sings a coloratura*)

moreover we are all out of tea
get hold of some tea
and sew the buttons
on my winter coat

(*To* FATHER) You keep exerting yourself
but nothing changes

(*Half-sings a coloratura*)

just as I keep exerting myself
but nothing changes

DOCTOR. If one can
afford
such a misfortune
a degeneration
from inside
outwards

QUEEN (*to* DOCTOR). You yourself have said
isn't it horrible
to sing the same part
over two hundred times
To be hounded
through all the world's opera houses
goaded
by *Magic Flute* coloraturas

DOCTOR. It is a pinnacle
an absolute pinnacle

(*To* FATHER) a pinnacle
my dear sir

FATHER. A pinnacle

DOCTOR. Genius
is a disease
a development like that

of a practicing artist
is a pathological process
that the public follows
with its undivided attention
the crowd observes
a voice
a coloratura voice
like your daughter's
my dear sir
is observed like a tightrope walker
by the crowd
which watches it in perpetual fear
that it will fall
it's as if we weren't even dealing
with a human being
it's all nothing but
a sensation

(*To the* FATHER) Such a voice
is a precious object
my dear sir
and hardly to be encountered every day
Thousands of them are trained
but in the end
we marvel at only a single one of them

FATHER. I myself had
a miserable childhood
whereas my daughter
was always spoiled rotten

DOCTOR. But only until the moment
when she began studying
at the academy

FATHER. She got
a free ride
a full scholarship
from her very first year

The president of the academy
knew that
he had a talent
to be reckoned with
in my daughter
(*Takes a sip from his bottle*)

DOCTOR. But it must be
enormously satisfying
your certainty
of possessing a mechanism
for a daughter
or a daughter for a mechanism
a famous
and incomparable mechanism
that bewitches
the theater-going world
my dear sir

FATHER. She is uncivil
and inconsiderate
and unteachable

DOCTOR. But just think of
your daughter's beauty
it's without parallel

MRS VARGO (*to* QUEEN). Your father shouldn't drink so much

QUEEN. Well the doctor has also
said his piece on that
namely that
you can't change nature

(*Half-sings a coloratura*)

everybody's always saying
the same thing
over and over again

DOCTOR. If only the two of you
could make up your minds

to go your separate ways
at least for a little while
if only your father
would separate from you
for his health's sake

(QUEEN *half-sings a coloratura*)

If only you could separate
from your father
for your art's sake
because constant nervous tension
when we cannot help terming it senseless
weakens the voice
then one day all of a sudden
you'll no longer be able to sing
coloraturas
with such astonishing facility

QUEEN (*to* MRS VARGO). Put on more white
lots of white
my face
must be a completely artificial face
my body
an artificial one
everything must be artificial

DOCTOR. As you know Mrs Vargo
this place
is a puppet theater
no people act here
only puppets
Here everything moves
unnaturally
which is the most natural
thing in the world

(QUEEN *half-sings a coloratura*)

The thickest possible layer of white
Mrs Vargo

don't be stingy
with the make-up
don't be stingy

(FATHER *takes a sip from his bottle*)

Thick white
really thick white

FATHER. Make the white thick

DOCTOR. It accentuates
her artificiality
it accentuates
her natural artificiality

QUEEN (*to* MRS VARGO). Are the seams sturdy
is it all sturdily stitched together
I am constantly worrying
that
when I raise my arm
the costume will tear
make sure that it can't tear at the seams anywhere
Mrs Vargo
it's appalling
suddenly
the costume tears under my arm
and the audience bursts into laughter
it tears
make sure that it can't tear at the seams anywhere
I suddenly make this movement

(*Very quickly raises her right arm, her costume noisily tears under that arm. Screams*)

Once again it has torn
once again it has torn
whenever I raise my arm
lift my arm

DOCTOR. Now Mrs Vargo

QUEEN. You see Doctor
    time and again I say
    sew it all sturdily together
    and it tears

DOCTOR. This is a disaster
    right before your entrance
    your costume has torn

QUEEN. It's the same thing every time
    right before my entrance
    it tears
    this is just silly
    this is vile
    Mrs Vargo
    time and again I say sturdy seams
    make the seams sturdy
    then I raise my arm
    and the costume tears

DOCTOR. Immediately
    before your entrance

FATHER. This is inexcusable
    Mrs Vargo

MRS VARGO *tries as quickly as possible to sew up the tear under the right
arm of the costume;* DOCTOR *assists her*

DOCTOR. Haven't you got
    any heavy-duty thread
    Mrs Vargo

QUEEN. How many times I have said
    pick yourself up
    a spool of heavy-duty thread
    but the same thing always happens
    the costume is stitched together with
    the cheapest ordinary thread
    and naturally tears
    at the most sensitive spot

FATHER. This is why my daughter is
    so nervous
    this why in certain circumstances
    she messes up a coloratura

DOCTOR. And the entire performance
    is imperiled
    Mrs Vargo

QUEEN. Why in the world haven't you always
    sewn up my costume
    so that it won't tear
    so that I can move about in my costume
    as I please
    this must be the hundredth time it has torn

DOCTOR. As if this tearing of costumes
    were acceptable at the opera

    (*To the* FATHER) of course this has got
    to make your daughter nervous

QUEEN. Always the same routine Doctor
    I raise my arm
    and the costume tears
    this is what
    is driving me crazy
    nobody understands
    my nervousness
    and so this tearing of my costume drives me
    crazy
    nobody knows what I put up with
    how incredibly unreliable the people around me are
    everybody here is unreliable
    these theaters and opera houses are teeming
    with unreliable people

DOCTOR. Here nothing holds sway but dilettantism

FATHER. Along with schadenfreude

DOCTOR. Schadenfreude naturally

MRS VARGO *is finished sewing.* QUEEN *slumps forward in despair, but then immediately rights herself*

QUEEN. It's horrible Doctor
no really
it's horrible
(*Very quickly raises her left arm and her costume very noisily tears*)

DOCTOR. A catastrophe
a catastrophe
Mrs Vargo

(MRS VARGO *sews up the tear under the left arm as quickly as possible*)

You must hurry
do you hear me Mrs Vargo
you must hurry
The overture

MRS VARGO. The overture
I was in such a hurry
I didn't even hear the overture
all of a sudden the Three Ladies
are onstage

FATHER. Always too late
and always at the last minute
a catastrophe every time
this is inconsiderate
my child

QUEEN. And on top of all this
to have a father
who doesn't understand a thing
and who secretly hates
what one does

DOCTOR. You must hurry
Mrs Vargo

(QUEEN *half-sings a coloratura*)

In today's opera houses
there is a constant

atmosphere of catastrophe
in theaters in general
nothing functions right
quickly Mrs Vargo
the Three Ladies
are already onstage

QUEEN. The Three Ladies
the Three Ladies

FATHER. The Three Ladies
are already onstage
my child

MRS VARGO (*sighs*). Done

DOCTOR. At the last minute

FATHER. At the last minute

MRS VARGO. Now none of it can
ever tear again
ma'am

DOCTOR. Concentration
nothing but concentration
Concentration
is the most crucial thing

(QUEEN *half-sings a coloratura*)

Her coach should do his afternoon coaching
a bit earlier in the day

(QUEEN *half-sings a coloratura*)

Then the question is
whether

(QUEEN *half sings a coloratura*)

MRS VARGO (*to* QUEEN). Raise your arm
to put your mind at rest

QUEEN *half-sings a coloratura, raises her right arm and then her left*

DOCTOR. You see
nothing is tearing

the whole thing is sturdy now
Mrs Vargo
has stitched it all together
as sturdily as possible
I personally observed
how sturdily she stitched up the seams

FATHER. The Three Ladies
are already onstage

DOCTOR. In fact the serpent has already been slain

(QUEEN *half-sings a coloratura*)

What an unpleasant tenor voice
an utterly unbearable Tamino

(QUEEN *sings a coloratura*)

An utterly unbearable tenor
an utterly unbearable conductor

(QUEEN *rises and steps forward and raises her head as high as possible*)

And the most significant opera
in the history of opera

QUEEN *makes for the door*

FATHER. The crown
don't forget the crown

MRS VARGO (*in horror*). The crown
naturally the crown

(*Takes the crown down from the clothes rack and sets it on* QUEEN'*s head*)

DOCTOR (*to* MRS VARGO). Fasten it on
so that it can't fall off

(MRS VARGO *fastens the crown and buckles the belt around* QUEEN'*s waist*)

Queens of the Night
have been known
to lose their crowns

FATHER. My lovely child

Exit QUEEN *with* MRS VARGO

DOCTOR. Just imagine
if on the stage
if right in the middle of the stage
your daughter's costume tears
under the arms
first under the right arm
and then under the left
undoubtedly a catastrophe
I regard this
trial arm-raising as an
unconditional necessity

(FATHER *turns up the loudspeaker*)

To be obliged
to perform a part
that one loathes
because one has talent
genius in certain circumstances
my dear sir
or because one is forced
to do so in every conceivable circumstance
for example by a father
is horrible

(*The recitative "Oh tremble not, beloved son" is heard from the loud-speaker*)

The theater
and in particular
the opera
my dear sir
is hell

The aria is heard from the loudspeaker

DOCTOR *and* FATHER *motionlessly listen to the remainder of the aria*

CURTAIN

AT THE THREE HUSSARS

QUEEN OF THE NIGHT, FATHER, *and* DOCTOR, *seated at a circular table*
Two side-tables with lamps
WINTER *in the background*

DOCTOR. An outstanding performance
 The mise en scène
 was excellent
 Apart from the conductor
 Such apathy
 towards the score
 Artificiality

 (QUEEN *beckons* WINTER *over*)

 Astonishing
 the audience's
 incapacity to react
 Poverty of imagination
 Downright crippling stupidity

 (QUEEN *says something unintelligible to* WINTER, *standing immediately behind her. Exit* WINTER)

 Mistimed cues
 constant anxiety
 literally
 uninterrupted anxiety
 Like at Covent Garden
 Like at Covent Garden
 How easy it is
 to disrupt a production

to the point of insufferableness
no exactitude
my dear sir
Aptitude on the part of the actors
of the singers
but no exactitude
it's no use
it's absolutely no use

QUEEN (*to* FATHER). You hear
you don't see
but you do hear

DOCTOR And he hears
everything
the most insignificant things
with incredible reliability
A person who can't see
hears incredibly clearly

FATHER. Today's performance
was about ten minutes shorter
than the first one

DOCTOR. This incessant anxiety
believe me
outstanding seats
Naturally
regarding Fritz Busch
no

QUEEN. Every time I think
this is the last time
that I'll put up with this
that I'll go through with this
yet again
and yet again
and yet again
one fine day there'll be no more yet agains
ever again

Enter WINTER *with a bottle of wine; he pours a sip for* DOCTOR, QUEEN *and* FATHER; *then he tops off* DOCTOR's *glass and exits*

DOCTOR. What we miss
  is the precision
  the exactitude
  the inconsiderateness
  the extremity of artificiality
  like the score
  but what we read
  in the newspapers
  is of an appalling naivety
  since
  something that has not been studied
  and therefore not been fathomed
  is described there
  such effrontery
  my dear sir

  (*Enter* WINTER *with the entrees, which he serves*)

Diminution
my dear sir
parsimony
artificiality

(*To* WINTER) If you Winter
have come to grasp
the fact that everything
is exceedingly questionable
that one cannot
rely on anything
that everything is grounds
for distrust
and for contempt
If you perform
with eyes wide open
and perform an inconsiderate dissection
you are present
at a philosophical state of affairs

WINTER (*to* QUEEN). An absolutely extraordinary success
madam
The newspapers

DOCTOR (*interrupting*). Lies Winter
all lies Winter
Organs
of incompetence
each one of them a maw
that unremittingly
spews
vulgarity
ignobility

(*To* WINTER) You know
Gevrey Chambertin
not too cold
not too warm

(*To* QUEEN) on the other hand the world is such a wasteland
without newspapers

(*To* WINTER) please bring the gentleman
some white-bread
toast

(*Exit* WINTER)

The air
in the opera house
is atrocious

QUEEN. I am always worried
that the fire curtain
is going to come crashing down

DOCTOR. Your old nightmare
about being crushed
by the fire curtain

Enter WINTER *with* FATHER'*s toast*

DOCTOR (*to* WINTER). Listen to this
Madam

is still forever worrying
that she will be crushed
by the fire curtain
You remember

WINTER (*serving* FATHER *his toast*). Madam has always
talked about this

DOCTOR. It's true that
at the Metropolitan Opera
the fire curtain did once fall down
during a performance
but nobody was injured

(*Exit* WINTER)

I believe
it was during a performance
of *Fidelio*

QUEEN. With Kirsten

DOCTOR. With Kirsten Flagstad

FATHER. Twelve years ago

DOCTOR. A performance
conducted by Fritz Busch

FATHER. Who was substituting
for Bruno Walter

DOCTOR. Indeed
I remember
Busch was substituting
for Walter

QUEEN (*calling out*). Winter
Winter

(*Enter* WINTER)

Bring some mineral water
Winter

(*Exit* WINTER)

Every time I say
this is the last time
call it off
don't make any more appearances
bow out
for good

DOCTOR. If you are talking about
retiring
at the pinnacle
bowing out
at the pinnacle
of your vitality
of your art
of your disgust with art
(*Laughs*)
well you haven't
reached that pinnacle yet

Enter WINTER *with the mineral water*

QUEEN (*to* WINTER). If only I could confide in somebody
but there is nobody
I can confide in
my days of being a confidence trickster's dupe
are over
and done with

(*To* WINTER, *as he pours the mineral water*)

This I believe
I believe that that is mineral water
Winter
nothing else
I believe nothing else
absolutely nothing else

(*Looks* WINTER *in the eye*)

nothing else whatsoever
just

that what you're now pouring me
is mineral water

Exit WINTER

DOCTOR. A blind person naturally
gets tired
more quickly
and more intensively
than other people
But the loutishness of the crowds
is a given
There is nobody
who is a more intensive
witness
(*To* QUEEN) of your art

QUEEN. Then
after the performance
when everything is over
this insatiable appetite

DOCTOR. When the restaurant in question
is as celebrated
as the Three Hussars

QUEEN (*calling to* WINTER, *who is offstage*). Did you hear that Winter
When the restaurant in question
is as celebrated
as the Three Hussars

DOCTOR. The meal isn't just a meal
it's an extravaganza

QUEEN. This remark is
typical of you Doctor

DOCTOR. The consommé
and a philosophical topic
The beefsteak tartar
and

the idea of self-annihilation
for example

QUEEN. The difficulty
of always singing exactly right
in completely different conditions
of always singing the same role
exactly right

DOCTOR. Fluctuations in temperature
fluctuations in consciousness
naturally

QUEEN. Is it more taxing
or not as taxing
in cold water
as in warm water
is it more taxing in Paris
than in Buenos Aires
or vice-versa

DOCTOR. Or vice-versa

FATHER. My daughter
is fully conversant with
the fluctuations
in nature

DOCTOR. A step too many
or too large a step
a lapse of attention
of the most laughable sort
a lapse of attention on her partner's part
and everything falls to bits
my dear sir

FATHER. She imagines herself
in the craziest situation

DOCTOR. One time it is
an Italian

the next time a Spanish
the next an English
the next a German conductor
(*Laughs*)

FATHER. She has made herself
into a specialist

DOCTOR. A specialist

FATHER. As her anxiety
and her monstrousness
as her fluency
and her insecurity
and her inconsiderateness increase
so do her fees

DOCTOR. Naturally
her fees are increasing

FATHER. But now
her villas her numerous houses make her
unhappy

DOCTOR. What one wants
to begin with is
what one subsequently doesn't want at all

DOCTOR *and* FATHER *laugh*

QUEEN. At the Three Hussars
it is mandatory to eat
fried beef and onions in gravy or
a beefsteak tartar

DOCTOR. Fried beef and onions in gravy or
a beefsteak tartar

QUEEN. It's food that prepares
itself
that mixes
crushes

itself
This is something that Winter
understands
(*Shouting out to* WINTER) Isn't it Winter
it's something that you
understand

DOCTOR. A reliable man
    who never steps out of character

FATHER. Also a Scorpio
    like me

QUEEN. My father always sits
    in the twelfth row
    in the middle of the twelfth row
    he always sits
    in the same seat

FATHER. I hear best
    in the twelfth row

QUEEN. Nobody
    sits on either side of him
    he needs
    the two seats on either side of him
    for his arms and hands
    (*Laughs*)

DOCTOR. A person like
    your father
    has an uncommonly well-trained sense of hearing

QUEEN. He hears everything

DOCTOR. Naturally

QUEEN. A coloratura that isn't exactly right
    bothers him for days on end
    on these days he says nothing
    holds his tongue

DOCTOR. When one has staked one's entire fortune
  on such a voice
  and everything
  has come to fruition

QUEEN. He always used to yearn
  for me to sing the Queen of the Night
  at Covent Garden
  and by now I have sung
  at Covent Garden twenty times

FATHER. Twenty times

DOCTOR. Once we have achieved something
  even something of the highest order
  we see
  that it is nothing

FATHER. Nothing
  nothing

DOCTOR. In the end
  nothing
  It is sheer torture
  my dear sir
  and one's intellect
  is a formidable one

QUEEN. Since my father
  got the armbands
  I haven't worried about him
  as much

DOCTOR. Society
  is extremely inconsiderate
  if a person evinces a weakness
  this weakness is
  taken advantage of
  everything is based on that
  (*To* QUEEN) When you are walking up and down
  in the park

before a performance
aren't you thinking all the while
that you might suddenly
fail to deliver
that all of a sudden you
won't be able to sing
your coloraturas
That when you step into the opera house
you will unleash a scandal
as you suddenly
lose command
of your art
I believe
artists exist
in perpetual fear
of the instantaneous loss
of their artistic powers
a singer
worries that he will suddenly no longer be able to sing
an actor
that he will suddenly
forget his lines et cetera
without a doubt I myself would
be incessantly afflicted by this fear
and would conceivably be unfit
to be a practicing artist
Science
once one is conscious of it
is soothing
Medicine
is absolutely unacquainted with
the concept of fear

(*To* FATHER) May I pour you
some wine
my dear sir

(*Pours* FATHER *some wine*)

Medicine
But what is there to explain
when of course nothing whatsoever
can be explained
when nothing whatsoever

QUEEN. Before the performance
I naturally
avoid myself
I distract myself
I listen
I eavesdrop
Distraction

DOCTOR. But naturally
distraction is impossible

QUEEN (*looks at* FATHER). Naturally
I get out of his way
I simply avoid him
once I've avoided him
I calm down
(*To* FATHER) It's all been settled
you are going off to the mountains
I am determined to make this tour alone
If it's something important
he doesn't hear
suddenly he loses his hearing
as well
(*Suddenly cries out*) Winter

(*Enter* WINTER)

A telegram Winter
write this down
(WINTER *readies pen and paper*)

Royal Opera Stockholm
Royal Opera Stockholm

(WINTER *writes*)

Did you get that

(WINTER *nods*)

Royal Opera Stockholm
Owing to sudden
owing to sudden

(*To* DOCTOR) listen to this Doctor
Owing to severe sudden

(*To* WINTER) owing to sudden severe illness
fulfillment of obligation
fulfillment of obligation
did you get that

(*To* DOCTOR) listen up
Listen up Doctor

(*To* WINTER) fulfillment of obligation impossible
Deeply regret cancellation et cetera
Send it off
at once
now

Exit WINTER

DOCTOR. But surely you're

QUEEN. Not actually ill
  you were about to say
  naturally
  I am not actually ill
  not in the least

  (*Laughs*)

  but I shan't be traveling to Stockholm
  not to Stockholm
  not to Stockholm

  (*Suddenly*)

  nor to Copenhagen
  nor to Copenhagen either

  (*Cries out*)

Winter

(*Enter* WINTER)

Send a telegram to Copenhagen
as well
write this down

(WINTER *writes*)

Royal Opera Copenhagen
Owing to sudden severe illness
fulfillment of obligation impossible
deeply regret cancellation et cetera
send off both telegrams at once

Exit WINTER

QUEEN (*to* DOCTOR). I shall travel with my father
  to the mountains
  To the mountains Doctor
  no coloratura
  nothing
  I know that my father
  cannot stand
  the awful stench of the people
  who sit next to him at the opera
  he hates the perspiration of the opera-goers
  it stupefies him
  and to such a powerful extent
  I think
  because of his alcoholism

DOCTOR. Naturally
  an alcoholic finds
  the perspiration of his fellow human beings
  especially at the theater
  or at the opera
  quite appalling

QUEEN. I have never yet
  called off an appearance
  except suddenly

DOCTOR. But this time for once
  the lie
  is suddenly
  a quite-possibly
  fatal illness

QUEEN *and* DOCTOR *laugh*

FATHER. Being contradicted is something she can't put up with
  She can't put up with being contradicted

DOCTOR. One must have strength
  to cancel
  to call off something
  that has become habitual
  to cancel an appearance onstage
  or

QUEEN. Or

DOCTOR. Or in the middle of such an appearance
  for example in the middle of the Revenge Aria
  to stop singing
  let one's arms drop
  ignore the orchestra
  ignore the other singers
  ignore the audience
  ignore everybody
  to stand there
  and do nothing
  and stare at everybody
  stare at them do you understand
  and suddenly stick out one's tongue

  (QUEEN *and* DOCTOR *laugh*)

To start by canceling engagements formally
  by telegram
  but then
  suddenly
  super-suddenly

for example at the Metropolitan Opera
or at Covent Garden
during the most striking passage naturally
to unleash a scandal
derail a performance
to clap one's hands
and stick out one's tongue
and exit the stage laughing
laughing
laughing do you understand
laughing

QUEEN *and* DOCTOR *laugh*

FATHER. My daughter is one of a kind
she sings
the most complicated and the most beautiful
coloraturas in the world
she is justifiably famous

DOCTOR. But of course that doesn't mean
one can't indulge oneself
in a prank every now and then

(QUEEN *and* DOCTOR *laugh*)

Your daughter
is the most celebrated one
she has
no peer

QUEEN. Suddenly

(*Laughs*)

on the audience

(*Laughs*)

no

(*Looks at* FATHER)

not in front of him
in front of him no

DOCTOR. Why don't you just
   say what you want to say
   Your father obviously
   will accept
   whatever you do
   given that we're all
   in quite a frolicsome mood by now

QUEEN. In a frolicsome mood

   (*Calls out*)

   Winter
   Winter

   (*Enter* WINTER)

   Winter
   what does one do
   when one wants to say something
   and can't say it
   because at least somebody
   is sorry for somebody

   (*Looks at* FATHER)

   Winter

   (WINTER *is at a loss for a reply*)

   To spit
   in the audience's face

   (*Loudly laughs*)

   Winter
   bring it now
   you know

   (*Exit* WINTER)

   Coloratura-machine
   Coloratura-machine
   do you hear me Doctor
   Coloratura-machine

   (DOCTOR *laughs*)

Considerateness
when there is absolutely no occasion for it
none whatsoever
I dream about that
I'm always picturing that
unleashing a scandal
at the apex of my pinnacle
it's monstrous
but natural Doctor
as perverse as can be
but as natural as can be
or suddenly
going insane
at my pinnacle
parents are bearers of guilt
not inspirers of confidence Doctor
to be thrust by one's parents
into a single monstrous
never-ending imposture
When we have sacrificed ourselves
to our discipline Doctor
totally sacrificed ourselves
The great artist at the pinnacle of her art
I know
What a staccato
what a staccato

FATHER. You should have heard
    my daughter in Florence
    The newspapers wrote
    that with her every entrance
    her art was attaining
    a higher level of perfection
    the highest demands
    Doctor
    the highest demands imaginable
    it is because of these that each and every one of us

must exert himself ever harder
to such an extraordinary extent Doctor
especially artists
who now must exert themselves
as they never used to have to
nowadays artists are
put to the test
as never before
in no case may any consideration
be shown
artists show no consideration
for the public
and the public likewise
shows no consideration for them
Anybody who has attained his goal
is naturally
fatally unhappy

DOCTOR (*to* FATHER). Because you see
nothing
or almost nothing
you hear all the better
my dear sir
a person who sees poorly
hears well
just as a person who hears poorly
sees well
in certain situations my dear sir
but good ears
can naturally never
take the place of bad eyes
or vice-versa

(QUEEN *laughs*)

If only you could see your daughter
she is lovely to behold
my dear sir

When it's a matter of keeping
all these people
whom she loathes
at arm's length from your daughter
the crowd of people keeps getting more alarming
we have of course for the longest time
been arriving and leaving exclusively through the back doors
when we arrive or leave
we aren't arriving or leaving alone
everything we do is
under surveillance
only when we take refuge in a private room
at the Three Hussars for example
and are behind locked doors
but we are always stared at my dear sir
You yourself are noticing this most terrible of all conditions
possibly not with such clarity
we contrive to sneak out
but the audience always drags us back in
if we breathe a sigh of relief my dear sir
the audience mobs us
at the very next corner
Today your daughter's voice
was the most perfect of all voices
Listen up my dear sir
above all we mustn't
forget about the Brunetti chisel
the double rachiotome

(*To* QUEEN) I promised your father
that I would continue my lecture
on postmortem dissection
at the Three Hussars

(*To* FATHER) don't forget about
the dural forceps

(QUEEN *coughs*)

Above all your daughter

must take care not to catch a cold
the human body
is always on the brink
of every illness
in constant dread
in mortal terror

(QUEEN *coughs*)

We wake up
and think
we are doomed
one pain
my dear sir
one painful movement
and we believe
we are at the end

(*To* FATHER) it is a single step

(*Enter* WINTER *with a bottle of champagne*)

The desire
to be dead
whence our fear
in face of the end

(WINTER *opens the bottle; a pop is heard*)

Every given moment
is always the most propitious one
every given moment is
always propitious

(WINTER *pours the champagne*)

When we are among actors
or singers
my dear sir
we are among intriguers
It's a matter
of sheltering a creature like your daughter
such an artistic creature

from the artistic world

(QUEEN *coughs*)

(*To* WINTER) What time is it anyway Winter

WINTER. Half past one

DOCTOR. Half past one

QUEEN. Half past one

Exit WINTER

DOCTOR. Intensity
intellectual inconsiderateness
in every case
a lethal process
my dear sir

(ALL *drink their champagne*)

If we experience
these conditions
and circumstances for a very long time
and suddenly drop dead

FATHER. Drop dead

DOCTOR. We see a theatrical artist
we hear a trained voice
a coloratura soprano
my dear sir
on a dung heap
my dear sir
culture is a dung heap
on which theatricality
and musicality
flourish
it really is a dung heap
my dear sir

(*Pours them all champagne from the bottle*)

One can prolong this unnatural condition
that we call existence

or human nature
artificially
my dear sir
but this prolongation by no means a necessity
on the other hand I do intend to continue
my scientific work
to complete the book that I have been working on
for the past twenty years
one of these days
by then everything will undoubtedly have been torn to pieces
your daughter's existence

(QUEEN *coughs*)

of all existences is useful
to this work
that has completely engrossed me
to a twelve-volume opus
on the human body my dear sir
useful to an extreme degree
probably it is the existence of your daughter alone
that will allow me finally and conclusively to complete
this essay that I had already abandoned
years before I met
your daughter
and you my dear sir

(QUEEN *coughs*)

Our modus operandi is naturally
a dilettantish one
on the other hand everything falls to pieces
everything deteriorates
in your daughter's orbit
consistency at its most extreme has no tolerance
for propinquity
right now she is singing
as no one has never
sung before
Hectic hastiness

my dear sir
nothing but hectic hastiness
along with the craziness
that is inextricable from this hastiness
May I have your attention please
my dear sir
one opens the pericardium
as one makes near the cardiac apex
a tiny incision
with forceps and intestinal scissors
or with the cerebral scalpel
an incision that one extends
my dear sir
along both sides
in a V-shaped pattern
One should note the contents
of the pericardial cavity

(QUEEN *coughs*)

Normally one finds
a small volume
of opaque liquid
in pathological cases one may find
a serous or purulent exudation
blood
or transudation
hydropericardium
my dear sir
In dealing with concretio pericardii one must dissect the heart
along with the adhering pericardium
One uses its resemblance
to the right fist
as a point of reference
And so to the cardiac incision
my dear sir
one grasps the anterior wall
of the right chamber
one draws the heart

slightly downwards
and thereby acquires
a straight line

(WINTER *appears and remains in the background*)

The so-called Rokitansky incision
facilitates the opening
of the left ventricle
my dear sir
one grasps the
apex which is situated much farther to the front
between the third and fourth fingers
of the left hand
and proceeds with index finger and thumb
into the opening of the left ventricle
and draws the entire heart thus fixed
downwards
The aorta lies
immediately beneath the apex
in the septum
Rokitansky's method of incision
has the advantage
of preserving the aorta pulmonaris
but the septum membranaceum is destroyed
as is the conductive system

(QUEEN *beckons* WINTER *over.* WINTER *approaches her from behind*
QUEEN *whispers something in his ear. Exit* WINTER)

As for the excision
of the tongue
and the pharynx
one removes the block of wood
by which the neck
is being stretched taut
first of all
using the cartilage scalpel
one dissects the hypodermis
of the throat until it is mostly exposed

then using the lingual scalpel
one penetrates beneath the skin

FATHER. Penetrates beneath the skin

DOCTOR. One lays the scalpel flat against the skin
and guides it carefully

FATHER. Carefully
(*Coughs*)

DOCTOR. Forward into the median plane
until one runs into the lower jawbone

(QUEEN *coughs*)

Then one raises the scalpel
in one's grip
and enters the oral cavity
with a clearly palpable jerk
my dear sir
and cuts through the floor of the oral cavity
along the horizontal
mandibular ramus
it is a classic structure
my dear sir

(QUEEN *coughs*)

mark my words
a classic structure

FATHER. A classic structure

DOCTOR. One proceeds
in the same way on the other side
(*To* QUEEN) Your father undoubtedly once had the makings
of an outstanding practitioner
many people suffer
all their lives
as a consequence of having
been obliged to discontinue some vehemently embarked-on course of
study
all of a sudden

A good anatomist
needs to have a healthy physique
Next one pulls the skin of the throat
inside-out and upwards
One grasps the tongue
with the second and fourth fingers
and pulls it downwards
with the thumb and index finger

(*Enter* WINTER *with a bottle of champagne*)

By now the pharyngeal structures are only connected
to the rear wall of the pharynx
which must now be cut through

(WINTER *opens the bottle of champagne*)

To this end one lays the lingual scalpel
flat
and by sight
or by touch
my dear sir
by touch
or by sight
one locates
the boundary between the hard
and soft palates

(*A pop is heard*)

thrusts through
and presses on all the way to the rear wall of the pharynx

(QUEEN *coughs.* WINTER *pours everyone champagne*)

Now one guides the incision
outwards in an arc
and all the way to the spinal column
then one cuts through the fascia praevertebralis
all the while keeping the edge of the scalpel perpendicular
to the spinal column
and making the dividing cut first to the left
then to the right

> (*To* WINTER) Winter
> it's getting late
> if you pour us another bottle

WINTER. The lady

DOCTOR. Fine Winter fine

Exit WINTER

> While constantly pulling
> the tongue
> through which one lifts the pharyngeal viscera
> from the spinal column

QUEEN *coughs*

FATHER. Lifts them from the spinal column

DOCTOR. Now using the intestinal scissors one cuts
> paramedially
> up top
> through the tonsillar ring
> and enters the esophagus
> in the median plane
> in doing which one holds the scissors
> at a slightly sloping angle
> and rotates them only once one is inside
> my dear sir
> and cuts through the esophagus
> in the median line
> Now one can excise
> all the pharyngeal organs
> en bloc
> In cases of lymphatic leukemia
> the tonsils can be
> extremely enlarged

> (*To* QUEEN) If your father
> hadn't fallen ill
> fallen ill
> really much too young
> and not also then gone

almost totally blind
we would now be dining
with a medical authority

FATHER. A medical authority

DOCTOR. A head like the head
of your father
is at bottom
a thoroughly medical head
And you can see for yourself
how keen
his interest
in medicine is
even though he already knows everything
he is always in the mood
for a refresher course
a refresher course
in special procedures
in the field of medicine
Believe me
such unflagging interest
is nowhere to be found
in physicians
in them we encounter
nothing but arrogance

(*To* FATHER) Before one
sets about dissecting the abdominal organs
one checks to see
whether or not less subtle changes
have taken place in the site of the abdominal organs
such as for example adhesions
between the liver and the intestines

The QUEEN *coughs*

FATHER. Between the liver and the intestines

Enter WINTER, *who walks up to the small side-table at stage left and turns off its lamp and vanishes*

DOCTOR. Or between the gall-bladder
and the intestinal loops
but most important of all is the comportment of the greater omentum
which in inflammatory processes
in the area of the stomach
of the intestines
of the gall-bladder
of the uterus et cetera
is warped towards the process
an unmistakable hint
violent distension of the stomach
in cases of arteriomesenterial intestinal stoppage

(QUEEN *coughs*)

a distension that can be so extreme
that the stomach extends all the way to the symphysis
A violent dilation of the large intestine
megacolon
Hirschsprung's disease
my dear sir
Recessus duodeno jejunalis
Recessus intersigmoides
Recessus retrocoecalis
Recessus ileocoecalis
Recessus paracolicus et cetera

QUEEN *coughs*

FATHER. Recessus paracolicus

QUEEN *coughs. Enter* WINTER, *who turns off the lamp on the side-table in the background and vanishes. It is slowly getting dark*

DOCTOR. On to the dissection of the liver
listen up
my dear sir
normally the surface of the liver is
smooth
There may be
alterations of this surface texture

Zahn grooves
Grooves caused by constriction
In cases of hepar lobatum one finds grooves
cicatrized indentations
my dear sir
Postal-package shapes
in the liver
in the depths of the grooves
one sees caseated gummas
tuberosity et cetera

FATHER. Caseated gummas
postal-package shapes

DOCTOR. Postal-package shaped
caseated gummas
grayish-red ones
in cases of parenchymatous degeneration
dark brown ones
in cases of senile atrophy
pale yellow ones in cases of fatty liver disease
green ones in cases of jaundice
nutmeg-like ones in cases of congestion
To carry out this dissection one takes the cerebral scalpel
and makes the principal incision
in other words one cuts in
at the place where the curvature of the liver is
most pronounced
on both the left
and the right lobes

(QUEEN *coughs*)

while taking care not to cut them apart

FATHER. Not to cut them apart

(QUEEN *adjusts* FATHER's *armbands*)

These armbands
are a source of comfort

DOCTOR. Actually
   the law forbids a person
   who is not completely blind
   to wear armbands on both arms
   and your father is not completely blind

QUEEN *coughs*

FATHER. Not to cut them apart

DOCTOR. Not to cut them apart
   The structure of the liver
   arises from the fact
   that there is a discrepancy
   between the center
   and the periphery of its acinus

FATHER. What about the dissection of that certain area

DOCTOR. One spreads the legs of the corpse
   my dear sir
   takes up the cartilage scalpel
   gives a slight downward tug to the penis
   with one's left hand
   thereby stretching taut the skin of the symphysis

FATHER. Stretching it taut

DOCTOR. And beginning at the extreme left
   cuts downward
   with one's right hand in an arc
   in an arc
   my dear sir
   all the way to the level of the rectum
   and anus
   and pulls the penis and scrotum
   aside to the left
   (QUEEN *coughs*)

   One makes the same incision
   on the right side

with short sawing motions
cuts in two
the spongy cellular tissue
all the way to the free end of the symphysis
and there inserts the cartilage scalpel
and cuts through in an arc
the connective tissue of the pelvic floor
Having reached the median line
one effects the same division
on the other side
not in a single incision

(QUEEN *coughs*)

lest one damage
the urethra
which is near the symphysis
the penis
and scrotum are stretched
drawn upwards
through the opening thus made
and the two arc-shaped incisions
are united with a single diagonal incision
By this point the genitals are attached
only by the tissue of the promontory
my dear sir
from which they are to be detached
A procedure whose demonstration
requires the utmost circumspection
With regard to the stomach
one pulls down the entire small intestine
and Colon transversum
and initially contemplates the stomach
from the outside

QUEEN (*to* FATHER). The doctor
    is famed as an authority
    throughout Europe

he is highly respected
his books
and his articles
have been translated
into every
language
(*Coughs*)

FATHER. The world always
expects something
extraordinary
from an authority
there is nothing more strenuous
than being an authority

DOCTOR (*to* FATHER). All my life
I have longed for a career
in the background
but by nature
I am unfit for one

QUEEN. For the rest of the night
I shall be incapable of getting
my coloraturas
back out of my head
my dread of
and aversion to
everything
having to do with
grand opera

DOCTOR (*to* FATHER). To think that everyone
be he intellectual
or artistic
always makes himself
into a standard-bearer
of infamy
my dear sir
To be sure for a long time
a creature like your daughter was successfully

sheltered
shielded
my dear sir

(QUEEN *coughs*)

from a smut-bespattered public
from its lethal
incompetence
The theater
and in particular the opera
is no place
for a natural human being

(QUEEN *yawns*)

When we add
the feeblemindedness
that holds sway among this artistic breed
my dear sir
to the vulgarity
of the spectators
we arrive at madness

(QUEEN *coughs*)

and at ignorance
my dear sir
we are too intelligent

(*The stage slowly darkens*)

(*Turning to* FATHER) but you
my dear sir
fail to notice this
because you have been perpetually
and for quite a long time now
an entire decade
I believe
or even longer
constantly
living
in the kind of darkness

that is now
descending
Such an existence
is undoubtedly
a competent one
Few are they who exist
with such intensity
Light
is a misfortune

(*The stage is completely dark*)

Like on the public stage
my dear sir
thanks to which everything is
supremely insecure

QUEEN (*suddenly loudly crying out*). Winter
Winter

(*Enter* WINTER, *but he cannot be seen.* QUEEN, *after a pause*)

Did you send the telegrams
the telegrams to Stockholm
and Copenhagen

WINTER. Naturally madam

DOCTOR. It's good
that you sent the telegrams
that comes as a relief to me
I am relieved
I am quite relieved

QUEEN (*after a pause*). Exhaustion
nothing but exhaustion

Glasses and bottles are overturned onto the table

THE END

THE CELEBRITIES

BASS. I have achieved everything
　　　I have sung all the great roles
　　　in all the great opera houses
　　　Ochs under Kleiber
　　　with Schwarzkopf as the Marschallin

The Dummies

RICHARD MAYR

RICHARD TAUBER

LOTTE LEHMANN

ALEXANDER MOISSI

HELENE THIMIG

MAX REINHARDT

ARTURO TOSCANINI

ELLY NEY

SAMUEL FISCHER

The Actors

BASS, *a baron*

TENOR

SOPRANO

ACTOR

ACTRESS

DIRECTOR

CONDUCTOR

FEMALE PIANIST

PUBLISHER

FIRST SERVANT

SECOND SERVANT

The BASS's *summer residence*

First Prologue
THE PERFIDY OF THE ARTISTS

A dining hall with stark white walls

Apart from the SOPRANO, *whose place next to the Lotte Lehmann dummy is empty, all the actors are sitting next to their respectively appropriate dummies around a large round table, eating roasted pheasant and duck, and drinking*

Stage right, FIRST SERVANT; *stage left,* SECOND SERVANT; *both waiting on the feasters*

A Bösendorfer grand piano

A grandfather clock

Loud laughter as the curtain rises, then

BASS. Head over heels
    head over heels

CONDUCTOR. Head over heels

ALL (*only vaguely in unison*). Head over heels

PUBLISHER. Head over heels

BASS. Into the orchestra pit

ACTOR and ACTRESS. Head over heels

BASS (*has his glass filled by* FIRST SERVANT). The very moment
    he raised his baton
    head over heels

ACTRESS and FEMALE PIANIST. Head over heels

BASS. And during *Falstaff*
    of all operas

Just imagine it
Falstaff
(ÁLL *laugh*)
Falstaff
head over heels into the orchestra pit
That was the end of his career
naturally

FIRST SERVANT (*to* BASS). Shall we serve more food my lord

BASS. But of course
obviously

(SERVANTS *serve more roasted pheasant and duck*)

That was the end of his career
naturally
A talent of the first rank
who couldn't hold his own

CONDUCTOR. An unprecedented talent

PUBLISHER. A true artist

DIRECTOR. But an unfortunate fellow

BASS. An unfortunate fellow
a truly unfortunate fellow

CONDUCTOR. And an honorable man
honorable

DIRECTOR. Honorable

BASS. Thoroughly honorable

TENOR. A lifelong diabetic

BASS. And on top of all that
he was a lifelong diabetic
An unfortunate soul
without question an unfortunate soul

(*Looks at the clock*)

Dear old Gundi

(*Raises his glass and has* FIRST SERVANT *refill it*)

and I
rehearsed *Un ballo in maschera*
under him
Un ballo in maschera imagine that
under him
at Antwerp
The last time I sang under him
was at Glyndebourne
a disastrous performance

(*Eats a large piece of pheasant*)

Old Klemperer
used to say of him
that he was as musical as a milch cow

(*Drinks*)

a milch cow
That was the last time
that I saw Schuricht
the last time I saw Ebert
also an unfortunate soul like our dear friend
'thirty-seven
the pinnacle

CONDUCTOR. The absolute pinnacle

DIRECTOR. Ebert Schuricht Busch Kleiber Klemperer
It's positively unrepeatable

(*To* PIANIST) Wasn't it also in that year that
you hosted a Mozart evening
It was the evening of the catastrophic storm

BASS (*holds out his glass, and* FIRST SERVANT *refills it*). *Così* literally fell
into the water

CONDUCTOR. And Helletsgruber
caught pneumonia and was finished

BASS. In front of Hitler
    all of it in front of Hitler

PUBLISHER. Nietzsche foresaw all of this
    Mankind would have been bound to listen to Sils Maria

DIRECTOR. Nowadays even Glyndebourne
    is just a music factory
    albeit not quite so gigantic

BASS. Nowadays singing is done from a conveyor belt
    everybody sings and acts from a conveyor belt

    (*Picks up a pheasant bone*)

    a single colossal exercise in mass production
    it's pseudomusical

    (*Looks at the clock*)

    Gundi is standing me up
    She's an attention-grabber
    One cannot sing Ochs
    two hundred times with impunity
    two hundred times
    Between Salzburg and Bayreuth
    the whole thing is slowly but surely
    wearing out
    Of course I'm constantly saying to Gundi
    do the sensible thing
    bail out of your contract
    any day now your voice is going to be worn out
    But she's inconvincible

PUBLISHER. And a charming person

BASS. An utterly
    pathological soul
    And the greater the talent
    the more total is its annihilation

    (*Picks up another pheasant bone and gnaws at it*)

    Mankind has it in

for genius
Take a good look at all these talents
highly gifted talents
talents more highly gifted than any that came before them
all completely worn out
and ten years ago they were rising stars
No staying power
no economy
no ethos

TENOR. Discipline is a foreign word nowadays

BASS. Absolutely

PUBLISHER. A foreign word my lord
Nowadays the word discipline is a foreign word

BASS (*to* ELLY NEY). My dear Elly Ney
what would have become of you
if you had not practiced
your eight-to-ten hours a day

(*To* TOSCANINI) My highly honored Maestro Toscanini
whom am I addressing thus
I am addressing the total comprehension of music in its entirety
Nowadays young people haven't the faintest idea of
what music is
They embark on a course of study in music
and conclude it
but they have no idea whatsoever
of what music is
Just put one of these young careerists through their paces sometime
You'll get the shock of your life
all of them are letter-perfect
letter-perfect

DIRECTOR. Nowadays everybody is letter-perfect

BASS. Letter-perfect
but they haven't a clue about music

(*To* TAUBER) My dear Tauber
Cross my heart

(*Looks at all the guests in turn*)

I promise not to insult anybody
to sing Schubert
well anyway
Singers charge by the note to sing
and instrumentalists do exactly the same
But it may well be the case that society
will put an end
to this state of affairs
to this perverse fortune-cultivating at the concert podium
and in the theater
that over the short or long run
society
will put an end to this nightmare
An end ladies and gentlemen

(*Drains his glass and has it refilled right away*)

a sudden end
Nowadays art as a whole is
nothing but
a gigantic exploitation of society
and it has as little in common with art
as musical notes have with banknotes
Nowadays the great opera houses like the great theaters
are merely great banking houses
in which so-called artists amass gigantic fortunes

PUBLISHER. Truly spoken my lord

BASS. But a colossal failure of the banks
hence a colossal failure of the opera houses and the theaters
is in the immediate offing

(*Picks up another pheasant bone*)

But the so-called great protagonists sense this
because in reality they are nothing but speculators

and will bring their little lambkins safely into the fold
The public is one big puffed-up imbecile

(*To* TOSCANINI) my dear Maestro Toscanini
today I listened to your recording of *Cosi*
from back in 'thirty-seven
and compared it with the recording made by our unfortunate
disastrously unfortunate friend
I must say
But let the dead rest in peace

(*Raises his glass and has it refilled by* FIRST SERVANT)

The engagement in Buenos Aires
was his first engagement
after his terrible car accident near Barcelona
Knappertsbusch somehow secured him the job
old Knappertsbusch
he had relied on having
a chair or at least a stool to sit on
poor fellow
because on account of his spinal injury
he could no longer conduct while standing up
of course he had also already been much too slow
much too sluggish

(*Gnaws ostentatiously at his bone*)

CONDUCTOR. That was noticeable in his tempos
they were sluggish
very sluggish

BASS. Which is unsuitable for Mozart
But back in 'fifty-two
I heard a good *Magic Flute* conducted by him
in Mannheim

(*Drinks*)

Black ice in the Barcelona area
a rare occurrence

(*Gnaws ostentatiously at the bone*)

PIANIST. I myself once drove through
    black ice in Barcelona

BASS. There's also quite a nice

    (*Drinks a hefty gulp*)

    philharmonic society there
    I have never been much taken with Spain
    I had plenty of opportunities to go to Madrid
    and sing Ochs there
    That's always a bit tricky in Spain

PUBLISHER. Where you are of course quite a patron
    and connoisseur of the arts

BASS. I know it's about time I visited the Alhambra

    (*Gnaws ostentatiously at the bone*)

    The car skidded
    and flipped over
    both batons lay
    in fragments in the middle of the road
    he had always carried two batons with him

DIRECTOR. A bad omen

BASS. His wife
    a Pschorr
    like Richard Strauss's wife
    got a concussion during the accident
    He had a go at using
    two batons at once you know
    All joking aside
    the man had to be in a cast for two-and-a-half years

    (*Gnaws ostentatiously at the bone*)

    It naturally ate up his entire fortune
    he'd been born into a rich family
    in Vienna's Cottage District
    He was left in the end with just the little timber mill
    on the Wallersee

which of course all of you are familiar with
even as children we always called it
the art mill
because artists had always made art
in that timber mill

(*To* TOSCANINI, *after draining his glass*) In that timber mill my dear
  maestro
I made your acquaintance
George Szell was there too
You remember
You gave a demonstration

(*Gnaws ostentatiously at the bone and throws it onto his plate*)

of how to conduct *Macbeth*
to our unfortunate fellow
I had planned on bringing back to our friend
a little morsel from *Der Rosenkavalier*
it was a cloudy thundery afternoon
Szell's Rolls Royce was parked in front of the mill in the swamp

(*Picks up a piece of pheasant*)

The curtains had been pulled back
I couldn't believe my eyes
the great Toscanini was demonstrating the tempi
for *Macbeth* to our friend
That little latticed mill-window

PIANIST. It's just so nice in the country

BASS. As you can well imagine
  I could have been knocked over with a feather
  Toscanini in the mill
  You were showing him the tempi for *Macbeth*
  I immediately realized
  that they were for *Macbeth*
  Several times you stamped your foot on the floor of the mill
  because our friend hadn't understood you
  Of course he went on to conduct *Macbeth* at the opera

he tried to copy
what you had demonstrated to him
but he kept getting it wrong
one time he would be too fast
another time he'd be too slow
You literally stamped your foot several times on the floor of the mill

(*Gnaws ostentatiously at a bone*)

The whole mill shook
as the great Toscanini stamped his foot
But he understood nothing
I observed every single detail through the mill window
Eventually you gave up
You threw down the baton
it was evidently our friend's baton
on the fireside seat
and sat down on the fireside seat
and furiously pulled at your hair

(*Drinks*)

At first I was wary
˙of stepping into this scene
but I screwed up my courage and stepped in

PIANIST. Into that enchanting little mill

BASS. Meeting Toscanini
a colossal event

ACTRESS. A pinnacle

BASS. An absolute pinnacle
without a doubt
And there's something else I remember
how while you were demonstrating the tempi for *Macbeth* to our
    friend
Szell the great George Szell
(*To* TOSCANINI) was standing in the background
by the tiled stove in the corner
completely motionless in the background

(*Licks his fingers*)
Toscanini and Szell
and our friend
and me
(*Drinks*)
Szell wasn't moving a muscle
Then I walked in
and something remarkable happened

(*Point-blank to* TOSCANINI) You took no notice of me whatsoever
my highly honored maestro
you took a look out the window
you were completely exhausted
with your hair all unkempt from pulling at it

(*Looks at all the guests in turn and laughs and gnaws at the bone again*)

And then you said your goodbyes
but you didn't deign to address a single word to me
That was the beginning of our friendship
my dear maestro

(*To* RICHARD MAYR) That evening I gave Richard Mayr
an account of my experience
He was then singing Ochs for the last time

(*Point-blank to* RICHARD MAYR) Your last summer

(*Point-blank to* TOSCANINI) You certainly took great pains over our
    friend
but he never became
a conductor of any originality
Undoubtedly Szell
had profited from your instruction in *Macbeth*

(*Gnaws at the bone*)

PUBLISHER. Genius must take care
    not to nurture mediocrity

DIRECTOR. You're right about that
    you're completely right about that

PUBLISHER *laughs.*

BASS (*gnaws at his bone*). After his spinal injury
he could no longer conduct while standing up
only while sitting down

ACTRESS. Poor fellow

BASS. But on this occasion there was no chair
nor even a stool
nothing

PIANIST. He would have had to see to such things himself

TENOR. Naturally himself

BASS. Himself
himself
one must always see to one's own affairs oneself
And even in South America
He tried to raise his baton
and sit down
in other words he did raise his baton
and sit down
and he fell head over heels into the orchestra pit
head over heels

DIRECTOR (*loudly laughing*). Head over heels

PUBLISHER. Head over heels

TENOR (*laughing*). Head over heels

ALL (*laughing and shouting in unison*). Head over heels

BASS (*interrupting the laughter*). His first appearance in three years
two-and-a-half of them in a cast
a job secured by Knappertsbusch

(DIRECTOR *laughs*. PUBLISHER *laughs*. PIANIST *laughs*. ALL *laugh*. BASS
interrupting the laughter at a bellowing volume)

and then the man fell into the orchestra pit
during *Falstaff*

CONDUCTOR. Making public appearances in South America
is always risky

BASS. I could tell you lots of stories about that

(*Drains his glass and immediately has it refilled*)

all of which
or at least most of which
end with a death

(*Looks at the clock*)

So I've just sung Ochs for the two-hundredth time
and we're all commemorating this milestone
and who should be missing
but her

DIRECTOR. A typical child of our time
highly talented

BASS. But completely undisciplined

CONDUCTOR. But what a Fiordiligi
She is my discovery
I heard her when she was still just a girl
in the Mariazell Basilica
Hail Star of the Sea
She sang one of the most beautiful Marienlieder I have ever heard
I was virtually electrified then
I started by sending her to our esteemed Hilde Güden
at my own expense
You know the rest of the story
an incredible career

BASS. But an endangered one
you've got to admit that

(*Gnaws at his bone*)

CONDUCTOR. To be sure

BASS *drains his glass and has it refilled*

PUBLISHER (*to* SAMUEL FISCHER). My dear colleague Samuel Fischer
is an uncle of hers

DIRECTOR. You'll notice that the most important artists
are all related to one another

    the most celebrated ones are related
    to all the other most celebrated ones
    The exceptions prove the rule

PUBLISHER. Incidentally our esteemed no-show
    is also a relative of Thomas Mann's
    and the latter as I have just found out
    is related to James Joyce

PIANIST (*exclaims*). To James Joyce
    to Joyce
    You don't say

ACTRESS (*almost hysterically*). Related to Joyce literally

PUBLISHER. Related to Joyce literally
    Joyce and Mann are relatives
    And Joyce I have discovered
    is related to Rilke

PIANIST. Then of course Mann is also
    related to Rilke
    if Joyce is related to Mann
    and Rilke to Joyce

PUBLISHER. That's a sensation

ACTRESS. A sensation

DIRECTOR. Sensational

CONDUCTOR. Incredible

PUBLISHER. So many people are related to Rilke
    that it can't even be said
    how many people Rilke is related to

    (*To* BASS) In any case your lady friend
    will appear in our new biography of Rilke
    which I am planning for the autumn
    and in our new biography of Joyce as well
    and also in the new biography of Wittgenstein
    that I am planning

I myself am writing a book
about the most celebrated artists
of my own time

BASS. Writers
even when they are scholars
are specialists in exaggeration

(*Raises his glass, looks at the clock and has his glass refilled*)

There are artists
mainly musicians
or stage performers
who are of course all basically music makers
who plunge from one misfortune into the next
like our dear colleague

CONDUCTOR. Take Patzak
you remember Patzak
an absolute darling of the public
a voice

DIRECTOR. Like a crowing rooster's

PUBLISHER. Which is the determining factor for celebrity

DIRECTOR. Really an abrasively hideous voice

CONDUCTOR. But Patzak's voice exerted
a fascination. like that of no other

DIRECTOR. Patzak and Ferrier
an absolute pinnacle

CONDUCTOR. Naturally under Walter's baton

DIRECTOR. People who are crippled in some way always
exert a fascination

PUBLISHER. Absolute beauty does not fascinate

DIRECTOR. Crippledom always
exerts a fascination
In every kind of art

be it painting
be it literature
indeed even in music
Crippledom fascinates us

PUBLISHER. Witness
Patzak with his crippledom
a genuinely hideous abrasive crowing rooster's voice on the one hand
at the same time the most highly trained most perfect most fascinating
    voice on the other

DIRECTOR. That hideous crowing rooster's voice
and that crippled hand
they sent shivers down your spine

CONDUCTOR. To perform *Fidelio* with Patzak
that was a real delight
and with Flagstad
Patzak had the most extraordinary voice
that I had ever heard
but not the most beautiful
not the most beautiful

TENOR. The most precise voice

BASS. The most precise voice

CONDUCTOR. Patzak was the most precise singer of them all
The most precise singer with the most precise voice
and with the most precise sense of hearing

DIRECTOR. The most precise sense of hearing without a doubt

PUBLISHER. His crippled deportment

(BASS *beckons* FIRST SERVANT *over and has his glass filled*)

summoned forth by his crippled hand
made Patzak capable of the most extraordinary artistry

BASS *looks at the clock*

DIRECTOR. It is always a crippling deformity
that gives the impetus
to fascination

PUBLISHER. Genius
  is a crippling deformity

  (BASS *gnaws at a bone*)

  Patzak
  and in particular Patzak's deformity
  is the subject of a twenty-page chapter
  in the book by Adorno
  that I am bringing out this autumn
  a history of music to end all histories of music
  Adorno analyzes Patzak's deformity
  and Patzak's obtuseness
  and arrives at the most startling conclusions
  The crippling deformity
  of Patzak's hand
  is indispensable to his artistry
  Patzak would have been nothing
  without his crippled hand

  (*Exclaims*)

  No great man is without his crippling deformity
  be it visible or invisible
  All great men are crippled
  all greatness is crippled

DIRECTOR. The art of cripples is the highest kind of art
  the most exceptional kind

CONDUCTOR (*loudly interjects*). Cripples enjoy an intimate relationship
  with harmony

DIRECTOR. What an exceptionally intimate relationship
  with nature they enjoy

PUBLISHER. Which is why they enjoy such a colossally intimate
  relationship with art and
  understanding of art

DIRECTOR. The great the important the celebrated artists
  have always been cripples

PUBLISHER. Adorno has proved that this is a fact

(BASS *throws his bone on to his plate*)

The crippling deformity in question
can as Adorno has proved
be a physical deformity
but also an intellectual deformity
Goethe Schiller Heine Schopenhauer Kant
all of them cripples through and through cripples
even genius of the political kind is crippled
Genius is always crippled

(BASS *has his glass refilled*)

Just think of Shakespeare
of Dostoyevsky
of Flaubert Proust et cetera

BASS. Beethoven

PUBLISHER. Beethoven obviously
Mozart Bach Handel Wagner

DIRECTOR. Not to mention all the great performers
think of Paderewski Paganini Chopin
Furtwängler Casals Cortot

CONDUCTOR. Nikisch Walter

PUBLISHER. The greatest conductors are always cripples
Mental cripples or physical cripples

CONDUCTOR. Furtwängler is a textbook example
all his interpretations flow from his crippling deformity

DIRECTOR. This much is clear
it is to cripples alone that true genius divulges itself

PUBLISHER. We might as well be saying that artists
the greatest artists are in a class by themselves
when we say that the greatest cripples are in a class by themselves
That we are studying a single musical score composed by crippledom
when we are studying the musical scores of the geniuses

DIRECTOR. When you think about it
  Bach was crippled

PUBLISHER. So was Leonardo

CONDUCTOR. Even if these crippling deformities are not immediately
    perceived
  they're still there
  The extraordinary individual is always crippled
  Everything that takes place within him
  is a crippling deformity

PUBLISHER. That is no thesis
  it's a fact
  The exclusive causes of creativity are
  a crippling physical deformity or a crippling mental deformity

BASS. When will we be able to read Adorno's book anyway

PUBLISHER. I'll be bringing it out this autumn
  A magnum opus
  it's the magnum opus of the second half of the present century

BASS (*summons* FIRST SERVANT *by clapping, shouts*). When Madame the
    distinguished vocalist arrives
  possibly via the garden
  lead her here straight away
  straight away

  (FIRST SERVANT *fills* BASS'*s glass*)

  She is sawing at the branch
  she sings on
  She is sawing at the branch
  she sings on

PUBLISHER. She is admirable

BASS. Gundi has surely
  thought up something
  for this little party
  she's thought up something surely

  (*Drinks*)

But it was *her* idea
to invite you all here today
to a party in honor of my two-hundredth Ochs
Two hundred Ochses
But it's a lovely role

PUBLISHER. It's the *Faust* of Hofmannsthal
Hofmannsthal's *Faust*

BASS. Ochs is extremely popular in America
She's thought up something
something clever
something exceptional surely
something unusual that's just like Gundi
Hopefully she's not drunk again
She does tend to get drunk
after her last exit of the evening
after the opera is over
A clever person

PUBLISHER. And no less charming than clever

BASS. A little cat
You don't really know her
not really ladies and gentlemen
She is a cat I tell you a cat
She has surely

(*Gnaws ostentatiously at a bone*)

dreamed up something clever
Our unfortunate fellow was smitten with her
but she spurned him
spurned him

(*Drinks*)

spurned him
spurned that unfortunate highly musical fellow
He who broke his backbone in Barcelona

CONDUCTOR. The really remarkable thing about this career of hers is
that it has occasioned one misfortune after another
with each new misfortune being greater than the last one

BASS. One could be forgiven for supposing
that the man in each of these affairs
was engaged for the sole purpose of plunging into a new misfortune
But these misfortunate souls are the very people
who never give up

DIRECTOR. Truly spoken

BASS (*drinks*). I once knew this woman a colleague
who kept breaking her fingers
Guess what she was
A pianist naturally

(ACTRESS *laughs*)

Just stop playing Bach all the time
She had trouble playing the *Art of the Fugue*
I had always said to her
but she was the most mulish person I had ever known
You're just going to keep breaking your fingers over and over again
And she kept breaking her fingers over and over again

PUBLISHER. Many an artist walks with eyes wide open right up
to the abyss
and plunges into it

CONDUCTOR. These people attract misfortune
From all quarters these people are warned
but they always fumble their way into the abyss

BASS. It was an absolute catastrophe for his widow
He had wanted
to be buried at Henndorf am Wallersee
which after all isn't just next door to Buenos Aires
But it in the end he was buried
in snuggest proximity to his little timber mill

DIRECTOR. All of us made it possible

ACTRESS. All of us

ALL (*in only vague unison*). All of us

CONDUCTOR. I gave the eulogy
  It isn't easy
  to find the appropriate words

CURTAIN

Second Prologue

THE ARTISTS GET RID OF THEIR ROLE MODELS

As before

BASS (*exclaims*). There are no chance events
   (*Has his glass is filled by* FIRST SERVANT)

DIRECTOR. In a mathematical world that has been completely thought
      out
   and that is also fully coextensive with nature
   there cannot be any unique chance events

PUBLISHER. A world in which we are nonetheless constantly
   being taken unawares by chance events
   taken unawares and it goes without saying
   taken down

CONDUCTOR. The creative individual
   who must live solely in his imagination throughout his life
   But the truth is a different truth
   The widow knows
   what she was doing
   when she sent her husband across the Atlantic

   (*To* ELLY NEY) But you didn't understand our colleagues much better
   than I do
   dear Elly Ney

TENOR. What is she up to now anyway
   the widow that is
   Didn't she use to dabble at playing the harp

CONDUCTOR (*laughs*). At playing the harp
   at playing the harp

She even once played
in the great hall of the Musikverein
when her husband was conducting

DIRECTOR. There is nothing more horrible
more repulsive
than these artistic marriages

BASS (*gnaws at a bone*). Truly spoken

DIRECTOR. One half of each such marriage
annihilates the other
They're marriages
of feeblemindedness and addlebrainedness

CONDUCTOR. A welter of shipwrecked artistic marriages
A welter of great men made into laughing-stocks by their wives

DIRECTOR. Any two talents in such a marriage
no matter how great they are
annihilate each other
first one of them annihilates the other
and then vice-versa
Either the wife is submissive
or she is annihilated
or the husband is submissive
or he is annihilated
in every case both spouses are annihilated
Both of them always achieve
what they had in mind from the beginning
the annihilation of their spouse
the humiliation the defamation of art

PUBLISHER. The self-annihilation of artistic couples
is a total self-annihilation

BASS (*exclaims*). Truly spoken

DIRECTOR. The artist has to stand alone
against the world
to be a solitary figure
standing against everyone and everything

PUBLISHER. He must unflaggingly expose himself to insults

CONDUCTOR. Yet artists are the most easily offended people anywhere

BASS. Truly spoken

DIRECTOR. Artists are society's true victims

PUBLISHER. And the artistic marriage
is the most ridiculous thing ever

DIRECTOR. The artistic marriage
is a funeral for talent

CONDUCTOR. The death of genius

BASS. Chaliapin constantly had to cancel appearances on account of his
wife's numerous intestinal stoppages

CONDUCTOR. I had a colleague
who married one of his colleagues
we were together at the academy
These small towns annihilate young people
first they drive them to despair
and then into a marriage
and annihilate them
The man who conducted *La Cenerentola*
at the age of twenty-two
a sensation
He got married
and from that point on he only went downhill
Usually an illness
a terminal illness
as a consequence of the insane act of matrimony
all of them the most unfortunate relationships
but never acknowledged to be such
Nobody ever talks about that
about the awfulness
In Bad Segeberg
between Hamburg and Kiel
I ran into my colleague for the first time in years
he was looking for an Evangelist for the Passion

in those days there was only a single Evangelist in all of Europe
Helmut Krebs

(*Starts to laugh, then checks himself*)

just imagine
said my colleague in a perfectly cheerful tone
I've been trying to hire Krebs
and the doctor tells me I've already got him

(ALL *laugh*)

Already got him
already got him

ALL *continue laughing*

BASS. The doctor says

CONDUCTOR. Your colleague says

BASS. I've already got him

(*Looks at the clock*)

Still no sign
of our golden child

CONDUCTOR (*to* TOSCANINI). Suddenly slowing down
quite suddenly slowing down you know
super-suddenly don't you know Toscanini

PUBLISHER (*quoting*). Seriousness must be merry
pain must shimmer with seriousness don't you know
Has music not got a whiff
of combinatorial analysis about it
and vice-versa
Figured harmonies
Figured acoustics
are part of combinatorial analysis

BASS. I have yet to meet a human being
more ambitious than Gundi

CONDUCTOR. She is without a doubt the most headstrong

BASS. Gundi is headstrong

CONDUCTOR. And the most gifted
  She gets
  what she wants
  She has a crystal-clear idea
  of what she wants

BASS (to LOTTE LEHMANN). She's always saying
  that you the revered Lotte Lehmann
  are her role model
  At least once a day
  she listens to a record
  with your voice on it
  Her regard for you
  is immeasurable

DIRECTOR. What Shakespeare undoubtedly
  Dostoyevsky
  Heinrich von Kleist
  are for writers
  the greatest most creative performer
  is for performers
  the performer of all time

CONDUCTOR. The greatest performer of all time

BASS. For Gundi Lotte Lehmann was
  and is
  the greatest

  (*Point-blank to* LOTTE LEHMANN) Even in her sleep
  while dreaming
  she speaks of you in terms of the utmost reverence

PUBLISHER. Whereas in the ordinary person's case
  his cognitive faculty
  is the lantern
  that lights his path quoth Schopenhauer
  in the case of the genius it is the sun
  that reveals the world to him

BASS. Surely she's
thought up something clever
for today

CONDUCTOR. Harmony
in a world full of disharmony

BASS (*to* SERVANTS). More food
more drink

SERVANTS *serve everybody more food and drink*

DIRECTOR. The most beautiful of artists
as well as the most skillful

PUBLISHER. Numerators
are the mathematical vowels
Numbers
are numerators

(*To* ALL) Novalis
Combinatorial analysis
leads to numerical improvisation
and teaches the numerical art of composition
the mathematical basso continuo
Pythagoras
Leibniz
Language is a mathematical instrument of ideas
The poet
rhetorician and philosopher
play and compose grammatically

BASS. In ten years
I have achieved everything
that you see here
exclusively
thanks to my talent
and to my staying power
and to my refusal to compromise

(*To* SERVANTS) Serve the ladies and gentlemen

(SERVANTS *serve*)

To my talent
to my energy

(*To* RICHARD MAYR) people demand the very best from
a bass
especially when he is a basso profundo
I have achieved everything
I have sung all the great roles
in all the great opera houses
Ochs under Kleiber
with Schwarzkopf as the Marschallin

(*Looks at the clock*)

Gundi is something else
she's standing me up

CONDUCTOR. A person of great intensity
hypernervous
in her extreme
in her supremely extreme concentration

DIRECTOR. A couple of glasses of wine
because the opera is over

BASS. Over
over

CONDUCTOR. You must
cut her some slack my lord
allow her to let herself go for a bit let off a little steam let her hair
down

PUBLISHER. Artists
especially the most intense ones
need to be alone from time to time

DIRECTOR. It's quite possible that right now she is writing her letter
to her mother

BASS. Gundi always has some excuse
But today
when I've really been looking forward to this little party

It's not every day
that a man sings his two-hundredth Ochs

CONDUCTOR. The best Ochs
the best Ochs ever

BASS. You're making me blush
(*Looks at the clock*)

CONDUCTOR. She's probably taking her obligatory detour

BASS. The obligatory detour

DIRECTOR. She has thought up
something special for today my lord

BASS. Thought up something
thought up something

CONDUCTOR (*taps his glass with a knife and stands up and raises his glass
to* BASS). And so once again my lord
my dear friend
to your two-hundredth Ochs
Ochs for the two-hundredth time

(ALL *raise their glasses*)

To his health
health

ALL. Health

ALL (*only vaguely in unison*). health
health
health

ALL *drain their glasses*

CONDUCTOR. You are not only the most celebrated Ochs
You are also the greatest one

DIRECTOR. The greatest

PUBLISHER. Undoubtedly

BASS. You're making me blush

CONDUCTOR. No more words
   It isn't easy
   to find the appropriate words
   (*Point-blank to* BASS) The world of opera
   can consider itself lucky
   to have you

BASS. You're making me blush
   (*To* LOTTE LEHMANN *and* RICHARD MAYR) but the absolute pinnacle
   Rosenkavalier-wise
   is undoubtedly you two
   Lotte Lehmann and Richard Mayr
   That has never been repeated
   But I can say
   that I have managed quite successfully
   to cultivate my own modest talents

   (*To* MAYR) To sing under the tutelage of such a mighty role model as
      you
   the supremely honored Richard Mayr
   I too of course hail from a family of brewers
   My grandfather used to drive a four-in-hand carriage
   to the opera at Munich
   a four-in-hand carriage
   He was a Wagnerian naturally
   and a cousin of Richard Strauss's wife
   also a Pschorr
   a fool for opera
   a Wagnerian naturally
   Not a fortnight passed
   in which he didn't
   drive his four-in-hand carriage his four-in-hand carriage to the opera
   At first we children had no great liking for opera
   but I would have been no true grandson of my grandfather
   nor a true scion of a family of brewers
   if a passion for opera hadn't eventually
   erupted from me

in the truest sense of the word
erupted from me
naturally at the same moment
at which I discovered my voice
during a Sunday outing at Lake Starnberg
at Lake Starnberg
that's how it happened
My grandfather told Strauss about it
And Strauss told him
to send me to him
and so I went to Strauss

(*Point-blank to* MAYR) And Strauss recommended me to you
and you made me into what I am today
I believe I have
achieved something of note

CONDUCTOR and DIRECTOR (*in unison*). You can say that again

TENOR. He himself is a role model
    The baron himself is a role model

PUBLISHER (*exclaims*). A role model the baron's a role model

CONDUCTOR. I've never heard a better Figaro

DIRECTOR. And your Iago

TENOR. And his Rocco

CONDUCTOR. Better than Edelmann

BASS. I knew Edelmann well
    I met Edelmann through Emanuel List
    at Frida Leider's house in Berlin
    I believe it was in 'fifty-nine
    The only really perfect opera since Mozart
    is of course *Der Rosenkavalier*

PUBLISHER. A musical magnum opus
    a magnum opus of music
    (*To* CONDUCTOR) Am I not right

CONDUCTOR. You can say that again

BASS. But one mustn't be too old
  for Ochs
  not too young
  but not too old either

  (*To* RICHARD MAYR) You were thirty-five then
  at your pinnacle
  when you sang Ochs
  at your pinnacle

PUBLISHER. Talent demands of society
  its absolutely undivided attention
  just as society demands the absolutely undivided attention
  of talent

BASS (*exclaims with great pathos*). But talent isn't everything

CONDUCTOR. Talent is just one of those things

BASS. Knappertsbusch once said
  everybody's got talent
  everybody is talented

PUBLISHER. On the contrary talent
  must be annihilated from the outset
  so that the artist can emerge
  The annihilation of talent in the artist
  is a prerequisite for his existence

DIRECTOR. Talent is a stumbling block
  talent is a *chopping* block

PUBLISHER. Truly spoken

BASS. The first time I sang in front of an audience
  here
  at the Festspielhaus
  in 'fifty-nine can you believe it
  everybody was there
  everybody
  Krauss Szell Klemperer Krips and so on
  It was then that I first heard Lisa Della Casa
  and I was really impressed with her

She was my Olympia by the way
my Olympia
after the first ten measures I fainted dead away
The Magic Flute
Within these hallowed halls believe it or not
dead away after just the first two measures
I don't remember any more
how I came out of it
The next thing I knew I was looking up at the gridiron
and the stagehands were looking down at me
from quite high up as you know
they were all looking down at me
because I had fainted dead away
It was of course an absolutely insane idea
my singing in front of those celebrated people
insane and completely half-baked
half-baked
suddenly I couldn't hear my accompanist
who was sitting thirty meters away at the grand piano
I couldn't hear any more I just couldn't hear anything any more
and I looked up
and the stagehands were looking down at me
then I fainted
It was all over over over over over
Then out at the entrance Krips said to me
young man become a butcher
butcher butcher
I can still hear him saying butcher butcher
He totally annihilated me with those words
totally
to tell a young man
to become a butcher
at a moment like that
the sensitive Mozart conductor
how devious
how devious
And that's how talents are annihilated ladies and gentlemen

CONDUCTOR. But Krips couldn't annihilate your talent
  not yours my lord

BASS. I was absolutely floored
  annihilated

PUBLISHER. You are living proof
  of how mistaken Krips was

BASS. He walked on corpses

  (*To* CONDUCTOR) Then your unfortunate colleague
  God bless his soul
  took me aside and invited me
  to console myself by coming out to his mill in the country
  to his little timber mill

PIANIST. To the mill with the cute little windows

BASS. He said the whole thing wasn't all that bad
  and I went out to the mill with a couple of piano arrangements
  and he played *Die Winterreise* with me
  for an entire afternoon
  He really was an outstanding accompanist

CONDUCTOR. He could have been one of the best répétiteurs
  one of the best ever

BASS. Contrary to Mr Krips's opinion
  your colleague said to me
  I was an absolutely extraordinary talent
  if it were up to him he said
  I'd already have been engaged on the spot
  but he said he had absolutely no pull at any of the opera houses
  At the time he had just broken a leg
  in St Moritz

PUBLISHER (*exclaims*). In St Moritz

BASS. And believe it or not
  back then he
  the unfortunate fellow said to me
  I broke my left leg

on the doorstep of Nietzsche's house in Sils Maria
On the doorstep of Nietzsche's house

PUBLISHER. On the doorstep of Nietzsche's house
on the doorstep of Nietzsche's house

BASS. He would have hired me straight away

(*Point-blank to* RICHARD MAYR) You'll laugh at this he said to me
You are the ideal Ochs

(*To* CONDUCTOR) And so Krips hadn't quite managed to knock
the opera and the singing out of me
for weeks
I was the most depressed human being imaginable
Every time I hear Krips I think
he very nearly annihilated your life
And believe it or not ladies and gentlemen
two days after Krips died in Geneva
I passed him on the autobahn
all of a sudden I found myself passing a top-of-the-line hearse from
    Geneva
and in that top-of-the-line hearse was Krips
the late Krips
the late Krips
That can hardly be a chance event
certainly was no chance event
no chance event

PUBLISHER. Given that we are after all constantly
    being taken unawares by chance events
    taken unawares and it goes without saying
    overwhelmed

BASS. Whether Krips liked it
or not
I became a celebrated performer

CONDUCTOR. You can say that again

PUBLISHER. Celebrated
genuinely celebrated

DIRECTOR. A celebrity

BASS (*laughs*). I am a celebrity

DIRECTOR. But naturally
  there are also cripples
  whose artistry is not of the highest order

PUBLISHER. Naturally

DIRECTOR. Who despite their crippledom
  never exceed mediocrity
  who despite their crippling deformity are unable to get started on
    anything

PUBLISHER. Who are unable to capitalize on their crippledom
  like our friend who to the end of his life
  remained a mediocrity

  (*To* TOSCANINI) Even the instruction
  that you honored Maestro gave our friend in the little old timber mill
  was of no use to him
  obviously

DIRECTOR. Mediocrity is the straitjacket
  in which mediocrities are confined throughout their lives
  just as the genius is confined throughout his life
  in the straitjacket of genius

BASS (*to* TOSCANINI). And you my most highly honored Maestro
    Toscanini
  all those pinnacles at La Scala
  and in America
  to say absolutely nothing of your pinnacles here in Salzburg
  they were achievable only thanks to the greatest afflictions imaginable

  (*Glances to either side*)

  Every one of us has his own crippling deformity
  Artists maintain an impassible silence on the subject of their
    crippledom
  but without crippledom there is no art
  at least not in the concert hall or the theater

PUBLISHER. And without crippledom there is no literature

BASS (*to* MAX REINHARDT). And you my dear Reinhardt

> (*To* HELENE THIMIG) And you my dear Helene Thimig

> (*To* ALEXANDER MOISSI) And you my dear Moissi

> (*To* LOTTE LEHMANN) And you my most highly esteemed Lotte Lehmann

> All crippled
> Everyone has his own crippling deformity
> but it is not acknowledged
> the artist does not acknowledge his crippledom
> but he capitalizes on his crippledom
> Quite apart from our honored Elly Ney
> and our honored Richard Mayr
> our unforgettable Ochs von Lerchenau

> (*To* SAMUEL FISCHER) You could sing a song about
> what I'm talking about

DIRECTOR. When artists

> and it makes no difference whether we're talking about
> so-called creative artists
> or so-called performing artists
> who of course are creative in their own right
> are dead
> are dead ladies and gentlemen
> when they are dead
> the thing that all their lives they have kept silent about kept secret
> their crippling deformity
> comes to light
> their mental or physical deformity whichever
> The genius is an utterly pathological and crippled human being
> and an utterly pathological and crippled character

> (*Exclaims*)

> Ask the doctors
> what comes to light

when they cut into an artist's corpse with
their scalpels

BASS (*looks at the clock*). Gundi
is standing us all up
she's standing up
the most celebrated people

PUBLISHER. She is a star my lord
the latest absolute star my lord

BASS. She promised me
that she would be punctual
Singing Ochs for the two-hundredth time
that's nothing to sneeze at

CONDUCTOR. You haven't an inkling of what star sopranos
are like my lord

BASS. Probably she's getting drunk with her manager
now that *Cosi*'s over

PUBLISHER. A star
keeps the whole world on tenterhooks
you've got to come to terms with that my lord

BASS (*looks at the clock, then says to* ELLY NEY). But now even though
Gundi isn't here
may I make a request of our highly esteemed Elly Ney
It is the desire of everybody present

(*Rises*)

to hear Elly Ney

(*Raises his glass to Elly Ney. Exclaims*)

to Elly Ney
to Elly Ney

(ALL *drink to* ELLY NEY. *The* BASS *exclaims*)

A long life
to our Elly Ney
to our greatest female keyboard artist

(Drains his glass, walks up to ELLY NEY, *helps her out of her chair and leads her carefully and slowly to the Bösendorfer, and it is quite clear that* ELLY NEY *is a dummy as he says)*

Our chief role model
has always been
Elly Ney

PIANIST *(shrieking hysterically)*. My chief role model

BASS. As Richard Mayr is my chief role model

TENOR. As Richard Tauber is mine

DIRECTOR. As Max Reinhardt is mine

ACTOR. As Alexander Moissi is my role model

ACTRESS. As Helene Thimig is my role model

PUBLISHER. As Samuel Fischer is my role model

CONDUCTOR. My role model was always Toscanini

BASS *(places* ELLY NEY's *hands on the keyboard and says)*. Schumann
   naturally Schumann

PUBLISHER. Schumann naturally

PIANIST *(with great pathos)*. A glorious moment
   to think that I am still permitted to experience this

ELLY NEY *softly plays Schumann's* Fantasie, op. 17

PUBLISHER. It is
   as if Schumann himself
   were playing using Elly Ney's hands
   The genius of Schumann
   using the hands of the greatest female keyboard virtuoso of all time

DIRECTOR *(to* MAX REINHARDT*)*. A touching scene Mr Reinhardt
   isn't it

PUBLISHER. If only Hofmannsthal could see this
   if only Hofmannsthal could experience this

ACTRESS (*to* HELENE THIMIG). Isn't this the pinnacle
Ms Thimig

CONDUCTOR. The pinnacle

ACTOR. Absolutely

PUBLISHER (*to* LOTTE LEHMANN). It's just as you describe in your
memoirs
a once-in-a-century publication
a magnum opus

PIANIST. Entirely different from Clara Haskil

ACTRESS. Schumann has always been
my great love

Offstage, the SOPRANO *announces her approach with a series of thumps and
loud shrieks*

BASS (*alarmed*). It's Gundi

ALL (*gazing in terror at the doorway of the room, as* ELLY NEY *insensibly
continues playing*). It's Gundi

SOPRANO (*standing in the doorway with a half-empty champagne bottle in
her hand, in a menacing tone*). Where is she
where
where

(*Notices* LOTTE LEHMANN *sitting at the table*)

Ah there she is
The Lotte Lehmann
my great role model Lotte Lehmann

(*Slurring her words*)

My role model
Lotte Lehmann
The Marschallin

(*Exclaims*)

The Marschallin
She's sitting right there

(*Walks up to* LOTTE LEHMANN *and hits her over the head with the champagne bottle; the head crashes onto the table, and the* SOPRANO *hits it several more times with the champagne bottle*)

There's your Marschallin for you
there's your Marschallin for you

(ALL *are deeply alarmed, and* ELLY NEY *continues playing calmly and at an even tempo.* SOPRANO *scrutinizes the whole company*)

What are you waiting for
what are you waiting for

(*Screams*)

What the hell are you waiting for
The celebrities
Your bugbears

(*Raises her arm in preparation for delivering another blow to* LOTTE LEHMANN'*s head and rousingly exclaims*)

You've got to smash them
to smash them
smash them to death
your role models
smash them to pieces
to pieces

(*Hits* LOTTE LEHMANN'*s head and screams*)

like this
like this

ACTRESS *picks up a large candlestick from the table and smashes* HELENE THIMIG *to pieces with it without saying a word.* ALL *have now suddenly acquired the confidence to smash their role model to pieces*

SOPRANO. Smash them
smash them
go on
Go on smash them

(*Hits* LOTTE LEHMANN *on the head*)

In a flash, DIRECTOR *draws a knife and stabs* MAX REINHARDT *in the back*

TENOR *seizes* RICHARD TAUBER *by the throat and strangles him*

At the same time, with a single blow of his fist, CONDUCTOR *smashes* TOSCANINI *to pieces*

PUBLISHER *draws a pistol and shoots* SAMUEL FISCHER *in the back of the neck*

PIANIST *leaps to her feet and succumbs to a fit of screaming and lunges at* ELLY NEY, *who is still equably playing the piano, and grabs her head from behind and pounds the keyboard of the Bösendorfer several times with it with her hands.*

BASS (*punches* RICHARD MAYR *and says*). You dog

SERVANTS, *standing against the wall, stare at the scene*

BASS *to* FIRST SERVANT, *seizing him by the throat with both hands*

CONDUCTOR *to* SECOND SERVANT, *seizing him by the throat with both hands*

BASS. Death to the witnesses
    to the witnesses
    Death to them

BASS *and* CONDUCTOR *throttle* SERVANTS *until they collapse*

PUBLISHER *has leapt to his feet and made for the now-shut door, and having reached it, turns around and stares at the scene; then he takes a few steps back into the room and walks up to* SAMUEL FISCHER, *whose head is lying on the table, and once again shoots him in the back of the neck*

CURTAIN

Scene I

THE PERFIDY OF THE ARTISTS

A drawing room; a broad, roofless terrace

The walls are hung with painted portraits of the role models

Each of the actors is sitting in an armchair beneath the portrait of his role model

Enter FIRST *and* SECOND SERVANTS

FIRST SERVANT. It's going to rain my lord

BASS (*with a pair of binoculars hung around his neck*). Rain
Nonsense rain

SECOND SERVANT. There's going to be a thunderstorm

BASS. Nonsense
the weather couldn't be nicer out there

(*Looks outside*)

Clear skies
Wind speed zero
Not a leaf is stirring
in all creation
not a leaf

FIRST SERVANT. That just goes to prove my point my lord

BASS. Nonsense

(*To the others*) Perennial killjoys
First thing in the morning
these naysayers are already at work

(*Gets up, walks out on to the terrace and holds his index finger in the air
Shouts back at the others*)

Nothing
absolutely nothing
The performance will take place
I have rarely been wrong
rarely
If anyone is ever wrong
it's the meteorologists
If the meteorologists say
it's going to rain
you can be sure that it'll be sunny
You have to be mad
to listen to the meteorologists

(*To* SERVANTS) Why don't you bring my guests
something to drink
they're all just sitting there drinkless
A lovely day like this
and nothing to drink
that's bound to make everybody sad
So go make some now

(*Claps his hands and takes a deep breath*)

Summer air
just on the verge of being autumn air
It's summer air
that's just on the verge of being autumn air

CONDUCTOR. We're all rather exhausted
    Six concerts in four days

BASS. And Gundi's bearing the brunt of it

(*Walks up to* GUNDI *and kisses her forehead*)

My poor child
But now
there's nothing like getting away
away
a change of scenery

SOPRANO. I've gotten used to being busy
    The day after tomorrow it'll all be over

BASS. There's still today's performance
then it'll all be over
On a day as splendid as this one
the performance naturally will take place
I hate these outdoor operas

SOPRANO. Palm-trees cypress-trees peasants jackasses
nothing else
and windows giving onto the endless expanse of the ocean

BASS. It will do you good Gundi

(*Sits down*)

When I close my eyes
I fancy
I'm already there
Sea air
No opera
no general manager
no supernumeraries
no audience

(*To* CONDUCTOR) and are you off to St Moritz again

CONDUCTOR. Not this year
I have to undergo a back operation

BASS. Your old complaint right

CONDUCTOR. Once the doctors get hold of you
A specialist from Zurich
A back specialist

PUBLISHER. Zurich is the hometown of back specialists

CONDUCTOR. And kidney specialists

PUBLISHER. Kidney specialists
and back specialists

CONDUCTOR. Then I'll be recording some records
Rheingold in Berlin
at the same time as *Cosi* in Paris
and *Un ballo* in Chicago

SOPRANO. If it comes to that

CONDUCTOR. Which it will do of course
everything has gone to pieces all over

SOPRANO (*to* CONDUCTOR). But are you feeling any pain at the moment

CONDUCTOR. I am never pain-free at any time
The doctor says
I'm crazy to keep conducting

BASS. I've never seen the mountains
as clearly as I can now
Points outside
Look
there
the Untersberg
every cleft is visible
You'd think you could
literally count the trees

(*Peers through the binoculars*)

With my binoculars I can very easily
watch the chamois
for hours on end
so I sit here in my wing chair
an heirloom from my maternal grandmother
and watch the chamois
throw in a piping hot cup of tea
and I forget everything else
No other activity
revivifies me more fully
than watching the chamois
Being able to live in this spot
is a godsend
But naturally such a beautiful location spoils
one's intellect
And genius is mutilated in such a landscape

(*Lowers the binoculars*)

PUBLISHER (*with closed eyes*). Body Soul Mind
   are the elements of the world
   as Epos Lyra and Drama are the elements of poetry

BASS. That's Schopenhauer
   if I'm not mistaken

PUBLISHER. No it's Novalis

BASS. Naturally Novalis
   naturally

   (*Rises and walks out on to the terrace and peers out through the binoculars
   and lowers the binoculars again*)

With a little effort
it is quite possible
to see the chamois with the naked eye
There some peasants are walking
I can see some peasants at the foot of the mountain
They've got rucksacks
walking sticks and rucksacks
I see two laborers from the marble quarry
with their tools
A chamois

   (*Extends his arm and points into the distance.* ALL *gaze out*)

There
there
the chamois
there
now it's gone

   (*Peers through the binoculars again. Enter the* FIRST *and* SECOND
   SERVANTS *with bottled spirits, which they immediately serve*)

It really is a wonderful feeling
to drink milk from the cows in front of my house
every morning
to drink completely unspoiled milk
from completely unspoiled cows
and to eat cheese and bread made by the peasants on my doorstep

(*Takes a deep breath*)

I enjoy this state of affairs
My lungs need this air
the lungs of a bass
which without this air will go to the dogs

(*Takes a deep breath*)

It's as if with every breath I were inhaling
nature in its entirety

(*Raises his index finger into the air*)

Wind speed zero and holding

(*Steps into the drawing room*)

(*To the* SOPRANO) I'm sure
the performance will take place
This speculation that there'll be a storm today
is unfounded
I hate nothing more
than these outdoor operas

CONDUCTOR. They've become all the rage everywhere

BASS. Not to mention
that outdoor music
is of debatable value
it's invariably substandard
the wind dishevels the music in the air

CONDUCTOR. Time and again nothing but the pathological will
to want to be original
Pretty soon there won't be a backyard in this town
that hasn't hosted an opera performance

DIRECTOR. Outdoors it isn't even a work of art

CONDUCTOR. It's now considered normal
to use every nook and cranny of the city as a stage

FIRST *and* SECOND SERVANTS *serve sandwiches*

BASS (*to* FIRST SERVANT). Well what have we here

(After taking a bite from a sandwich)

The best sandwiches
in existence
made personally by the countess
made fresh daily by the countess

CONDUCTOR *(after taking a bite from a sandwich)*. Phenomenal

BASS. A tradition
   the afternoon salmon sandwich
   the salmon sandwich in the afternoon
   That was my last Ochs yesterday evening
   Emanuel List sang him five hundred times
   At the Metropolitan alone I sang Ochs
   a hundred and thirty times
   with the most celebrated partners
   Reining Schwarzkopf et cetera

CONDUCTOR. Bing said
   you were the best Ochs
   that he had ever heard at the Met
   And Bing is unquestionably
   the best general manager of an opera company there has ever been

   (To PUBLISHER*)* Bing's memoirs are a standard work

PUBLISHER *shrugs*

CONDUCTOR *(to* BASS*)*. When one is oneself a baron
   an actual baron like you
   and sings Ochs
   that's authenticity

DIRECTOR. An actual baron
   who moreover happens to be literally and certifiably
   related to the real Ochs von Lerchenau
   the actual historical figure

CONDUCTOR. There is indeed a thoroughly uncanny resemblance
   between you my lord
   and the historical figure

BASS. People do of course say
    that I am related to the actual Ochs von Lerchenau
    but nothing's been proved
    people say it
    the historians aren't of one mind on the question
    Von Lerchenau did indeed hail from a family of brewers
    like me
    von Lerchenau is no invention of Hofmannsthal's
    his actual historical existence has been proved beyond a doubt

CONDUCTOR (*to* BASS). How ever did you find this magnificent summer
        residence
    When did you settle here

BASS. In 'sixty-nine
    Back then it was still possible
    with the fee
    for my thirty-eighth Ochs at the Met
    A windfall
    But don't forget
    the whole thing when I bought it was
    a ruin
    a ruin

    (*Muses*)

    By Siepi's own report I know
    that for a single evening he once got
    twenty thousand dollars
    here
    in Salzburg
    The management paid him in cash
    as he wished
    He could sing with ease and relaxation
    But that was of course a one-time thing

DIRECTOR. The artist of modest needs
    is a mythical creature
    A great artist is demanding
    and he can never demand enough

because his art is absolutely priceless
There is no sum too high
to be paid to a significant artist
let alone to the greatest artists
to the most significant the most extraordinary
the most celebrated ones
The State whines and moans
but what is the State without high art
Muck quite simply nothing but muck

PUBLISHER (*quoting musingly*). In the State everything is dramaturgy
in the nation everything is drama
The life of the nation is a drama

BASS. One has only to bring a publisher into the house
and the world instantly turns into a world of the mind

DIRECTOR. The State exists
but it lives only through its artists

CONDUCTOR. Beautifully spoken

DIRECTOR. But our moronic politicians
and our querulous journalists
can't comprehend this
or they don't want to comprehend it

CONDUCTOR. Our moronic politicians comprehend nothing

DIRECTOR. The politicians in charge of our State
are in a quite genuine sense the gravediggers of the State
Our members of parliament are killing our State
that is the truth
Every four years the people vote
their gravediggers into parliament
they elect well-behaved morons to be gravediggers in parliament
The highest-paid gravediggers
are sitting in parliament

CONDUCTOR. Politicians are by their nature
opposed to artists

A lifelong deep-seated enmity
you must know
Artists see through politicians
and see through nothing but morons
puffed-up morons

PUBLISHER. But the politicians have power

DIRECTOR. Politicians have the power
to ruin the State
politicians ruin the State who else would
Every single one of these creatures becomes a politician
in order to ruin the State
Parliament is a den of cutthroats
a den of cutthroats
When a politician makes his entrance
it's the entrance of a genuine gravedigger of the State
What artists and scholars have built up
is ruined by politicians
Every day artists create the world anew
and politicians ruin it

BASS. Truly spoken

PUBLISHER (*quoting*). Only an artist
can divine the meaning of life

BASS (*to* PUBLISHER). Novalis I presume

PUBLISHER. Naturally Novalis
who else

BASS (*peering through his binoculars*). These tranquil soundless afternoons
in which absolutely nothing is stirring
are made for meditation

(*Stretches out his legs*)

To stretch out one's legs
stretch them all the way out

(*Lowers the binoculars and closes his eyes*)

and recapitulate one's life

or one's existence
a thoroughly mathematical procedure
And to make art
with one's eyes closed
to make music for oneself
to let the whole panoply of instruments
play and sing

DIRECTOR (*with eyes closed*). Closing one's eyes often effects
a complete penetration of the world
of all matter

PUBLISHER (*with closed eyes*). To have the courage
to penetrate everything
the entire drama

BASS. From my grandfather
whom I loved as I did no other human being
and who has remained the most important human being in my life
I acquired the ability
to remove myself from the world
from time to time
I am quite simply gone

SOPRANO. If he'd never had his grandfather
what a natural human being our friend would be

BASS. Talent
mathematics
physics
geophysics
nature in its entirety
I got from him

SOPRANO. In our house at the seaside
he talks about his grandfather
even during the night

DIRECTOR. He simply hails
from a thoroughly creative family

CONDUCTOR. Families in the brewing business are exceedingly creative
    Just think of the Strauss family
    or of Richard Mayr
    We owe almost the entire history of music
    to brewers

BASS (*rises and walks onto the terrace*). Last year they nearly built
    me a skyscraper
    They wanted to extend the sprawl of the city
    all the way here to my front doorstep
    At the last minute I managed
    to prevent the catastrophe
    There were already surveyors on the site

    (*Turns around*)

    A skyscraper can you believe it
    forty-two stories high
    between my summer residence and the Untersberg
    Even now I often wake up at night
    from this nightmare
    I had just arrived at the Met
    for my first Iago with Mirella Freni
    when my caretaker wrote to me
    that a skyscraper was set to be built right outside my windows
    Detained in New York for six weeks
    and the whole time
    even when I was onstage the image haunted my mind
    a forty-two-story skyscraper looming right outside my windows
    upon my return
    I managed to prevent the whole thing

    (*Gesturing towards outside*)

    I managed to bribe the mayor
    and the city council
    I also pulled strings with the chancellor of the republic
    and even the president of the republic
    I blackmailed the management of the festival
    I made it clear that if the skyscraper were built

I'd never sing another note
The skyscraper wasn't built
It was then that I saw quite distinctly
how powerful an artist can be

CONDUCTOR. What would the festival be without you my lord

DIRECTOR. Nothing but mediocrity would be possible

BASS (*suddenly, peering through the binoculars*). There there
there

(*Points into the distance. All gaze outside, rise, and walk on to the terrace.*
BASS *still pointing*)

The eagle
over there the eagle
the eagle is circling
look there
the eagle

ALL *look at the eagle*

CONDUCTOR. An actual eagle

DIRECTOR. That sure is one colossal bird

ACTOR and TENOR (*in perfect unison*). The king of the skies

ACTRESS. A real live eagle

SOPRANO. To think that eagles still exist

PUBLISHER. For the first time I'm seeing
an eagle
until today I'd known them
only from books of natural history

ALL *look aloft at the eagle*

BASS. When the wind speed is zero
the eagle circles
in front of the Untersberg

(*Raises his index finger into the air*)

Wind speed zero
absolute zero

CONDUCTOR. How distinctly one can see everything

ACTRESS. Every tree

SOPRANO. Everything is distinct

DIRECTOR. Superdistinct

BASS. I had to do a fair bit of shopping around
    to find this place
    at first I was planning
    to build my own house
    but then
    on account of my commitments
    I decided
    to buy an old building
    Then I found this castle
    It belonged to the prince-archbishop
    in the eighteenth century
    The place oozes with tradition
    It's a protected historical site

    (*Surveys his surroundings*)

    And with all these works of art here
    these precious objects you now behold
    it cost me only an average half-year's income
    But those days are long since over

PUBLISHER (*quoting*). He who now has no house

BASS. Our publisher
    our quoter

CONDUCTOR. Is that the only eagle
    there is here

BASS. The only one
    he always traces the same circles

DIRECTOR. Always the same circles
    just as the great artist
    always traces the same circles

PUBLISHER. The true artist
  is invariably a creator of an art that is always the same
  Just think of Mozart

CONDUCTOR. Two measures and it's Mozart
  Or Beethoven
  he is always the same
  with only minor modifications

PUBLISHER. Intimate modifications
  You will observe this phenomenon
  in all significant artists
  they all produce nothing but a single work
  that they always modify intimately incessantly imperceptibly

DIRECTOR. This is precisely what makes them great

PUBLISHER. Only a second-rate artist incessantly makes
  obvious modifications
  and hops in one direction one time and in another the next
  Genius is always obdurately the same
  Outwardly unwavering
  inwardly and outwardly obdurate

BASS. When I bought this castle
  I was unaware of the eagle's existence
  of the fact that an eagle dwelt here
  It was clear to me from the beginning
  that I would have to have a house in the country
  I have been living in the country
  since long before it became fashionable
  to live in the country
  in any case I have always lived in the country
  as much as I possibly could
  Even lungs as unslayable as mine
  decay in the big city
  A bass alternates between catching his breath in the country
  and exhaling his voice in the great opera houses of the world

CONDUCTOR. What a panorama
As if it were already history

BASS. Emanuel List once said to me
stay in the country half the year
and the other half sing in the big city
to rake in the money
But let's sit back down shall we

(ALL *reenter the drawing room and resume their seats*)

This place is at its loveliest
after the end of the festival
when all the hoopla has died down
When I am alone with my servants
here I can rehearse my roles without being disturbed
and pace up and down here in the drawing room and on the terrace
The most difficult roles are as easy as can be in these environs
look

(*Points at the portraits of the role models*)

Here among all these role models on the wall

(*Points at the portrait of* RICHARD MAYR)

The most significant Ochs
and the most significant bass of his time

(*Points at* LOTTE LEHMANN)

the greatest Marschallin of all time
A native of Berlin a German
like all the darlings of Viennese opera

DIRECTOR. Even the great Burgtheater actors
were Germans

BASS. Even our esteemed love and latest Kammersängerin
is German
albeit not from Berlin
but rather from Küstrin

(*To the* PIANIST) And of course our enchanting lady piano virtuoso
is also German

from Mecklenburg

(*Looks out at the terrace*)

I've been offered
thirteen million
an American millionaire
wanted to buy the whole thing outright
But this house is not for sale
While the eagle circles overhead
I pace back and forth in the marble quarry
and rehearse my roles
or I stroll down to the Salzach

DIRECTOR. This town quite simply possesses
a magical attractive force

PUBLISHER. Magic

CONDUCTOR. It's the atmosphere

BASS. I really wanted
to be an actor
and of course I actually did start out as an actor
at the theater in Josefstadt
But then

DIRECTOR. Then you were quite simply too intelligent
to be capable of developing as an actor
An actor must be intelligent
but he mustn't be *too* intelligent
Should he
suddenly
out of the blue become what he can't in certain circumstances prevent
himself
from becoming
namely a scholar
he will cease to be a sufficiently good actor
A good actor is a lifelong natural
if he loses his natural talent

his naturalness
he is lost as an actor
Then they try their hand at directing like me
When an actor has lost his innocence
he tries his hand at directing
The greatest actors haven't yet lost their innocence
even at an advanced old age

BASS. Actors look down upon opera singers
and vice-versa
at the same time they marvel at each other

ACTOR. To enter a poetic text quite impartially
as one would enter an unknown forest
to enter such mysterious natural scenery
in search of a clearing

DIRECTOR. That is quite a subtle characterization
He who renounces nature
also withdraws from art
the highly artistic individual is a wholly natural individual
Genius cannot explain what it itself is
We hear and feel at the same time
and from the one more than from the other

CONDUCTOR. When I was very young I wanted to become an actor
but my father the doctor
wouldn't allow it
He never even got over the fact
that I had opted for music
Music my father always used to say
is hardly a proper occupation
it's a time-filler
a painkiller

ACTOR. Being celebrated
is what it's all about

BASS. All of us sitting here
are celebrities

we may even be the most celebrated celebrities
we *are* the most celebrated celebrities

PUBLISHER (*quoting*). Everything is sorcery
or nothing
The rationality of sorcery

BASS. Every single one of us
has reached the top

FIRST SERVANT (*entering*). Telephone my lord

BASS (*rises*). Excuse me
(*Exit*)

SOPRANO (*with eyes closed*). Just between us here now
a piece of news
that I heard earlier today
He has been appointed to a professorship
Appointed to a professorship by the president of the republic
He mustn't know about it
Not today not yet
He'll get too excited
this will be the biggest surprise he's ever had

(*After a pause*)

He's got everything
but he still isn't a professor

CONDUCTOR. An honorary one

DIRECTOR. Since when have you known this

PUBLISHER. Honorary

SOPRANO. Since yesterday

DIRECTOR (*to* CONDUCTOR). Hasn't it already been three years
since you became a professor

SOPRANO. And I know for a fact
that the mayor is going to appoint him
our honorary mayor

PUBLISHER. Honorary mayor of this city
  which owes so many pinnacles to him

SOPRANO. But please
  let's keep this all strictly sub rosa

  (*Looks at the portrait of* LOTTE LEHMANN)

  Lotte Lehmann once maintained to me
  that her greatest source of pride
  was the fact that at the tender age of fifty
  she had been appointed a professor
  an honorary professor

TENOR. Oh come now
  every person of any standing
  is a professor in this country

PUBLISHER. An honorary professor

SOPRANO (*raising her finger to her lips*). Shhhhh

BASS (*returns*). It was only the roofer

  (*Sits down and stretches out his legs. After a pause*)

  People reproach me
  they say this is luxury
  But for a world-renowned bass
  Just think of Reinhardt
  who bought the Leopoldskron Palace

  (*Muses*)

  Sitting out there on the terrace
  drinking milk eating bread

  (*To* PUBLISHER) I am a trusty consumer of your products
  I have read almost all your publications
  Joyce Heinrich Mann et cetera
  I certainly know a thing or two about world literature

CONDUCTOR. That's most unusual
  For a singer

and what's more a bass
to be an aficionado of literature

BASS. Just think of Proust
He's a must-read author
I have read all of Proust

(*To* SOPRANO) Gundi keeps me supplied with the heavyweight stuff

CONDUCTOR. Think of Walter of Nikisch
they all read a lot
highly educated people
Schuricht for example

BASS. They say a lack of education
is a prerequisite for being a singer

PUBLISHER. But the exception proves the rule

DIRECTOR. Everybody's cut from the same cloth

(*It is getting dark*)

To say nothing of the general managers of theaters
the most educated of whom are undoubtedly those of the opera houses
General managers dread nothing more
than getting involved in a conversation about literature
and dramaturges are by and large idiots

PUBLISHER. It's a statistical fact
that general managers of theaters
read only three or four books a year
one book per quarter
this is a statistical fact

BASS. And the top two of these three books
are the railway timetable and the land register
From time to time I send the servants away
then I am alone with Gundi
we read a book apiece
and make plans
In the evening the smell of the swamp down below on the terrace

(*It is beginning to drizzle*)

and letting a good aphorism
melt on one's tongue

(*To* PUBLISHER *point-blank*) be it an aphorism from Novalis
or from Schopenhauer
German philosophy
is an inexhaustible treasury for a thinking human being
And Gundi cooks
You simply can't imagine
what it's like
when you've just gotten back from New York
and you're jumping straight into a pair of lederhosen
a little hike a spot of work in the garden
It's contrast
that keeps me alive contrast

DIRECTOR. Contrast is everything

CONDUCTOR. Contrast is everything

BASS (*to* PIANIST). Now and then a visit to our lady pianist's house
I knock at her window
a spot of Schumann a spot of Romanticism don't you know
The entire world is here in little
a genuinely beautiful and pleasurable natural environment

(*Looks out at the terrace*)

It's getting cloudy

PUBLISHER. This fall I am publishing
a book by an American professor
who is actually from Vienna
A phenomenal piece of writing
The whole time I've been here I've been thinking
which of us is which character type
described by Sontheimer
that's the scholar's name
A magnum opus
it's all very logically set forth in this book
which I am going to publish in a first edition of eighty thousand copies

These days the general reader appreciates such findings

(BASS *raises his binoculars and remains motionlessly gazing out through them until the end of the scene*)

This work
which must be described as a magnum opus
marks the resumption of our series entitled *Sex and Character*
Incidentally it was from Weininger
that I got the idea of quite simply entitling the series *Sex and Character*
Weininger like all great students of human character was Viennese
Freud Weininger you know who I'm talking about

(*To* BASS) When our host stepped out on to the terrace a little while
    ago
to point out the eagle to us
I thought one of us must also be an eagle
or at any rate a rooster
a rooster do you hear me
a rooster or an eagle
and an array of other animal creatures
for each of us resembles a particular species of animal creature
So I sat there the whole time and thought
which of us is essentially which species of animal
There has never been a more informative book on human beings
than this one
Freud was nothing but a precursor
the whole body of previous sexological and characterological research
    nothing but a precursor
If I were now to ask you all

(*The rain starts becoming heavy*)

which animal's head are you wearing

(*The rain becomes even heavier*)

You must buy the book
Instinct and space
have much in common
says Novalis
It will be one of our biggest-ever commercial successes

The rain becomes even heavier

FIRST SERVANT. It's raining my lord

SOPRANO (*delightedly*). It's raining

BASS. In fact it's pouring

PIANIST. It's really pouring

Loud thunder

DIRECTOR. The meteorologists were right

BASS. From time to time the meteorologists are right

Even louder thunder

CURTAIN

Scene II
THE REVELATION OF THE ARTISTS

The dining hall

ALL, *with the heads of animals, merrily tipsy, sitting, eating, and drinking around the table*

SERVANTS, *with rats' heads, are waiting on the feasters*

BASS (*with an ox's head*). Then he became a privy councilor
   a privy councilor
   can you believe it a privy councilor
   and a performer of Mozart to boot
   a veritable festival artist

ALL *laugh*

CONDUCTOR (*with a rooster's head*). A masterclass
   at the academy as a retirement plan

PUBLISHER (*with a fox's head, to* CONDUCTOR). Most highly honored
      sir
   is it not true
   that artists
   are society's stepchildren
   stepchildren

BASS. Dig in everybody
   dig in
   it's all here
   everything's here
   everything

PUBLISHER. You know Böhm
   not everything Böhm does
   is outstanding

CONDUCTOR. The most exceptional talents
  are from the East Indies
  I've got a Burmese pupil
  a genius I tell you
  Asia in general is
  a huge reservoir of talent
  quite extraordinary musical gifts
  I tell you
  the entire Orient is still undiscovered

BASS (*to* ACTRESS, *who has a cow's head*). Dig in why don't you
  dig in
  help yourself

  (*Summons* SERVANTS *by clapping*)

  And at the proper moment
  dessert

  (*To* PIANIST, *who has a goat's head*) Those were the days
  when Clara Haskil
  used to sit where you're sitting
  In that very chair towards nine o' clock
  she would always have her attack of migraine

CONDUCTOR. The bane of instrumentalists
  is their susceptibility to illness
  it's always some illness or other
  that prevents them from totally devoting themselves
  I repeat totally devoting themselves to their calling their art
  How much better Arrau for example would be
  if he weren't always getting those neck pains

BASS (*laughing*). Pianists
  especially female pianists
  get cramps in their fingers
  Cellists get arthritis

PUBLISHER. And violinists I know for a fact
  have got it in their elbows

CONDUCTOR. Exactly
  in their elbows

TENOR (*bursts out laughing*). In their elbows

BASS. What they lack in their fiddle bows
  they make up for in their elbows

CONDUCTOR. And conductors
  have got it in their spinal columns

BASS. The singers have got it in their lungs
  and if not in their lungs
  then in their very throats
  (*Opens his mouth wide*)
  Look
  (*Points into his throat*)
  There at the back
  there
  The so-called gold in the throat
  is often nothing other
  than cancer of the larynx
  (*Summons the servants by clapping*)
  So what's for dessert

FIRST SERVANT. Ice cream my lord

BASS. Ice cream
  no ice cream for me
  Ice cream when we're almost all vocal-cord artists
  vocal-cord artists

DIRECTOR. An excellent term for describing
  singers and actors
  vocal-chord artists
  vocal-chord artists

BASS. Ice cream for the vocal-chord artists
  Bring on the ice cream
  Serve up the ice cream
  ice cream galore
  Ladies love eating ice cream
  don't they

SECOND SERVANT. And cream-cheese strudel

BASS. Ladies and gentlemen
    cream-cheese strudel
    Cream-cheese strudel
    made personally by the countess
    cream-cheese strudel made with her own hands

CONDUCTOR. Hence literally noble cream-cheese strudel

SERVANTS *return to their places away from the table*

BASS. It is a well-known fact
    that Chaliapin
    ate ice cream every day
    Caruso on the other hand once had to take
    a year off on account of a serving of ice cream that he had eaten
    at the Vienna Naschmarkt
    and this at the pinnacle of his career

DIRECTOR. It's said that
    this serving of ice cream indirectly caused
    his death

BASS. It is the scourge
    of the singer

    (*To* PIANIST) My dear
    how ever is your left leg doing

    (*To* OTHERS) She can't play any of the pedals
    She's been playing a full week without pedals
    She gave in to our esteemed colleague
    Claudio Arrau
    and went with him on a ski trip
    to the Engadin where she promptly broke her leg

DIRECTOR. Ski trips are the scourge of stage actors

CONDUCTOR. You're telling me
    You're telling me
    As if there could be anything more moronic than a ski trip
    ski trips are a mass delusion

a mass delusion
and yet everyone makes a pilgrimage to the mountains
with their skis on their back
just to break their legs

PIANIST. The difficult thing is
not to get out of practice afterwards

CONDUCTOR. There's no escaping the fact that not everything
can be played without the pedals
Such that for quite some time now you have been
a pedalaplegic

ALL *laugh*

BASS. We hope your pedalaplegia
is by no means long-lasting

CONDUCTOR. It's precisely for her use of the pedal
that she is celebrated

BASS. We'll all keep our fingers crossed for her
keep them crossed
very tightly

(DIRECTOR *raises* PIANIST's *right hand and crosses index fingers with her*)

Everybody's got to keep the artists' fingers crossed
keep their fingers perpetually crossed
Perpetually crossed

(*Bursting into laughter*)

Perpetually crossed

SOPRANO (*with a cat's head*). A pianist's legs
are at least as important
as her fingers

SERVANTS *serve cream-cheese strudel*

BASS. The true artist
is incessantly in conflict
with his art

PUBLISHER (*quoting*). The authentically industrious
    are stimulated by difficulties

BASS. Truly spoken
    The authentic artist takes the road
    that no one else takes
    the most difficult road of all

ACTOR (*with a dog's head*). He is perpetually
    in a conflict situation

BASS. In return for which it's only right and fair
    that he should see that he is handsomely paid
    But of course taxes eat it all up
    it's all eaten up by taxes
    You won't believe how much was taken
    from me in taxes last year alone
    I was left with at most
    a tenth of the gross
    So it's entirely natural
    for the guarantees demanded by artists
    to assume gigantic proportions

DIRECTOR. An artist is an ideal artist
    when he is also a good businessman
    otherwise he will unfailingly
    at all times walk into a trap
    The opera houses are traps

BASS. Traps that artists walk straight into
    all great stages are basically traps
    Anybody who knows this covers his back
    with horrendously huge guarantees
    Emanuel List once said to me
    always demand three times as much as the top fee
    in other words at least three times as much
    as your predecessor got
    And so when I sang Ochs at the Met
    I demanded three times as much as List

three times as much as List
and List got the top fee
the top fee that's ever been paid at the Met
The most expensive Ochs
that's ever sung at the Met

DIRECTOR. The managements try by every conceivable means
to oppress the artists
the artists in turn are intimidated by
the managements'
blackmailing

BASS. Opera-singing can be quite literally
a big business
The general managers give in
they pay the demanded fees
The general managers blackmail the artists
why shouldn't the artists also blackmail the general managers
The artists must recoup their losses
The theaters especially the opera houses
throw millions out the window every year
The art of singing has never before
been at such a premium
My tactics which I owe to List
But the days of this ideal situation
are numbered
soon the pipeline will be shut off
Right now we've got to squeeze out of them
what's left to be squeezed out

(*Drains his glass, which is then immediately refilled*)

(*To* CONDUCTOR) My most highly honored colleague
compared with you I'm just small fry

(*Looks around the room*)

This tiny bit of luxury
when I can no longer afford this tiny bit of luxury
List stopped singing out of the blue
but not because his doctors had recommended

that he should stop
List had quite simply had enough
He suddenly felt that he'd had it up to his neck with the entire singing
    profession
up to his neck in the truest sense of the idiom
No advance notice
nothing else
he exited the stage

CONDUCTOR. List had a very high level of intelligence
I remember
one time when I was conducting *Fidelio*
at Covent Garden with List
and Helena Braun and Frantz
suddenly
before his big aria

BASS. Which you in defiance of tradition didn't cut

CONDUCTOR. No never
I never cut arias
suddenly before his big aria

BASS (*half-singing*). If you haven't got gold in your pocket

CONDUCTOR. Yeah that one that one

BASS. Suddenly his voice was gone right
I know

(*Half-singing*)

Life plods along
so sadly

CONDUCTOR. I would have been delighted to conduct a *Fidelio* with
    you in it
but it just never worked out

BASS. What a pity
a real pity
But perhaps an opportunity will yet arise

CONDUCTOR. The performance had to be interrupted
But when I went to List's dressing room to ask him what happened
List told me
his voice had come back
List laughed and told me
that now his voice was back he laughed
do you understand he laughed
But by then the audience had all left

DIRECTOR. A medical phenomenon

CONDUCTOR. All of a sudden his voice was gone
All of a sudden it was back again
List attributed it all to
a sedative tablet he had taken the day before
it was the day on which List was knighted
along with Bing incidentally
before this ceremony at Buckingham palace
His doctors denied that there was any connection

PUBLISHER. Doctors always deny that there is any connection

(*Quoting*)

The art of medicine says Novalis
is undoubtedly the art
of killing

BASS (*to* TENOR). My esteemed colleague
are you by any chance also familiar with this
with the voice suddenly disappearing
and suddenly coming right back

TENOR (*hoarsely, while mutely pointing at his larynx*). Today I've got no
voice at all
a cold
perhaps a cold
perhaps
I'm not quite sure

BASS. Then you really shouldn't be eating ice cream
that's just mad
He's got to sing this evening

and he's eating ice cream

(*Exclaims*)

It's madness
utter madness

(*To* FIRST SERVANT) Confiscate the distinguished vocalist's ice cream
Confiscate it
That's just totally mad
It's madness

ACTRESS *bursts out laughing.* PIANIST *bursts out laughing.* ALL *burst out laughing as* FIRST SERVANT *confiscates* TENOR'*s ice cream*

BASS (*to* TENOR). Have some of the cream-cheese strudel my esteemed
    colleague
it soothes the vocal cords
Eat some
eat some

(*To* OTHERS) He's an old pro
but without a voice even the greatest old pro can't sing

(*To* TENOR) Do you actually often eat ice cream

TENOR *shakes his head*

BASS. Remember Caruso
remember Caruso

(*To* OTHERS) Young people think
they can indulge themselves in everything

(SERVANTS *serve coffee*)

Young artists let
everything hang by a thread

DIRECTOR. As I keep on telling them
all these highly talented actors

BASS. Dig in ladies and gentlemen
dig in

DIRECTOR. Who I rehearse my plays with
for all their talent they waste their lives in the most foolish manner
some of them squander themselves on drink

others squander themselves on whores
and the most talented among them squander themselves completely
    on both
drink and whores
First I think
there's a talent
out of this talent I can make a Homburg
or a Hamlet
and then at rehearsals
he turns out to be a total wreck
I can't make a Homburg or a Hamlet
out of a wreck
The most gifted of them attach themselves to some average slut
who's far too lousy even for the suburban theaters
and ruin themselves in no time flat
Not even a genius is immune
to being ruined by a slut like that
First I hear a splendid voice and I vow to myself
with this voice
that this utterly extraordinarily beautiful and gifted individual belongs
    to
I shall rehearse Hamlet
and half a year later a ruin shows up
for the dress rehearsal
It's insanity the things all these young people get up to

CONDUCTOR. Once you turn forty
    you're in safe territory
    then you stop letting everything hang by a thread

BASS. What you mean
    is that then you start
    letting everything hang by a lasso

SOPRANO (*reprovingly*). Now now

BASS. Young people
    are shoved into the meat grinder
    by their unscrupulous teachers

by all these unscrupulous singing teachers
all these opera houses are
a single giant melodramatic meat grinder

DIRECTOR. Artists are such delicate creatures
one tiny case of sore throat
can throw an entire opera season into chaos

CONDUCTOR. You're right about that
Bing once told me
how happy he was
after three years of preparation
to be able to start his best season ever
then all of a sudden
on the evening of the first performance
Birgit Nilsson got a sore throat
and the whole season went to pieces
a mishap like that makes an entire opera season collapse

BASS. I once happened
to spoil a performance
It made headlines
I was supposed to be singing Ochs at Paris
at the same moment when I was guilelessly sitting
at the Cavaletto in Venice
Edelmann leapt into the breach for me
I've always been grateful to him for that
But you've got to be already world-famous
to get away with something like that
To be engaged to sing Ochs at the Paris Opera
and to forget about it

(*Bursts into loud laughter, exclaims*)

Servants servants

(*To* OTHERS) How refined
to have oneself waited on by rats

(*To* CONDUCTOR) Between you and me
the whole time I've been thinking

we're all animals
I think I'm sitting opposite a rooster
as though you were sporting a rooster's head
And Gundi were sporting a cat's head
an actual cat's head

(*Laughs*)

And our pianist a goat's head
a goat's head

(*Laughs*)

(*To* PUBLISHER) You sly fox

(*To* OTHERS) You aren't angry at me
for not telling you
what you all look like to me now

PUBLISHER (*quoting with a raised index finger*). Elements of a fairy tale
Abstraction weakens
Reduction strengthens

BASS (*to* SERVANTS). Now pour us some champagne

SERVANTS *fetch the bottles of champagne and open them*

BASS. Here we drink real champagne
not Sekt
champagne
champagne
I am no Sektarian

(*Looks around, nobody is laughing*)

Champagne makes everything bearable

(*Looks around the table.* ALL *burst into raucous laughter that instantly stops when the first cork pops*)

The rats are pouring champagne
The rats are pouring champagne

(*Drinks*)

How refined

ALL *drink*

BASS (*to* SOPRANO). Meow
meow

(*Barks at* TENOR. *Grunts at* DIRECTOR. *Bleats at* PIANIST. *Moos at*
ACTRESS. *Raises his glass*)

To the management
to the management

ALL (*raise their glasses*). To the president
To the president of the festival
Long may
he live

ALL (*in only vague unison*). Live
live
live

BASS. A characterful wine
Eh what do you think

CONDUCTOR. Excellent

DIRECTOR. Excellent

TENOR. Excellent

PUBLISHER. Phenomenal
I believe you are
all currently figures of indisputably international renown
at the pinnacle of the internationality of your celebrity

BASS. Fabulous
that's just fabulous
an absolutely capital formulation

DIRECTOR. Our publisher
is a stylistic treasury
everything he says
is a quotation
He is a quoter

(*Raises his glass and exclaims*)

To the quoter
to our quoter

(*Raises his glass higher*)

ALL (*raise their glasses and exclaim*). To our quoter

DIRECTOR. An enormous power to fascinate
emanates from celebrity
from this very table
one might say
An opera singer is a genuine monarch of artistic high society
and the bass essentially
is its king

(*Raises his glass, encouraging the others*)

To the king of all opera singers
To the king of the opera

ALL *raise their glasses and drain them.* SERVANTS *refill them*

BASS. But how much it has cost me
to become
what I am
A young man of course never believes
he'll reach the summit
he keeps believing this
until he has reached the summit

PUBLISHER. You are undoubtedly
at the summit today my lord

DIRECTOR. The most celebrated figure in the operatic world
the most celebrated worldwide

CONDUCTOR. I still remember
your first evening my lord
I had the good fortune
to conduct that performance
A completely unknown singer
emerged from the wings
I was worried in the extreme

as you can well imagine
because the young man was a completely unknown quantity
It is of course asking a great deal
of a highly celebrated conductor
to require him to sign off on a totally unknown singer at the last
    minute
but that's what saved the performance

DIRECTOR. A felonious demand on the part of the management

CONDUCTOR. It was indeed a felonious demand on the part of the
    management
And there wasn't even a single rehearsal
believe it or not
not a single rehearsal
But then suddenly this Figaro
started singing as I had never heard a Figaro sing before

(*To* BASS) that was the beginning of your career
the beginning of your celebrity my lord

BASS (*to* CONDUCTOR). A stroke of luck ladies and gentlemen
to happen upon the greatest conductor of one's time
and thereby become great oneself

PUBLISHER. Here a publisher
can only be a gatecrasher
a gatecrasher
a gatecrasher

BASS. Did you hear that
A gatecrasher a gatecrasher

(*Raises his glass and says*)

Let's drink to the gatecrasher
to our gatecrasher
to our gatecrasher the publisher

PUBLISHER. Absolutely
absolutely a gatecrasher of the arts

ALL *raise their glasses and drain them*

BASS. And yet a person like our publisher
  spends most of his time
  dealing with authentic specialists in creation
  with absolutely high art
  which is my preferred term for poetry

  (*Point-blank to* PUBLISHER, *while having his glass refilled*) An entire
      head full of poetry
  the entire history of poetry in a single
  head
  I ask myself
  how can a person stand it
  I think to myself
  the head of a person like that
  would have to explode in the blink of an eye
  All those thousands and hundreds of thousands of
  works
  in a single head
  That's certainly not my idea of fun

  (*Suddenly summoning* SERVANTS *by clapping*)

SERVANTS *open bottles of champagne*

BASS (*imperiously*). Champagne ladies and gentlemen
  Champagne you rats

PUBLISHER. Poetry
  is beyond the reach of
  the performing classes

BASS (*pounding the table-top with both fists*). Champagne
  Champagne
  Champagne

CURTAIN

Scene III

THE VOICES OF THE ARTISTS

ALL *as in the preceding scene rising from their chairs and raising their glasses in a common toast as their increasingly and soon unbearably loud animal voices are heard from numerous loudspeakers mounted on every side of the stage, with the rooster's abrasive cock-a-doodle-doo sounding three times above all the other voices*

THE END

IMMANUEL KANT

. . . which isn't to say
That one must imitate life in the theater . . .
—Antonin Artaud

Dramatis Personae

KANT

KANT'S WIFE

ERNST LUDWIG

FRIEDRICH, *a parrot*

MILLIONAIRESS

CAPTAIN

ADMIRAL

ART COLLECTOR

STEWARD

STEWARD'S ASSISTANT

COOK

SHIP'S OFFICERS

SAILORS

PASSENGERS

DOCTORS

MALE NURSES

MUSICIANS

On the High Seas

FOREDECK

Two folding chairs, six non-folding chairs
STEWARD *is standing behind the folding chair at stage left and saluting*
Enter KANT *and his wife, followed by* ERNST LUDWIG (*carrying the covered cage containing* FRIEDRICH *in his right hand, and a bag of birdseed in his left*)
Steam-whistles sound

STEWARD (*springing to attention*). Good morning, Professor Kant

    (KANT *steps in front of him, appraises the folding chair*)

    Wind west-
    northwest
    Professor Kant

MRS KANT. It's cool today

    (*To* STEWARD) today you must cover up my husband
    especially well

STEWARD. Wind west-northwest
    Excellent weather conditions
    they're excellent Professor

    (*Steam-whistles sound*)

    Mrs Kant
    I have personally consulted the chief meteorologist

    (*Turning to* KANT) on your instructions Professor Kant

KANT. All possible degrees
    of eccentricity
    from those of planets
    to those of comets

MRS KANT. Last night my husband requested
   a second blanket
   but nobody brought him
   a second blanket
   He has suffered since his sixth year

   (*Steam-whistles sound*)

   from a tendency to catch colds

KANT. Nature works here
   as it does elsewhere
   through imperceptible declines
   imperceptible ones

   (STEWARD *and* MRS KANT *adjust* KANT's *folding chair. Steam-whistles sound.* KANT *observing the two of them*)

   I am talking about the precisely circular motion
   of the particle
   of the basic substance
   but also about the purposelessness
   of nature
   ladies and gentlemen

   (*Suddenly, while* MRS KANT *and* STEWARD *are adjusting* KANT's *folding chair, to* ERNST LUDWIG)

Don't remove the cover abruptly
don't do it abruptly
Friedrich's eyesight
is priceless
So-called scribes
and parrots
have the most sensitive eyesight
The true philosopher
in himself
Remove the cover
slowly
quite slowly
only little by little

(*Peremptorily*)

Set him down

(ERNST LUDWIG *makes as if to set the cage down in a non-folding chair*)

Not *there*
not in *that* chair
in the chair next to my chair
Friedrich must be immediately within reach

(*Points with his cane at the non-folding chair next to his*)

put him there

FRIEDRICH. There there

KANT. Naturally there

ERNST LUDWIG *sets the cage down in the non-folding chair next to* KANT's *folding chair*

MRS KANT. Such an intelligent
such a highly philosophical animal

KANT. Psittacus erithacus
the philosopher-in-himself
in itself
in-itself

FRIEDRICH. Psittacus erithacus

MRS KANT. He looked quite listless
this morning
but then my husband said his name
My husband said Friedrich Friedrich Friedrich

KANT. Friedrich

FRIEDRICH. Imperative imperative imperative

ERNST LUDWIG *starts to tug at the cover of the cage*

KANT (*striking him on the finger with his cane*). *No* not
like *that*
Cautiously
little by little

FRIEDRICH. Little by little
cautiously

KANT. Everybody's always making such
oafish gesticulations
and disturbing
and frightening him

MRS KANT (*to* KANT). Aren't you going to sit down

KANT (*as if he has not heard her*). Specifically
with a gentle touch
with sensitivity

(*Tugs gently at the cover of the cage*)

(*To* ERNST LUDWIG) You must tug
at the cover like this
carefully
extremely carefully
very carefully
only little by little
can the light
penetrate the cage
Psittacus erithacus
is the most sensitive of species

MRS KANT (*to* ERNST LUDWIG *in an accusing tone*). Ernst Ludwig
you've been with us for twenty-five years now
and you still don't know
how to take the cover off the cage

ERNST LUDWIG *joins* KANT *in tugging at the cover of the cage*

KANT. Like this
little by little

(ERNST LUDWIG *starts tugging slightly faster.* KANT *strikes him on the finger*)

Slowly I say

(*The two of them tug at the cover.* KANT *suddenly*)

Not yet
not yet

MRS KANT (*to* KANT). Do sit down

KANT (*steps up to his folding chair*). The farther
the diffused parts
of the primordial material
are from the sun
the weaker is the force
that makes them sink

(*Sits*)

Oh no

(*Tries to stand up but fails.* MRS KANT *and the* STEWARD *help him*)

Sometimes it seems to me that
I hear downright poorly
On the other hand
the more poorly I see
the better I hear
A one-of-a-kind race
for eyesight
America
my one and only hope

(*To* STEWARD) Is everything in order

(*Steam-whistles sound*)

on the high seas

STEWARD (*springing to attention*). Everything's in order
on the high seas

KANT (*sits back down after his folding chair is adjusted*). I must
have the ideal line

(*Licks his right index finger and holds it up in the air*)

West-northwest
The ideal line

STEWARD (*springing to attention*). West-northwest
The ideal line

FRIEDRICH. Ideal line ideal line

MRS KANT (*to* ERNST LUDWIG). Move Friedrich
up here right next to my husband

(ERNST LUDWIG *places* FRIEDRICH *right next to* KANT)

Only now that Friedrich
has been placed right next to him
will my husband find the ideal line

KANT (*as if searching for the ideal line, with outstretched arms*). The ideal
line
Now I've got the ideal line

FRIEDRICH. Imperative imperative imperative

KANT (*leaning back*). Back
to the origins of the celestial bodies
to the primordial material
My name is Leibniz he said
Down
into the fundus of history
Possibly
the constriction of the pupil
is traceable to overexertion

(STEWARD *swathes* KANT's *upper body and lower body in two blankets
each*)

The view
of the causes

(*Suddenly*)

Columbia University
is awarding me an honorary doctorate
they're *awarding* me one

(*To* STEWARD) There are no better
ophthalmologists
than the ophthalmologists
of Columbia University
It is no accident that I of all people have received

an invitation from the university
that has the best ophthalmologists in the world
Kant won't lose his eyesight
Between one and two in the morning
my wife reads to me
my *New Estimation of Living Forces*
An absurdity
on the high seas
but it helps me put up with the turbines
This hour of reading has become absolutely essential
The laws have no bearing
on any instances of motion
in the absence of a consideration of their velocity

(*Exclaims*)

Eccentric
Luxury fanatic

(*Suddenly*)

It's too deep
much too deep
(STEWARD *and* MRS KANT *adjust* KANT'*s folding chair*)

Eccentricity
is the noblest of distinguishing traits
among comets

(*Tugs slowly at the cover of the cage to the astonishment of* ERNST
LUDWIG)

Psittacus erithacus

(*Inspects* FRIEDRICH)

Everything is in order

FRIEDRICH. Imperative imperative imperative

KANT (*to* FRIEDRICH). The proceedings have commenced

FRIEDRICH. The proceedings have commenced

KANT (*to* ERNST LUDWIG). Sit down
you blockhead

(*To* MRS KANT) Do sit down my dear

(*With the assistance of* ERNST LUDWIG *suddenly covers* FRIEDRICH. *Then, licking his right index finger and holding it up*)

West-northwest
Full speed ahead

STEWARD (*springing to attention*). West-northwest
full speed ahead

MRS KANT *and* ERNST LUDWIG *sit down*

KANT. Jupiter
Mars
Mercury
Central force

(ERNST LUDWIG *stands up and adjusts the cover of the cage and sits back down*)

Eccentricity
because the sun in its axial rotation
falls far short of Mercury's
velocity

(*Cocks an ear towards* FRIEDRICH)

FRIEDRICH. Falls far short of Mercury's
velocity

KANT. Approximate
orbital velocity
Heat

(*To* MRS KANT) You shouldn't have eaten
the stew yesterday evening

(*To* ERNST LUDWIG) The conscience of the world
is dead in you
conclusively dead

MRS KANT. Ernst Ludwig's sister
is dead
writes her husband

KANT (*to* ERNST LUDWIG). Be of good cheer
　on the high seas
　there's no possibility
　of attending a funeral
　How old was your sister

ERNST LUDWIG. Thirty-seven

KANT. Thirty-seven
　As old as a cat's tongue is long
　as old as a cat's tongue is long

　(*Cocks an ear towards* FRIEDRICH)

FRIEDRICH. As old as a cat's tongue is long
　as old as a cat's tongue is long

MRS KANT *beckons* STEWARD *to her side and whispers something in his ear*

KANT (*simultaneously to* FRIEDRICH). The demons
　which are subject to nature
　The resistance of all parts
　the particle of the primordial material
　West-northwest

FRIEDRICH. West-northwest

MRS KANT (*to* STEWARD). Bring us the menu

　(STEWARD *starts to leave.* MRS KANT *calls him back*)

　Wait steward

　(STEWARD *turns around to face* MRS KANT. MRS KANT *while* KANT
　whispers something to FRIEDRICH)

　My husband would like some tripe
　Tripe
　do you understand

　(*Whispers something into* STEWARD's *ear*)

KANT (*now turned away from* FRIEDRICH *and speaking at the same time
　　as his wife is whispering*). A person who is going blind
　always has a superior sense of hearing

FRIEDRICH. Superior sense of hearing superior sense of hearing

KANT. Leibniz
  my name is Leibniz
  said Leibniz

Exit STEWARD

MRS KANT. This evening
  there's going to be an engagement party on board

KANT. An engagement party

MRS KANT. The millionairess
  is treating the couple to a marzipan torte
  that's three meters in diameter

KANT. I've got the ideal line

MRS KANT. Three meters in diameter
  exactly one hundred and seventy-six centimeters tall
  like the bridegroom-to-be
  do you know who the bridegroom-to-be is

KANT. The optical illusion
  of the nineteen comets is deceptive

FRIEDRICH. Deceptive

MRS KANT. The mineral collector from Gelsenkirchen
  is the bridegroom-to-be
  And do you know
  who she is
  A baroness from Clairvaux

FRIEDRICH.
  from Clairvaux

KANT. The specific density of the material
  is always the same

MRS KANT. The millionairess is traveling
  to America for the third time
  she's been working on raising the *Titanic*
  for twenty years

Her grandmother
went down with the *Titanic*
and with her grandmother sank
all the family jewels
The millionairess is from Ludwigsburg

FRIEDRICH. Ludwigsburg Ludwigsburg Ludwigsburg

KANT (*inquiringly*). From Ludwigsburg

MRS KANT. Coal coke metal

KANT (*to* FRIEDRICH). Psittacus erithacus

FRIEDRICH. Psittacus erithacus

MRS KANT. She makes linocuts
she has even once produced
an exhibition of her linocuts in America

KANT. The optical illusion
of the nineteen comets is deceptive

MRS KANT. She says
she knows you
What's more the captain has read
your *Eccentricity of the Planetary Orbits*
On the last evening
before our arrival in America
we'll be his guests
at the Chinese-lantern party
at his dinner table
along with the cardinal
and the admiral
and with Friedrich naturally
and Ernst Ludwig naturally

KANT. And Ernst Ludwig naturally

(*Enter* STEWARD, *who gives* MRS KANT *the menu.* KANT *suddenly, sitting up*)

That is too deep
much too deep

(*Steam-whistles sound*)
I must have the ideal line

(*The steward adjusts Kant's folding chair. Kant loses patience with* ERNST LUDWIG *and strikes him on the knee with his cane*)

Why are you sitting there
and gaping like that
help the steward

FRIEDRICH. Help the steward help the steward

ERNST LUDWIG *leaps up and helps* STEWARD

KANT. Do you think
I pay you to do nothing

(ERNST LUDWIG *has fallen to his knees before* KANT *and is swathing* KANT's *feet in the blankets.* KANT *is holding his cane with its bottom tip touching* ERNST LUDWIG)

Creatures like you are all paid
for just loafing about
We hired you to be our servant
Friedrich and I
but we're paying for the services of an idiot
you aren't even worth the silver headpiece coins
I've been giving you during the twenty-five years
you've been with us

(*To* MRS KANT) How long has Ernst Ludwig been my
and Friedrich's
and our employee how long

MRS KANT. Twenty-five years

KANT (*shouting*). Twenty-five years

(*To* ERNST LUDWIG) You are every bit as imbecilic as you were on the
first day
You still can't manage
to wrap my feet properly
and when I tell you
to stir my pap every morning

you never manage to do it
to say nothing of your performance of the rest of your duties
Friedrich deserved a better servant

(*To the* OTHERS) I'm constantly having to worry
that this idiot
who's been carrying my priceless Friedrich
behind me for twenty-five years and counting
will drop my Friedrich
and then my Friedrich will be dead
One fine day
he's going to drop him

(*Thwacks* ERNST LUDWIG *on his upper back and addresses him in a hectoring tone*)

and then it'll be time
for the likes of you to settle up
Right now time is on your side
but the day is already in sight
when everything will gang up on you
and on imbecility in general

(*Licks his right index finger and holds it up in the air*)

West-northwest
precisely west-northwest

STEWARD. West-northwest Professor Kant

KANT. Kant
on the high seas
They say that
Kant has
never left
Königsberg
Wherever Kant is is Königsberg

STEWARD (*with a bolster*). What about your bolster
Professor

MRS KANT. Give him the bolster

FRIEDRICH. Bolster bolster bolster

KANT. Give me the bolster

(STEWARD *places the bolster under* KANT'*s neck*)

The earth has something of its own
that may be likened to the diffusion of
the cosmic vapors and their tails

(*Turns to* FRIEDRICH *and whispers something in his ear*)

MRS KANT (*at the same time as her husband is whispering*). From time to
    time my husband
suddenly suffers
from the thinning of the air

KANT (*with his head raised*). The key date
will be a Tuesday

FRIEDRICH. Will be a Tuesday

MRS KANT (*immersed in the menu*). Are we arriving on Tuesday

STEWARD (*springs to attention*). If all goes well
we'll arrive on Tuesday

KANT (*licks his right index finger and holds it up in the air*). West-
    northwest isn't it

STEWARD. West-northwest Professor Kant
    (*Exit*)

KANT (*to his wife*). You shouldn't have eaten
the stew
When on the high seas
every rational human being
eats high seafood
You eat continental food

(*To* ERNST LUDWIG) Your fatty diet
is your curse

(*Cocks an ear towards the cage*)

Psittacus erithacus
is the most intelligent species
For example

seventeen years ago
I dictated the following sentence to him
There is no such thing
as a unique unconditionally universal
fundamental principle of all truths
Yesterday he repeated this sentence to me
verbatim
absolutely verbatim

(STEWARD *approaches with a stack of old newspapers*)

How old are those newspapers

STEWARD. Six weeks old Professor

KANT. Then they're fine
As a matter of principle I only read newspapers
that are at least four weeks old
six weeks old
is even better

(STEWARD *hands the newspapers to* MRS KANT)

These old newspapers
have a salutary effect
they occasion absolutely no irritation
Naturally
as far as the outside is world is concerned
I am
depending on the age of the newspapers
four or five or six weeks behind
The most recent events reported on in them
have long since been forgotten

(*To* STEWARD) At first
thirty years ago
my wife read to me
only from French papers
twenty years ago she suddenly switched to nothing but English papers
nowadays I only still read the German papers
I have never had any ambition

to read Portuguese papers
for instance

(*To* ERNST LUDWIG) Have you thoroughly mixed the birdseed
show it to me

(ERNST LUDWIG *leaps up and towards* KANT. KANT *points at the bag*)

Open it
I want to see
if you've thoroughly mixed the seed
Psittacus erithacus

FRIEDRICH. Psittacus erithacus

KANT. If he tacitly
   mind you tacitly condensed
   several propositions into one
   he would merely
   be deceitfully imposing the illusion
   of a simple fundamental principle

(ERNST LUDWIG *opens the bag and lets* KANT *peer into it.* KANT *inquiringly*)

Half-and-half

ERNST LUDWIG. Half-and-half

KANT. Professor Drahtgut
   maintained
   that the seed should be pulverized
   He was wrong
   Psittacus erithacus
   must partake of entire undamaged kernels
   By now the so-called zoologists
   have brought about the degeneration of the entire animal kingdom

(*To* STEWARD) On Sundays
   my Friedrich receives
   a toasted breakfast-roll
   he consumes it with the greatest gusto
   I once said that to Professor Drahtgut

My Psittacus erithacus
consumes a toasted roll
for breakfast I said
Drahtgut didn't believe me
And so I invited Professor Drahtgut
to breakfast
so that he could be convinced by the evidence of his own eyes
that Friedrich was capable
of consuming a toasted roll

FRIEDRICH. Drahtgut Drahtgut Drahtgut

KANT. That was the only time
  that I put Friedrich on display to a professor
  This man naturally had
  a devastating effect on Friedrich

  (*To* ERNST LUDWIG) You must inspect the seed
  for Friedrich
  inspect every single seed meticulously

  (*Exclaims*)

  To make sure he doesn't swallow any stones
  You'll recall
  that in Höchst
  you once slipped a stone

ERNST LUDWIG. A pebble

KANT. Nonsense a stone
  into the bag
  whether out of inattentiveness
  and hence completely accidentally
  or deliberately
  I do not know

  (*To* STEWARD) Friedrich would have
  almost
  choked to death on it

FRIEDRICH. Choked to death choked to death choked to death

KANT. You should have seen the pallor
   Friedrich's pallor

   (ERNST LUDWIG *makes as if to close the bag.* KANT *stops him from doing so and takes out a sample seed*)

   I always sample a seed
   from the bag
   ever since Ernst Ludwig
   slipped Friedrich a stone in the bag

   (*Sticks the seed into his mouth and chews thoroughly*)

   (*To* ERNST LUDWIG) Are these the Brazilian seeds
   or the ones from Guatemala

FRIEDRICH. The ones from Guatemala

KANT. In other words the Guatemalan seeds

   (ERNST LUDWIG *nods*)

   Actually the seeds
   from Guatemala
   are more wholesome
   than the Brazilian seeds
   more wholesome and cheaper

   (*Point-blank to* STEWARD) It happens quite often
   that something is more wholesome
   and at the same time cheaper
   The most expensive thing isn't always
   also the most wholesome thing

   (*He is quite visibly chewing again*)

   Seed from Guatemala
   for Friedrich

   (*Loudly, while suddenly spitting out the seed*)

   On a luxury liner
   We are after all
   on a luxury liner

   (*To* STEWARD) At first I couldn't

make up my mind
whether to opt
for the Coracopsis vasa

FRIEDRICH. Coracopsis vasa

KANT. Or for the Psittacus erithacus

FRIEDRICH. Psittacus erithacus

KANT. The Coracopsis vasa
lives even longer
Numerous specimens
have surpassed the age of sixty

(*To* FRIEDRICH) In two years
we'll celebrate your fiftieth birthday
Possibly
on the high seas
who knows

(*Looks around*)

I'll charter
an even much larger ship
just for that birthday celebration

(*To* STEWARD *with reference to* FRIEDRICH) He's happiest
when my wife is reading to me
and hence also to him
from the *Nürnberger Nachrichten*
that amuses him
he almost laughs himself to death then
The more serious the article is
the greater the danger is
that he'll laugh himself to death

(*Licks his right index finger and holds it up in the air*)

West-northwest
full speed ahead

STEWARD (*springing to attention*). West-northwest
Full speed ahead

KANT *to* MRS KANT. We can begin

(*Cocks an ear towards the cage. With reference to* FRIEDRICH)
His attentiveness
is superlative
No human being
is possessed of such powers of attention

(*Steam-whistles sound*)

I have delivered my most significant my most important lectures
to Friedrich
I know why whenever I deliver a lecture
Friedrich
is always at the very front of the audience
even in front of my academic colleagues

(*Steam-whistles sound*)

(*To the* STEWARD) That is why Friedrich
is Public Enemy No. 1
more than anyone else university professors loathe him
because he always sits
in the foremost place
The professors envy him
his attentiveness
Nothing escapes his notice
whereas virtually everything
escapes the notice of scholars
From the very beginning
I have always traveled
only with Friedrich
secretly
naturally
throughout Germany
It is said
that Kant has never
left Königsberg
but wherever Kant is
is Königsberg

Königsberg is
wherever Kant is

(*To* FRIEDRICH) Where is Königsberg

FRIEDRICH. Wherever Kant is

KANT. And where is Kant

FRIEDRICH. Kant is wherever Königsberg is

KANT (*exclamatorily*). Psittacus erithacus
Humankind
is monosyllabism
in itself
If the contrary of something
is affirmed
it is itself denied
If the contrary of something
is true
the something itself is false
Leibniz he said
Professor Leibniz

FRIEDRICH. Leibniz Leibniz

KANT. Leibniz was afraid
of Friedrich
Leibniz refused
to give a lecture in Königsberg
because he couldn't bear
Friedrich's presence
On account of Friedrich
Leibniz
turned me down

(*A man suffering from seasickness is led past* KANT *and his companions
by a* STEWARD)

Seasickness is
evidence
of everything

(*To* ERNST LUDWIG) From now on
buy only
the Guatemalan bird seed
stop buying the Brazilian

ERNST LUDWIG. Stop buying the Brazilian

KANT (*raises his head*). It's as though the wind
were changing direction
(*Licks his right index finger and holds it up in the air*)
Wind west-northwest

STEWARD. Wind west-northwest
full speed ahead
Professor

KANT. They say
that going ashore in America on a Tuesday
is bad luck

MRS KANT (*bursting into laughter*). For you
it's good luck
Immanuel
it's good luck for you
What's bad luck for others
is pure good luck for you

KANT (*musingly*). Surely the professors are expecting me
in black
But I'll disembark
in white
(*To all present*) We'll all
disembark in white
white
white
With the exception of Ernst Ludwig
who must disembark in black

MRS KANT. Ernst Ludwig in black
why Ernst Ludwig
in particular

KANT. Because his sister has died

MRS KANT. But Immanuel
surely he needn't disembark in black
just because of that

KANT. Possibly in this case
a black band
on his right arm
will suffice

MRS KANT. Where are we supposed
to get hold of a black suit for Ernst Ludwig

KANT. On a first-class luxury liner
like this one
even black suits in all sizes
can be scrounged up
on a luxury liner like this one
nothing is impossible

(*Directly to* MRS KANT) But you're right
a black armband will do
sew him a black armband

MRS KANT. But of course Immanuel

KANT. His sister's death
obligates him to wear
a black armband at minimum

(*To* ERNST LUDWIG) at minimum
at minimum

ERNST LUDWIG. At minimum

KANT (*to* ERNST LUDWIG). What did she die of anyway

ERNST LUDWIG. Of the garden shovel

KANT. Of the garden shovel

ERNST LUDWIG. The garden shovel
smashed her head to bits

KANT. An absurd death
   to have one's head smashed to bits
   by a garden shovel
   A single clumsy move
   and the garden shovel
   smashes one's head to bits

   (*To* STEWARD) As you know
   we're traveling to America
   for the first time
   to America
   I never had any desire
   to go to America
   A trip to America is an act of perversity
   I am basically taking this one only
   for my wife's sake
   She has dreamed
   of doing this all her life
   Now that Columbia University
   has made an honorary doctor of you
   you've got to go to America
   she said to me
   and I unhesitatingly acquiesced
   Can you believe it
   I acquiesced without hesitation
   I was planning on traveling with nothing
   just with my head and with Friedrich
   and with Ernst Ludwig naturally
   but now we've got a huge pile of luggage
   women always travel with huge suitcases
   A tasteless habit naturally
   For my part
   I'm content
   if I can change my clothes
   every two days
   Everything that is not
   is not

Everything that is
is
The principle of identity
you must be familiar with it

(*Cocks an ear towards the cage*)

Occasionally I think
he's dead as a doornail
but then I discover
that his intensity is at its highest pitch

(*To* STEWARD) When I hear nothing
absolutely nothing
his intensity is at its highest pitch
He mistrusts my wife
he abhors
the female sex
The fact is that my wife once unprecedentedly
made a snide remark about Friedrich
Nobody else has ever dared to do that
my wife once dared
to belittle Friedrich
In Sopot my wife
belittled Friedrich
but I brought my wife
to justice
before Friedrich
she was obliged to apologize to Friedrich
since then my wife hasn't been allowed
to comb Friedrich
a privilege
that my wife enjoyed for thirty years
Only Ernst Ludwig is permitted to comb Friedrich
Friedrich is combed
every day between five and half past five in the morning
One time my wife wanted to put nail polish on his talons
which would have almost driven me mad
only a woman can

think up such a piece of perversity
At night I lock up Friedrich's room
with my own hands I lock up
Friedrich's room at night
and Ernst Ludwig guards it
Here on the ship
we naturally have difficulties
with our living arrangements
I wouldn't have made the voyage at all
if I hadn't managed to get
an extra cabin for Friedrich
an almost fully soundproof cabin
as Friedrich absolutely cannot tolerate any noise at night
Psittacus erithacus
needs absolute nocturnal silence
the most difficult thing to obtain on a ship at sea
My wife fell in love with Friedrich
thirty years ago
I gave her an ultimatum
either or
she had been obliged to renounce Friedrich
Word of this affair had got around
in Königsberg
I sent my wife to Sopot for a year
during this period I was alone with my Friedrich
it was the happiest period of my life
(*To* STEWARD *suddenly*) Full speed ahead

STEWARD (*springing to attention*). Full speed ahead Professor

KANT. An operation
would prove everything naturally
an operation that enabled me to see
the inside of Friedrich's head
I would have complete proof

(*Directly to* STEWARD) This head keeps in storage everything
that has ever been said to it
there is no other head as completely organized as this one
If only I could see the inside of this head

and could keep hold of it
I would have complete proof

FRIEDRICH (*suddenly agitated*). Imperative imperative imperative

KANT. I pondered this American trip with Friedrich
very thoroughly and at great length
There would actually
be no risk
in sending
Friedrich by himself
to the world's universities
he is capable
of providing an unsurpassable summary
of everything I have ever thought

(*Cocking an ear towards the cage*)

It is merely out of arrogance
that science refuses to get involved
in such an adventure
On behalf of Kant
I shall summarize
for example
the principle of contradiction
I can hear Friedrich saying that

(*To* FRIEDRICH) What do you say
at the conclusion of your lecture

FRIEDRICH. I thank you for your attention

KANT. Everything that is
is
Everything that is not
is not
The world is the reverse side
of the world
Truth the reverse side
of truth

(*To* STEWARD *regarding* FRIEDRICH) He lives entirely
in my conceptual world

He abhors
what I abhor
He calls to account
what I call to account

(*Suddenly*)

What is the date of these newspapers anyway

STEWARD. The twenty-fifth

KANT. In other words the twenty-fifth of August

STEWARD. Naturally Professor Kant

KANT. Then today is
the twenty-fifth of September

(*To* MRS KANT) How my eyes long for
the next rainy day
This constant sunlight
almost completely blinds me
If my eyes were my sole consideration
I would spend the entire voyage
below deck
in my cabin
But I believe I'd be bound to suffocate
in the cabin
Friedrich also suffers
from a fear of suffocation
in his cabin

(*To* ERNST LUDWIG) Can't you see
that my feet are freezing

(*To* STEWARD *and his fellow-sitters*) He can't see it
He has the best eyes
and sees nothing

(ERNST LUDWIG *leaps up and swathes* KANT'*s feet even more tightly in the blankets*)

Servants
suffer from absolute blindness

even though
as has been proved
they have the best eyes
they see everything
and nothing

(*Kicks at the blankets and* ERNST LUDWIG *is obliged to swathe them all over again*)

FRIEDRICH (*loudly*). Imperative imperative imperative

KANT. Never in my life
could I have dreamed
of taking a voyage like this one
I'm taking it to save my eyesight

(MRS KANT *whispers something in* STEWARD's *ear*)

A tiny incision
in the iris
a trifling procedure

MRS KANT. You are bringing America reason
America is giving you eyesight

KANT. Kant is going
to America
to save his eyesight

MRS KANT. All America
is expecting you
The newspapers
are full of articles about you

KANT. Columbus discovered America
America has discovered Kant

(MRS KANT *whispers something in* STEWARD's *ear*)

Ernst Ludwig's right arm
is actually
fatter than
his left one

because he's been carrying
Friedrich's cage for thirty years and counting

(MRS KANT *bursts out laughing*. KANT *licks his finger and holds it up*)

West-northwest
full speed ahead

STEWARD (*snaps to attention, salutes*). Wind west-northwest
full speed ahead

FRIEDRICH. Full speed ahead

KANT. The president of the United States
will attend my first lecture
I believe he understands
a great deal about music
he's one of America's few musical personalities

(*To* STEWARD) Naturally I always employ
the indirect syllogistic method

MRS KANT (*to* STEWARD). Behind our house
we've built Friedrich
a house of his own
in which everything is tropical

KANT. Tropical
subtropical

MRS KANT. Every Saturday
Friedrich is in the tropics

KANT. The native habitat
of Psittacus erithacus
Guinea Angola
Lake Victoria you know

(*To* FRIEDRICH) Your native habitat

FRIEDRICH. Native habitat native habitat

KANT. Everything
whose contrary is false
is true

FRIEDRICH. I thank you for your attention

KANT (*suddenly to* STEWARD). Are there icebergs around here

STEWARD. There's no iceberg
  Professor Kant

MRS KANT *whispers something in* STEWARD's *ear*

KANT. Who says
  there isn't
  when they say there's
  no iceberg
  there's an iceberg
  Just think of the Titanic

FRIEDRICH. Titanic Titanic

KANT (*cocking an ear towards the cage*). All those people
  with their luxury
  who went down with the ship
  The dance band played
  while the whole ship was going under

  (*To* STEWARD) Aren't you ever afraid of going
  down with the ship
  Are you a swimmer

STEWARD. I'm a non-swimmer
  Professor Kant

KANT (*exclaims*). A non-swimmer
  He's a non-swimmer
  In your place I'd be worried
  night and day
  I'm a swimmer
  I've always been a good swimmer
  My wife is a non-swimmer
  Ernst Ludwig too can swim

  (*To* FRIEDRICH) And Friedrich can fly
  he can soar above us all
  if need be

MRS KANT *whispers something in* STEWARD'*s ear*

KANT. The first person here
  who will go under
  is Ernst Ludwig

  (*To* MRS KANT) I can just see you
  clinging to Ernst Ludwig
  and Ernst Ludwig
  dragging you down
  What a tragic ending

  (*To* STEWARD) Tell me
  how many lifeboats
  are here and ready to go

STEWARD. Twenty-two lifeboats
  Professor

KANT. Women and children first
  Ah

  (*Covers his eyes with his hands*)

  how my eyes ache
  In point of fact
  I didn't deserve
  glaucoma
  Eyesight
  is the most important thing
  without my eyesight
  my mind will also be lost
  adrift

MRS KANT (*has been studying the menu for some time. To* STEWARD).
  Make sure my husband's veal is minced
  No sauce
  no salad

KANT (*removes his hands from his eyes and gazes out at the ocean*).
  Everything is cloudy
  cloudy

cloudy
cloudy

MRS KANT. I'll have the steak as it is
peppered

FRIEDRICH. Peppered

ERNST LUDWIG *has stood up and is starting to remove the cover of the cage*

KANT (*furiously*). Don't you dare
remove that cover
The glaringly bright light
even bothers me
How much more will it bother Friedrich

ERNST LUDWIG *sits back down, places the bag of birdseed between his knees*

KANT. Entirely different thoughts
on the high seas
than on dry land

(MRS KANT *whispers something in* STEWARD's *ear*)

One's head affirms
what it has denied

(*Lingeringly cocks an ear towards the cage, then*)

Tuesday is my fateful day
which is also your fateful day

MRS KANT *whispers something in the* STEWARD's *ear. Exit* STEWARD *with the menu*

KANT (*to* FRIEDRICH). We belong together
no matter
what the world thinks
the world thinks
nothing but impudent twaddle

MRS KANT (*to* ERNST LUDWIG). Straighten
my husband's head

ERNST LUDWIG *leaps up and straightens* KANT's *head*

KANT (*to* MRS KANT). I believe
  I'm coming
  to America
  at exactly the right time
  Basically I am
  an opponent of Americanism
  I have always detested Americanism
  For decades I have refused to go there
  now I'm going to America
  In this case anyone would go
  Americanism
  is responsible for the end of the world

(*Irascibly to* ERNST LUDWIG) You're hurting me you know
  Haven't I taught you
  all those ways of gripping the head
  thirty years
  and the result is this catastrophe
  I once saw
  your sister
  a lovely child
  It's incredible
  that she was your sister
  Grace incarnate
  and you
  are brimming over with boorishness
  Your sister
  was extraordinarily sensitive
  and you're the antithesis
  (*Pushes him away*)

(*To* FRIEDRICH) We haven't managed to find anybody better
  than this blockhead
  Either
  he gives you the seed to early
  or too late
  People of this stripe

  (ERNST LUDWIG *sits down*)

have no sense of timing
they are totally impervious to any sense of anything
any sense of anything

MRS KANT (*leafing through the newspapers*). Always more assassinations
are you listening
The prime minister of Cambodia
has been assassinated

KANT. All my life I have been against newspapers
all my life I have gobbled them up

(MRS KANT *bursts out laughing*)

Why are you laughing

MRS KANT. It's this caricature

KANT. Everything is a caricature

MRS KANT (*bursts out laughing*). A completely inaccurate weather forecast
Bad weather is predicted
for the month of August

KANT (*bursts out laughing*). To pursue the chain of truths
all the way to its last link
The overthrow of all governments
is immediately imminent
Leibniz said Leibniz
my name is Leibniz

(*To* ERNST LUDWIG) Your kind's signature trait
is disobedience
which those who pay you
and your kind
have to take in their stride
Socialism
is lethal
Society has committed
suicide
in following the path of socialism
society has completely

misunderstood socialism
I am a socialist
the only true the only real socialist
everything else is an error
And communism
is a faddish delusion
Marx a ne'er-do-well
That poor feebleminded sap Lenin
completely misunderstood me
All those people
were nothing but born novelists
who never put to use their authentic genius
their talent

(*Suddenly laughs*)

May I speak to the cook
I must speak to the cook

(*To* MRS KANT) the cook must come here
he must come here

Enter STEWARD

STEWARD (*saluting*). Do you desire something Professor Kant

KANT. I must speak to the cook
  to the head chef
  I won't tolerate any caraway seeds
  in my caraway soup
  Get the head chef up here this instant

MRS KANT *whispers something in* STEWARD'*s ear. Exit* STEWARD

KANT (*to* ERNST LUDWIG). These ship's cooks are insidious
  there is nothing more insidious
  than a ship's cook
  On the high seas one must be on one's guard
  against the food
  that the ship's cook cooks

MRS KANT. But you've already spoken yesterday
  with the ship's cook
  with the head chef

KANT. I must speak with him every day
  I want to see him every day
  a dangerous transformation is always underway
  in such people
  and they are apt to start doing what they want all of a sudden

STEWARD *comes with* SHIP'S COOK

KANT (*to* SHIP'S COOK). Are you the chef
  the ship's head chef

SHIP'S COOK. At your service Professor Kant

KANT'*s wife beckons* STEWARD *over and slips him a banknote*

KANT (*looks at his pocket watch. To the* SHIP'S COOK). In soup
  we're dealing with a deadly substance
  don't you agree
  A deadly soupy substance
  literally a deadly soupy substance

SHIP'S COOK (*looks around, then repeats*). A deadly soupy substance

KANT. I know several kings
  who have died
  from an excess of caraway seeds in their soup
  You know
  what I'm driving at

  (*Cocking an ear towards the cage*)

  (*To* FRIEDRICH) It's good that you're provided for by seeds from Ernst
    Ludwig's bag

  (*To* SHIP'S COOK) Before I eat a spoonful
  my wife must eat a spoonful
  I've been insisting on this
  for fifty years

  (*Holding up his right index finger threateningly*)

Cooks are the most dangerous of all people
No caraway seeds in my soup

(*After a pause, during which everybody glances at one another*)

and no hair
You may go

Exit SHIP'S COOK

KANT (*calls out to him*). Chef
Chef

(SHIP'S COOK *turns around, remains stationary*)

How many caraway seeds are there usually
in one bowl of soup

SHIP'S COOK (*inquiringly*). In one bowl of soup

KANT. Don't say
how many
Keep on calmly cooking
Soon the fish of the Atlantic
will be absolutely inedible

(*To* STEWARD) Do you know that
the more of them that are caught
the more poisonous they are
My wife couldn't care less
that eels have already become inedible
Herrings are absolute life-shorteners

MRS KANT *whispers something in* STEWARD'*s ear*

KANT (*to* STEWARD). The problem
throughout the ages
has been the holes in the nets
A cousin of mine
introduced saltwater fish
into the Alps
He was the inventor of the refrigerator car
There is a monument to him in Innsbruck

(*Suddenly*)

But it has not yet been unveiled

(*Looks around*)

At every moment I think
the ship will burst
quite simply burst asunder
and we'll all go tumbling
to the bottom of the ocean

FRIEDRICH. Imperative imperative imperative

KANT. Every single life
is of the greatest importance
(*Looks around*)

MRS KANT. Perhaps it will be better
if he eats a puree

(*Steam-whistles sound*)

a finely whipped puree

KANT. Logic teaches
that nothing is more easily digested
than a puree
or tripe

Enter STEWARD's *assistant, who whispers something in* STEWARD's *ear.* MRS KANT *bursts out laughing and claps shut a newspaper. Steam-whistles sound*

STEWARD (*to* KANT). Dinner is served Professor Kant

Everybody rises and goes to dinner. ERNST LUDWIG *packs up the cage and exits last.* KANT *stops halfway to the stage exit, licking his right index finger and holding it high. Steam-whistles sound*

KANT. West-northwest

STEWARD (*saluting*). Wind west-northwest
full speed ahead

MIDDLE DECK

Several folding and non-folding chairs
MRS KANT *and* MILLIONAIRESS *are promenading together*

MILLIONAIRESS. There are many famous people
    on board
    Going incognito
    isn't doing them any good
    Word has already gotten around
    that Kant is on board
    (*Laughs*)
    If this trip doesn't get me to my goal
    the next one will
    My grandmother
    a born advertising poster
    coal coke metal you know
    with ambitions to be a pianist
    traveled on the Titanic
    with the entire coffer of family jewels
    (*The steam-whistles sound three times*)
    She had always said
    that she would die on the high seas
    The iceberg literally cut
    the *Titanic* wide open
    Lloyds must quite simply raise the *Titanic*
    I'll spare no effort
    to see the *Titanic* raised
    On his deathbed

my late husband made me swear to him
that I would stop at nothing
to see the *Titanic* raised
In any case it is Lloyds' solemn duty
Kant on board
Isn't this an enormity
It's said he's never left Königsberg
The lot of them are very witty people

(*The steam-whistles sound three times*)

I've spoken with the steward
We'll be dining at the captain's table
with the cardinal with the admiral
at the Chinese-lantern party
It's dreadful
I keep thinking about the iceberg
I didn't sleep a wink all night
after the cardinal's story
on the one hand I was all ears
on the other hand I was drinking whisky nonstop
The ship's doctor says that a couple of glasses in the evening
won't do me any harm
On a voyage like this
one must quite simply
surrender to the pleasures it offers

(*Suddenly, while inspecting* MRS KANT'*s dress*)

What a lovely dress
a proper dress to wear onboard
Every morning I'm in the greatest perplexity
when I think to myself
what am I going to wear again

(*The steam-whistles sound three times*)

on the one hand it's quite windy on deck
on the other hand it's awfully hot below deck
But I've never yet worn
the same dress twice on the high seas

It must be interesting
to be married to such an illustrious man
as Professor Kant
The steward says the professor is
an honorary doctor ten times over
I heard you'd met your husband on the Tristacher See
A sea marriage

(*Bursts out laughing*)

A sea marriage

MRS KANT. Yes on the water

MILLIONAIRESS. Your first voyage on the high seas
and on such a grand occasion
An honorary New York doctor
what a pinnacle

MRS KANT. My husband is an honorary doctor of Columbia University

MILLIONAIRESS. But of course that makes no difference
Just having any honorary doctor
at one's table
just having Kant in person
I'm just now realizing what that means
The cardinal is quite beside himself
with the thought that he's traveling on the same ship as Kant
Kant and the cardinal
I love America more than anywhere else
Don't you

MRS KANT. We're traveling to America for the first time

MILLIONAIRESS. To think that these days there are still people
traveling to America for the first time

(*Gazes out at the ocean*)

This vast expanse
this infinitude
Well
I firmly believe

Lloyds will raise the jewels
then I'll have gotten
what I wanted
After all I owe it to my husband
He had always wanted to become a shipbuilding engineer
a proper shipbuilding engineer
Well you know he came from
an actual proletarian family
Kant in person
It must be marvelous
to be married to a global celebrity
to Kant
Do you go to the masseur every day as I do
I get a daily massage from the ship's masseur
such a handsome physique
an elegant appearance
he's told me
he's basically a doctor
On account of a drawn-out case of pleurisy of his mother's
he hasn't been able to finish his MD
Oh well illnesses ruin everything
One day you're on the royal road
to developing a talent
to becoming a genius
and suddenly it's all reduced to nothing
because some illness has walked upon the scene
Every morning the ship's doctor comes
and takes my blood pressure
I've got my personal blood-pressure kit here with me
regardless of where I'm traveling to
I always have my personal blood-pressure kit with me
Doctors always work with the dodgiest instruments imaginable
Do you have dreams as absurd as mine
I dream that I'm walking along Fifth Avenue
and talking to a man and I ask him what time it is
and he turns out to be the Shah of Persia

(*Bursts out laughing*)

and he says
my dear
your garter has come undone
My garter I ask my garter
Indeed my dear your garter he says
and so I bend down
and in fact
my garter has come undone
Hey I say what are you of all people doing here on Fifth Avenue
But when I stand back up
I find myself on the Grossglockner
no kidding
People have the most absurd dreams on the high seas
or they suffer from insomnia
The cardinal has already vomited twice
Seasickness is something godawful
Have you at least got a decent cabin
I used to be terrified of travelling alone
a solo sea voyage quite simply terrified me
I traveled all over the world with my husband
and always by ship
always by ship as a matter of principle

(*Whispers in* MRS KANT'*s ear*) He was an epileptic

(*Again aloud*) I loathe flying
Ah I like it here on the ship
and being here on the ship suits my tastes
If I'm having bad dreams
I go up on deck
and think about Panama
you know what I mean sailors love oh yeah
And if my clothes are starting to fit too tightly
we do after all have a tailor on board
an actual Bohemian tailor
a genius in his own bailiwick
In a couple of days I'll have Lloyds deep enough in my pocket

to make them raise the *Titanic*
A pearl necklace just think of it
that Maria Theresia wore around her neck
and a heap of archducal rings
brilliants diamonds from all the imperial residences
Don't you find
the cardinal extremely good looking
He'd make a handsome pope
I'm sure one day he'll be pope
Then I'll be able to say
I traveled with the pope by ship to America
There are naturally bigger ships
but none of them is more comfortable
Luxury is comfortable
High-sea luxury is comfortable
I don't understand a thing about philosophy
but please do tell me what is your husband philosophizing about
    anyway
Is it literally incomprehensible
I'd so very much like to read something of your husband's
do you have anything by him that you could spare me
I'd certainly prefer not to meet Kant
without knowing a word written by Kant

(*Gazes out at the sea*)

My mother always told me
don't talk so much child
it weakens your organism

(*Suddenly*)

The *Titanic* has supposedly made more money
for the survivors' lawyers
than everything on the ship was worth
Are you also insured by Lloyds
Oh well
what a lovely afternoon

(*Suddenly curious*)

What is your husband's philosophy based on anyway
Oh yeah
Can you believe the mess I walked into
when I stepped into my cabin
I'd left the tap running
appalling
here it is two in the morning and I'm ankle-deep in water
it wasn't until four in the morning
that I managed to go to bed
The skittishness of people is astonishing
a change in the weather is in the air
Have you got your lanterns yet

MRS KANT. What lanterns

MILLIONAIRESS. Why the ones for the Chinese-lantern party

MRS KANT. I haven't thought about them at all yet

MILLIONAIRESS. I've always only ever had yellow lanterns
Yellow is my favorite color I'll have you know
it has been since I was a child
I love these onboard parties
Once when I was bound for Jamaica
with my husband
there was an incident
The party was already in full swing
and there was an explosion
The ship has exploded I thought
A panic just imagine a real panic
But it was only a firecracker going off
Your husband will enjoy it the party that is
You'll need at least six lanterns for it
That's two lanterns per person
Your husband you and your husband's assistant

MRS KANT. Ernst Ludwig

MILLIONAIRESS. Right Ernst Ludwig
Three times two is six

MRS KANT. You've forgotten about Friedrich

MILLIONAIRESS (*inquiringly*). Friedrich

MRS KANT. My husband's parrot

MILLIONAIRESS (*bursts out laughing*). Oh yeah the parrot
That'll be a real jaw-dropper
when the parrot walks in with two Chinese lanterns
a jaw-dropper

(*Gazes out at the ocean*)

I love moments like this
when I'm standing here
and looking out
Stay a while in New York
You must stay there a while
You must see Central Park
oh and all the lovely blouses on Thirty-Eighth Street
Broadway is no longer
what it once was
that's all dead and done with
The great actors are all in the cemetery
and the ones who are still alive are nothing
But I'm sure you have no interest in the theater
I don't go to the theater any more
it's got nothing left to offer
the theater is an anachronism
An acquaintance of mine
an author
and also a philosopher like your husband
has published a book
in which he proves that the theater
is an anachronism
Do you know Strindberg
There's a real man for you
everybody else is nothing
so I'm better off taking a hot footbath
than going to the theater

(*Suddenly lifts up the hem of her dress*)

Look

(MRS KANT *looks at* MILLIONAIRESS'*s right knee*)

My kneecap is prosthetic
It's a long story
It all happened quite suddenly
I was walking along the street three days after
our wedding day
forty-two years ago
and going to the jeweler's to pick up a napkin-ring
I had given my husband the napkin-ring as a present
you know an engraving
with the date of our wedding on it
As just as I'm about to enter the jeweler's shop
this man walks up to me and says watch out
watch out do you hear me watch out
I'm thinking he's a lunatic and I laugh
At that very instant the man hits me
in the knee with a metal walking stick
and dashes my kneecap to pieces with a single blow
It all happened so quickly
that the man escaped unidentified
The case has never been solved
At first the doctors made a wreck of me
In Europe of course basically only amateurs practice medicine
Then
after several unsuccessful operations in Viennese and Swiss clinics
I went to America
by then I had already resigned myself
to having a stiff leg for good
but at Columbia University
they fitted me with this prosthetic kneecap
look

(*Moves her leg to and fro in the air*)

It's completely normal

even though my kneecap is prosthetic
completely normal as if nothing had happened
The American doctors are geniuses I tell you

(*Lowers the hem of her dress and stands back up on both feet*)

Naturally I spared no expense
The experts are always expensive
If I'd stayed in Europe
I'd still be hobbling about with a stiff leg everywhere

(*They both sit down*)

but probably I would have long since killed myself
because I'm not the sort of person
to hobble about as a cripple all her life

MRS KANT. We have high hopes
    that my husband will get the help he needs
    in America

MILLIONAIRESS. America has helped out tons of people
    At first people are skeptical
    Anyone who doesn't know America loathes it
    Before I'd been to America
    I also loathed it

MRS KANT. My husband's eyes
    are getting worse every day
    The day
    is already in sight
    when he'll have ceased to see at all for good
    I'll have you know he's got glaucoma

MILLIONAIRESS. And your husband will be in the best hands
    for glaucoma in particular
    I know a professor there in Chicago
    who will make a tiny incision in the iris
    and your husband will see just as well as he did before
    nowadays glaucoma is no longer a serious problem
    Glaucoma has lost its terrors

MRS KANT. My husband is placing all his hopes
  in America
  in the American doctors

MILLIONAIRESS. I marvel at your husband
  a person who sees so much
  with such bad eyes
  The cardinal says
  your husband has thought much more and much more deeply
  than anybody else who's ever lived
  I never would have dreamed
  that I'd get to meet Kant in person
  Nor will anybody believe that I have

MRS KANT. Is your cabin as terribly drafty as ours

MILLIONAIRESS. Naturally
  All the cabins are drafty
  At night I put on a knitted cap

MRS KANT. That's a good idea

MILLIONAIRESS. After all drafts
  on the high seas always bothered
  my grandmother
  she was a passionate sea-voyager
  she took at least one sea voyage each year
  and a sea voyage around the entire world whenever possible
  that was an enormity in her day
  My grandmother was never
  without a knitted cap on board
  My child she always used to say
  if I didn't have this knitted cap
  Anyone who doesn't have a knitted cap on the high seas
  will come down with every possible illness
  they start out as perfectly harmless colds
  but they all eventually turn into chronic illnesses
  A single night without my knitted cap
  and I'd have caught my death of cold
  I assume my grandmother had her knitted cap on

when she went down with the Titanic
I can't picture her doing otherwise

(*Laughs*)

Oh yeah one can't protect oneself enough
So aren't you going to knit yourself a knitted cap like mine

MRS KANT. Certainly a knitted cap like yours
would do my husband a lot of good

MILLIONAIRESS. A knitted cap like mine
is the best protection
I must of course devote a considerable outlay
to the raising of the Titanic
So far Lloyds has been taking me for a ride
it's an uninterrupted struggle
to get hold of what you're legally entitled to
This is my third trip to America
on Lloyds-related business
but I'm not giving up
I made a solemn promise to my husband
when he was on his deathbed
Two lanterns per person
remember that
A parrot with two Chinese lanterns

MRS KANT. Ernst Ludwig will have to carry Friedrich's lanterns

MILLIONAIRESS. A screamingly funny fellow
Where in the world did you dig him up

MRS KANT. Without Ernst Ludwig
my husband would be lost
He'd never manage
to carry Friedrich himself

MILLIONAIRESS. A screamingly funny fellow
An intellectual trio

(*Bursts out laughing*)

An intellectual trio

MRS KANT. You're right about that

MILLIONAIRESS. Say somebody stuffs a fortune
   into a certain head
   for instance Kant's head right
   then at the very least the investor is going to learn
   what the point of the intellectual world is
   The intellectual world is
   a whole different world
   I grew up in the capitalist world
   I am a true child of capitalism
   My husband only ever addressed me as
   my capitalist child
   The first night at sea
   he always had diarrhea
   I've been observing your husband for days now
   it's fascinating
   What I find most striking
   is
   that your husband undoubtedly
   has a large shoe-size

MRS KANT. Thirteen

MILLIONAIRESS. That's exceptionally large

MRS KANT. It's an asset
   at clearance sales

MILLIONAIRESS. Yes exceptionally large sizes
   are absolutely an asset at clearance sales

KANT *and the others are approaching*

MRS KANT. Here comes my husband

MILLIONAIRESS. These footfalls herald the arrival of Kant

Both turn around. Enter KANT *with a sheaf of papers,* ERNST LUDWIG *with*
FRIEDRICH, *and* STEWARD *with blankets.* MRS KANT *and* MILLIONAIRESS
stand up

KANT (*promptly taking a seat on one of the folding chairs. Then, to* MILLIONAIRESS). My wife prizes conversation
of such universal breadth
as yours

MILLIONAIRESS (*laughing*). We understand each other
Professor Kant
We understand each other perfectly

MRS KANT *and* STEWARD *adjust* KANT*'s folding chair.* ERNST LUDWIG *has set down* FRIEDRICH*'s cage and the bag of seed and is swathing* KANT*'s feet with the blankets*

MRS KANT (*to* KANT). Will you be needing your headrest

KANT. Naturally my headrest
at midday I obviously need
my headrest

(*To* MILLIONAIRESS) The weather conditions are worsening

(*Licks his right index finger and holds it in the air*)

West-northwest

STEWARD (*springs to attention*). West-northwest Professor Kant

KANT *adjusts his eyeglasses and opens the sheaf of papers*

MILLIONAIRESS. My finest sea voyage
Professor Kant
To have such a lofty intellect on the ship
I'm in raptures
I've recommended
wearing a knitted cap for the prevention of colds to your wife
I knitted my cap myself
But you can also buy caps below deck

MRS KANT. Raise your head

KANT. Head raised

(MRS KANT *and* STEWARD *insert* KANT*'s headrest*)

Wait wait

that's just right
(*Looks straight ahead*)
Now I've got the ideal line
(*To* MILLIONAIRESS) Do you know Joseph Conrad

MILLIONAIRESS. Who's that

KANT. One of our greatest authors
a Pole

MRS KANT (*to* MILLIONAIRESS). Won't you be seated

KANT (*to* MILLIONAIRESS). Please do take a seat

ERNST LUDWIG *moves* FRIEDRICH'*s cage to a position immediately next to* KANT'*s folding chair and swathes* KANT'*s legs in blankets.* STEWARD *swathes* KANT'*s upper body in blankets*

KANT. Even on the high seas
conceitedness reigns supreme
One's mood is always changing
Eccentricity
Nature
is the quintessence of artificiality

MILLIONAIRESS. I showed your wife my knee
my artificial kneecap
my American kneecap
as my husband always called it
(*Exposes her knee*)
Look Professor Kant
here is my prosthetic kneecap

MRS KANT. American surgeons
fitted her with it
American doctors
are the best

MILLIONAIRESS. The best in the world
without a doubt

KANT (*gazing at* MILLIONAIRESS's *knee*). I see nothing
   You know I have glaucoma
   I see nothing
   almost nothing any more
   a pair of foundational propositions perhaps
   then darkness reigns supreme

MRS KANT (*to* MILLIONAIRESS, *who is pulling back down the hem of her*
   dress). He can see your knee
   but he can't tell
   that your kneecap is prosthetic

MILLIONAIRESS. For a man or woman of the mind
   the fear of going blind
   is the most appalling of all fears
   I have always thought
   better to be a leg short
   than an eye short

   (*Bursts out laughing*)

   Eyes are still pretty much never replaceable
   All joking aside
   as far as ophthalmologists go
   Columbia University really is
   the most celebrated place

   (*To* MRS KANT) I had a niece
   who went blind over the course of just a few days
   incurably
   the poor child
   One time I went out with her to pick raspberries
   in the Black Forest
   but the poor child couldn't find a single berry

   (MRS KANT *beckons* STEWARD *over and whispers something in his ear*)

   In European institutes for the blind
   the most indescribably appalling conditions reign supreme
   Tell me Professor Kant
   what is the basis of our more or less permanent fear of death
   our dread of the end

KANT (*flying into a rage*). Don't say the word end

MILLIONAIRESS (*nonplussed*). Oh well everybody's got their own goal to
reach

(*After a pause*)

Are you seasick Professor

KANT. You can quite easily see that I am see-sick
you can quite easily see it on account of my glasses

MILLIONAIRESS. I mean seasick
not see-sick

MRS KANT. My husband isn't seasick
he's never seasick

MILLIONAIRESS. Such intellects in particular always suffer
from horrible seasickness occasionally

KANT *leafs through his papers*

MRS KANT (*to* KANT). I'll knit you a cap

MILLIONAIRESS. Knit your husband
a red cap
a red cap will go well with his face
not a blue cap
not a green cap
a red cap
tightly knitted

(*Laughs*)

a cap with holes only
for the eyes and the nose

(*To* MRS KANT) I haven't the faintest idea
why I'm suddenly thinking
about the story of Little Red Riding Hood

(*To the* STEWARD) Hey why don't you fetch me
a double whisky
it's too lovely here
one must take advantage of such opportunities

(*To* KANT *and* MRS KANT) May I treat you two
to a whisky

MRS KANT. My husband doesn't drink

MILLIONAIRESS. Well that's too bad

(*Exit* STEWARD)

Soon it'll rain again
and everything will be dreary

(KANT *is jotting down notes on his papers*)

An artist I always used to say
or a scientist my husband must be
an artist or a philosopher
then I suddenly married Richard
dragged him out of the mud so to speak
But life on my side
was entirely too stressful for him
I wore him out
The air of luxury is too thin
for the proletariat
my father always used to say
Oh well I've been on my own for an awfully long time by now

(*Re-enter* STEWARD *with a double whisky for* MILLIONAIRESS.
MILLIONAIRESS *takes a long sip of whisky*)

Life is too short
to be allowed to slip away
don't you think so too Professor
I've always been a happy person
basically
What I'm saying is a platitude
but I am actually happy
With Kant in person
on a ship
bound for America

(*Takes another sip*)

For some people it's always a catastrophe

and for others it's a huge success

(*Raises her glass to the everyone in turn*)

To all your healths
Long may you live Professor Kant

KANT *cocks an ear towards* FRIEDRICH's *cage*

KANT (*to* ERNST LUDWIG). Nothing not a feather's stirring

ERNST LUDWIG. Perhaps he's sleeping

KANT. We were up too late last night
   Kant is one half of us
   the Psittacus erithacus is the other
   Probably the doctor's procedure
   exhausted him
   I summoned the doctor
   and had him auscultate Friedrich's head
   The doctor kept his opinion to himself

(*Cocks an ear towards the cage again*)

(*To* MILLIONAIRESS) Please allow me for simplicity's sake
to call you Millionairhead
Of course you may also address me simply as Professor

MILLIONAIRESS. You flatter me Professor Kant
   How ever have you managed
   to become so famous
   How do you keep all those philosophies of yours in your
   head

KANT. I have stored everything
   I've ever thought
   in Friedrich
   If I lose him
   I'll have lost everything

MILLIONAIRESS. I've always marveled
   at people
   who have written books
   naturally philosophical ones
   most of all

KANT. It all comes down to having an impact
  Anyone who has an impact on history
  in one direction
  as in the other
  on the whole of history
  do you understand

MILLIONAIRESS. My that's exciting
  (*Takes a forceful sip*)

MRS KANT *beckons* STEWARD *over and whispers something in his ear*

KANT. Every thought
  is the whole of history
  is past and future
  is everything
  do you understand
  A patriarchy naturally

  (*Cocking an ear towards* FRIEDRICH's *cage*)

  The doctors disarrange
  everything in a person
  kill everything in a person
  and in Friedrich most of all

  (*To* ERNST LUDWIG) Has he eaten

  (ERNST LUDWIG *nods*)

  How much

  (ERNST LUDWIG *indicates the amount on the bag of seed*)

  If a body's own development
  produces axial rotation
  then by rights all the spheres of the cosmic structure must have this
    rotation
  why then doesn't the moon have it

  (*Gazes meaningfully at everyone in turn*)

  (*To* MILLIONAIRESS *suddenly*) Tell me
  do you by any chance play the piano

MILLIONAIRESS. Where did you get that idea

KANT. It's just a question
everything about you suggests
you play the piano

MILLIONAIRESS. I like listening to music
is that it

KANT. That's it
I can plainly see it
That's it

MILLIONAIRESS. Where can one buy your books anyway
I'd like to buy everything of yours right away
Professor Kant

MRS KANT. Everywhere
all over the world

MILLIONAIRESS. I can hardly believe it
an event
a once-in-a-century event

KANT. Leibniz said Leibniz
I said Kant Kant
The causes are the heavenly bodies
planets
comets

MILLIONAIRESS. The most important thing
that has ever been thought
has been thought in your head
according to the cardinal
Ah it would be lovely
if he became pope
The world has never had
such a handsome pope
(*Suddenly to* KANT) What do you think of the Church

KANT (*while jotting down notes*). The ecliptic
is another

The direction as a surface
is another

MILLIONAIRESS (*takes a forceful sip*). A whole new system of thought
I think

KANT *cocks an ear at the cage and beckons* ERNST LUDWIG *over*. KANT *and*
ERNST LUDWIG *both cock their ears towards the cage*

MILLIONAIRESS. These animals
are very sensitive
I had a titmouse
that understood everything I said
suddenly it fell from its perch
before my very eyes
that made me really sad
To this day I still carry the dead titmouse with me
in spirit
a quite harmless perversion perhaps
(*Takes a forceful sip*)

KANT (*to* MRS KANT). Doctors induce
nothing but deteriorations of one's condition

A rustle of flapping wings is heard from within the cage

MILLIONAIRESS. Do you hear that

KANT (*shoves* ERNST LUDWIG *aside and listens*). He's woken up

KANT. He's woken up
possibly from a fainting fit

FRIEDRICH. Fainting fit fainting fit

KANT *tugs at the cover and briefly peers into the cage*

MILLIONAIRESS. That bird is the most important thing
that you own Professor Kant
the very most important

KANT *lets go of the cover*

KANT (*to the* MILLIONAIRESS). The system is a false system
the system is always a false system

STEWARD *makes as if to leave*

MRS KANT. Wait
    Fetch the podium
    My husband will give his lecture *now*

Exit STEWARD *after filling* MILLIONAIRESS's *glass*

FRIEDRICH. Now now now

KANT. Towards the ecliptic
    naturally
    perpendicularly

FRIEDRICH. Perpendicularly perpendicularly

MRS KANT. My husband gives
    his lecture
    without warning
    at a precisely determined
    unforeseen point of time

    (MILLIONAIRESS *takes a forceful sip*)

    In Würzburg he had only a dog
    for an audience

KANT (*to* MILLIONAIRESS). A brilliant lecture
    quite possibly my most brilliant lecture
    ever
    Kant has never left Königsberg
    This lie is widely believed

MRS KANT (*to* MILLIONAIRESS). My husband has asbestos arch-supports
    in his shoes
    he worries
    he'll catch fire
    if he doesn't have
    these arch-supports in his shoes
    when he's lecturing

MILLIONAIRESS. I've also always had a fear
    of electricity
    You just stick out your hand

and you're carbonized

(*Bursts out laughing*)

carbonized

(*To* MRS KANT) carbonized

FRIEDRICH. Carbonized carbonized carbonized

MILLIONAIRESS (*to* KANT). Aren't you also insured by Lloyds Professor
    Kant

FRIEDRICH. Lloyds Lloyds

MILLIONAIRESS. In your position
    I'd have taken out a huge policy
    on the parrot a long time ago
    Lloyds will insure pretty much anything
    Two three million
    in coverage for that untimely event Professor Kant
    Or maybe you should insure
    your own head
    your brain Professor Kant
    for a million
    what am I saying
    for ten million

    (*Takes a sip*)

    (*To* MRS KANT) In Duisberg they fitted me with a kneecap
    that wasn't rustproof
    I've always dreamt of this
    of being in closest quarters
    with a real expert

    (*Exclaims*)

    The light of eyesight
    for the light of reason

MRS KANT. Where is your husband buried anyway

MILLIONAIRESS. In New York
    By the evening after our arrival

I'll be with him
The first walk I always take in New York
is a walk to the cemetery to visit him

STEWARD *and his assistant are carrying a podium onto the deck*

MRS KANT (*crying out and leaping up*). The podium

MILLIONAIRESS *takes a sip*

MRS KANT (*points to a spot behind* KANT). Put it over there

(STEWARD *and his assistant set up the podium behind* KANT)

Immanuel
the podium

KANT. The podium
(*Stands up*)

ERNST LUDWIG *starts helping* KANT *to the podium*

FRIEDRICH. Ladies and gentlemen

KANT (*motions for the folding and non-folding chairs to be cleared away*).
Take it away
take all of it away
Away away

(STEWARD *and his assistant move the folding chairs and non-folding chairs away from the vicinity of the podium.* KANT *looks on as* STEWARD *and his assistant and* ERNST LUDWIG *set up the podium at the spot where he indicates he wants it to be*)

Good
good

(*Everybody steps back.* MILLIONAIRESS *has stood up.* KANT *stations himself behind the podium and is soon immersed in his papers.* ERNST LUDWIG *places* FRIEDRICH's *cage next to* KANT)

Peculiar acoustics on the high seas

(*Enter upstage the* CARDINAL, *followed gradually by several other passengers*)

Please sit down
Please do sit down

MRS KANT *sits down.* MILLIONAIRESS *sits down. Everybody else gradually sits down*

FRIEDRICH. Ladies and gentlemen
   Ladies and gentlemen
   Ladies and gentlemen

   (ERNST LUDWIG *opens the bag of seed, removes the cover from the cage completely, and feeds* FRIEDRICH)

   Ladies and gentlemen

MILLIONAIRESS *takes a long sip. Enter two passengers.*

The steam-whistles sound three times

KANT (*flustered*). Please sit down
   Please do sit down at once

   (*The steam-whistles sound three times*)

   Sit down

   (*The passengers sit down*)

FRIEDRICH. Sit down sit down

The steam-whistles sound three times

KANT (*after a fairly long pause*). It is impossible to speak of reason
   on the high seas

The steam-whistles sound three times

REAR DECK

A small drawing room

Dance music can be heard coming from an adjacent large drawing room offstage

KANT, KANT'*s wife*, MILLIONAIRESS, CARDINAL, *and* ADMIRAL *are dining around a table*

ERNST LUDWIG *and* FRIEDRICH *in a covered cage are at a small table at stage left*

Enter STEWARD *and his assistant*

The dance music grows louder

STEWARD *walks up to* CAPTAIN *with a bottle of champagne*

CAPTAIN (*reads aloud from the bottle*). Château Maginot
    Nineteen-seventeen

Murmurs of strong approval all around

MILLIONAIRESS (*exclaims*). But there's no Sunshine
    There's no Sunshine

CAPTAIN. There's no Sunshine
    That art collector's never on time
    (*The* STEWARD *opens the bottle and pours*)
    (*To* KANT) The finest weather conditions
    Professor Kant

MILLIONAIRESS. What a lovely Chinese-lantern party

ADMIRAL. I enjoy these Chinese-lantern parties

CAPTAIN (*pointing at* ERNST LUDWIG). A solicitous soul
   this type of servant
   is well-nigh extinct

MILLIONAIRESS. An authentic bird-protector
   He devotes his life completely
   to the animal

MRS KANT. Friedrich is almost fifty

ADMIRAL. An astonishing age
   for a bird

MRS KANT. In certain conditions
   Psittacus erithacus
   can live to be a hundred

CARDINAL. The native habitat of Psittacus erithacus
   is Guinea
   if I'm not mistaken

MILLIONAIRESS. You were the nuncio there
   weren't you

CARDINAL. Indeed I was

KANT. I gave Friedrich a sleeping pill
   Conscious participation
   in this Chinese lantern party
   would irritate him inordinately

ADMIRAL. Typical of someone with a head like a storage-bank

KANT. Or a storage-bank like a head

MRS KANT. Without Friedrich my husband
   couldn't exist

ADMIRAL. There is no doubt
   that one may grow used to such an animal

MRS KANT. My husband is no animal-lover
   that's something different

MILLIONAIRESS (*loudly*). I love animals
  more than anything else
  I have always
  loved animals

ADMIRAL. In America the love of our fellow creatures
  is extremely intense

CAPTAIN (*to* KANT). The finest weather conditions
  Professor Kant

  (*Raises his glass and glances at all the guests in turn*)

  Still no Mr Sunshine
  an old friend of the ship
  Since way back in thirty-seven
  Sunshine has been a regular on this ship
  The most celebrated art collector
  of all time
  A Goya specialist
  an anthroposophist
  a student of human nature
  a cosmopolitan

  (*Surveys all the guests*)

  My dear Professor Kant
  it is an edifying moment
  to have you here
  on my ship
  on the Praetoria
  and to raise a glass
  with all my guests this evening

  (*Everybody raises their glass and drinks*)

  I must say
  that this is the finest Chinese-lantern party
  that I have ever hosted

  (*Peers into the large drawing room, in which the music is now even louder,
  then*)

This Chinese lantern party will
go down in history
not only in nautical history
but also in the history of philosophy

MRS KANT *applauds*

MILLIONAIRESS (*joins her in applauding and exclaims*). To think that I'm
  privileged to witness

(*Exclaims loudly*)

the history of philosophy

CAPTAIN. Tomorrow morning
  at exactly eleven-twenty
  American time
  we'll be arriving in New York

Enter one of the ship's officers, who delivers a message to CAPTAIN

CAPTAIN (*after having read the message*). The problem with the engine
  has been fixed
  We had a problem with the engine

Everybody is completely motionless for an instant

MILLIONAIRESS. I didn't notice it at all

KANT (*raising his eyes*). I really didn't notice it at all

Exit the ship's officer

CAPTAIN. Everything is in order
  Everything is in order

MRS KANT. That hunch of yours
  about that strange sound

(*To* KANT) Do you see
  it really was something

(*To the others regarding* KANT) My husband has quite an extraordinary
  sense of hearing
  he had a hunch there was a problem with the engine

CAPTAIN. But please set your mind at rest
  everything is in perfect order
  (*Raises his glass*)

Everybody raises their glass and drinks. The dance music grows louder

MILLIONAIRESS. This is the most exciting sea voyage I've ever been on

MRS KANT. My husband is never wrong

CARDINAL. It's hardly a pleasant thing to think about
  going down with the ship

MILLIONAIRESS. A guardian angel
  is on board
  We have a guardian angel on board
  (*Drains her glass;* STEWARD *immediately refills it*)

ADMIRAL. It's absolutely impossible
  for a ship like this one to sink
  It is so well constructed
  that it can even run aground on an iceberg
  and not sink
  The age of the *Titanic* is over
  (*Raises his glass to everyone else in turn*)
  In honor of your presence Professor Kant

Everyone raises his glass in KANT's *honor and drains his glass. The* STEWARD
refills everyone's glass

CAPTAIN. Nowadays
  ocean liners are
  the safest means of travel

MILLIONAIRESS. Do you remember
  when the entire Manchester Philharmonic Orchestra
  sank off the coast of Argentina
  Since then there's been
  no Philharmonic in Manchester
  My brother-in-law was on board
  he managed to escape drowning

CAPTAIN. Sea travel hasn't witnessed a disaster
   on that scale in decades

MRS KANT. My husband was apprehensive

   (STEWARD *opens a second bottle of champagne*)

   about undertaking this sea voyage
   But I managed to set his mind at rest

MILLIONAIRESS. The stars are auspicious

ADMIRAL. Are you conscious Professor
   of the fact that your philosophy is the only one
   that the world is compelled to acknowledge
   has shaken it from the ground up
   the rest of them count for absolutely nothing

KANT. The ecliptic
   in defiance of reason
   proves all laws

ADMIRAL. The astonishing thing about it of course
   is its enormous impact
   but naturally this impact
   isn't astonishing at all

   (*To* CARDINAL) The Church naturally always
   assumes its ecclesiastical position

MILLIONAIRESS (*to* CARDINAL). Your eminence I have a question for you
   is it true that when a pope is elected
   white smoke ascends

   (*Everyone exchanges glances*)

   At the very instant
   at which a new pope is elected

CARDINAL. Yes
   white smoke
   actual white smoke

MILLIONAIRESS. Do you think
   that at the next papal election

a Roman
or a non-Roman will become pope

(*Suddenly enthusiastic*)

You would be the ideal pope
There has never yet been
a pope as super-elegant as you

Enter ART COLLECTOR

CAPTAIN (*exclaims*). Sunshine our art collector

(*Greets* ART COLLECTOR *and leads him to the table.* ART COLLECTOR *sits down after bowing in every direction*)

Our art collector
collects only the most valuable pieces of art

ADMIRAL. That is of course
a matter of interpretation

CARDINAL. Of course

CAPTAIN. A specialist in Goya
Velasquez
Rembrandt

MILLIONAIRESS. Rembrandt
I love Rembrandt

CAPTAIN (*to* ART COLLECTOR). Have you managed to buy the drawings

(*To the* OTHERS) He's a big fan of Kubin
You all know who Kubin was

ART COLLECTOR. The only exception
I make
is Kubin
otherwise I only collect old art

MILLIONAIRESS (*to* ART COLLECTOR). Tell me Mr Sunshine
don't I know you from Brussels
Let me think

(*Suddenly exclaims*)

Of course

but of course
you are a third cousin of mine
does Monfalcone mean anything to you

ART COLLECTOR. It's where my maternal ancestors hail from

MILLIONAIRESS. You see
You're a relative

(*Drains her glass*)

No matter where I go
I run into relatives
Each and every time I've traveled to America
I've run into some relative on the ship
I tell you chance encounters are the spice of life

ART COLLECTOR. Our relatives are
wherever things are beautiful
and wherever things are interesting

CAPTAIN. Mr Sunshine
is an Italian
but he has an American passport

(STEWARD *opens a third bottle of champagne*)

and a Portuguese one as well
If I'm not mistaken

ART COLLECTOR. And a German one

ADMIRAL. Do you specialize more in oil paintings
or in drawings

ART COLLECTOR. Oil oil
I exclusively collect oil
with very few exceptions
Toulouse Kubin as I've already mentioned

CAPTAIN *stands up and asks* MRS KANT *to dance with him and leads* MRS
KANT *into the large drawing room*

MILLIONAIRESS (*to* ADMIRAL). How were things in Persia
do tell me

(*Inquiringly*)

was it your first trip to Persia

ADMIRAL. My first trip to Persia

MILLIONAIRESS. Persepolis
weren't you thoroughly impressed by it
I am a column fanatic
In Persia I saw
the loveliest columns
Too bad though
that I couldn't read
what was written on them
Did you also visit the stone tombs

(ADMIRAL *shakes his head in the negative*)

You really should have seen them
they've been carved into the rock
carved into the living rock
Do you speak Persian

(ADMIRAL *shakes his head in the negative*. MILLIONAIRESS *drains her glass*)

One can't master everything after all

(*To* KANT) Isn't that right Professor Kant
one can't master everything after all
If only life weren't so short
Life is much too short

ADMIRAL. You're absolutely right about that my dear

MILLIONAIRESS. There's no end of things
one ought to see
Those lepers' faces in Shiraz
made a really powerful impression on me
those faces that had been
almost completely eaten away
I had never heard anything
about this reign of leprosy in Persia

There was this exorbitant luxury
on the one hand
and this dreadful poverty
on the other

ADMIRAL. A land of contradictions

MILLIONAIRESS. In Persia you're constantly worrying
you're going to come down with something fatal

ADMIRAL. In Tehran conditions of absolute chaos
reign supreme

MILLIONAIRESS. A horrible city

(*To* CARDINAL) Have you ever been to Persia your eminence

CARDINAL. To Afghanistan yes
to Persia no

MILLIONAIRESS. Naturally
after all there's no Christianity in Persia
Ever since I was in Persia
I've been unable to stand the sight of a Persian rug
Even before that I'd always had an aversion
to Persian rugs

(*To* ADMIRAL) As an admiral you've surely seen
the whole world
or at any rate the whole coastal part of it

ADMIRAL. The whole coastal part of it at any rate
Seafarers
have been everywhere
literally everywhere
They're familiar with everything

MILLIONAIRESS. Everything except the Alps
In the Emmental you'd be hopelessly lost

ADMIRAL. You're right about that my dear
the Emmental is more than a match for me

MILLIONAIRESS. I'm talking such a load of rubbish
and Professor Kant is sitting right across from me
I tell you
I've never been this interesting
on my way to America

KANT (*beckons* ERNST LUDWIG *over, calls out to him*). Ernst Ludwig

(ERNST LUDWIG *straightens the cover of the cage and comes to the table*)

Get
your glass

(ERNST LUDWIG *fetches his glass from his table*)

Can you hear anything
coming from Friedrich

(ERNST LUDWIG *shakes his head.* KANT *beckons* STEWARD *over and motions him to pour champagne into* ERNST LUDWIG'*s glass*)

Pour him
some champagne

CARDINAL. A loyal servant
of his master

ADMIRAL. The likes of him
are a dying breed
an irrevocably dying breed

KANT (*to* ERNST LUDWIG). When Friedrich wakes up
remove the cover
The ladies and gentlemen must see him

(*Regarding* CAPTAIN)

They should hear Friedrich
hear how he pronounces the word captain
impeccably

(*To* CARDINAL) And the word cardinal

(*And to* ADMIRAL) and the word admiral

(*And to* MILLIONAIRESS) And the word millionairess

(*Raises his glass and toasts* ERNST LUDWIG, *who toasts him back.* ERNST LUDWIG *returns to his place and eats and drinks some more and watches the scene at the table; now and then he cocks an ear towards the cage and peeks under the cover*)

Psittacus erithacus
needs a great deal of sleep

MILLIONAIRESS (*exclamatorily*). So you're a zoologist too
Professor Kant
I was completely unaware of that
A philosopher and a zoologist
combined

(*To* ADMIRAL) You have a really remarkable way of holding your fork
admiral
a really remarkable way

ADMIRAL. It's owing to a bullet wound
that I sustained in the Ardennes
at a secret conference

MILLIONAIRESS (*inquiringly*). An assassination attempt

ADMIRAL. An attempt
on the life of the Tunisian ambassador
who was killed
I myself
was only wounded
in my left hand
To this wound I owe
my Grand Cross of the Legion of Honor

MILLIONAIRESS (*inquisitively leaning towards* ADMIRAL). Oh yeah
the Grand Cross of the Legion of Honor
What were you doing in the Ardennes anyway

ADMIRAL. Attending a secret meeting
of the French and British governments

MILLIONAIRESS. So you were in the government

ADMIRAL. I was her majesty's counsel

MILLIONAIRESS. The queen of England's

ADMIRAL. Yes of course
　　I held this position
　　for six years

MILLIONAIRESS. How exciting
　　to be honest
　　I'm a pacifist
　　I am against war
　　I am against everything having to do with war

　　(*Looks at everyone else in turn*)

　　Everyone's got to be against war

　　(*To* CARDINAL) How about you your eminence
　　what brings you to America

CARDINAL. I'm delivering the inaugural lecture
　　for a professorship in equilibristics

　　(CAPTAIN *and* MRS KANT *re-enter and sit down*)

　　in Chicago
　　a favor for a friend
　　Moreover I have a high regard
　　for American doctors

MILLIONAIRESS. All invalids are drawn
　　to America
　　American doctors
　　have the best reputation
　　There are no good doctors
　　left in Europe

ADMIRAL. European medicine
　　isn't worth anything any more

STEWARD *opens the fourth bottle of champagne*

MRS KANT (*to her husband*). Do you see
　　the hopes of all invalids
　　are set on America

KANT. A body can right itself
   much more readily
   vis-à-vis many oblique surfaces
   than it can in relation to those
   that it encounters head-on
   and perpendicularly

MRS KANT (*regarding her husband*). My husband has always
   stretched his faculties to their very limits
   this is what has brought on his glaucoma
   if you know what I mean by that
   a case of glaucoma
   otherwise known as the green cataract

MILLIONAIRESS. One can't think as deeply for decades
   as Kant has done without being punished for it
   (*Drains her glass*)

CARDINAL. Nowadays the dreaded green cataract
   no longer leads to total blindness
   one's so-called ocular pressure
   can now be kept safely at bay
   thanks to modern medicine

MRS KANT. The ship's doctor told me the same thing

CARDINAL. An excellent man by the way

MILLIONAIRESS. A typical ship's doctor

ADMIRAL. Doctors are the true eccentrics
   of this historical epoch

CARDINAL. I can only agree with you on that point admiral

MRS KANT. My husband has always held doctors
   in contempt

CARDINAL. Contempt for doctors
   is quite common
   among thinkers

MILLIONAIRESS (*to* KANT). Who exactly was this Leibniz person
  you talk about so often
  You keep mentioning his name over and over again

KANT. Mr von Leibniz
  A close acquaintance of mine
  with whom I went on many long walks
  we never got tired
  from the very beginning
  we understood each other
  like no two other people

  (MRS KANT *beckons* STEWARD *over and whispers something in his ear
  and then slips him a banknote*)

  With Leibniz
  one heart one soul my dear
  two perpetually
  converging magnitudes
  We made each other's acquaintance in Sopot
  Newton
  was our employer
  if you know who Newton was

MILLIONAIRESS. I'm afraid I'm drawing a blank
  Professor Kant

  (*To* ART COLLECTOR) Goya was a genius wasn't he
  Did you know him

ART COLLECTOR. Not personally

MILLIONAIRESS. Rembrandt exerts
  such an incredible fascination on me
  The way he distributes his colors
  he always knows
  where to put the colors

  (*Holds her glass out to* STEWARD; STEWARD *fills it, and she drinks its
  contents at one go*)

  Do you know
  I'm planning a trip to the North Cape

it would be too lovely
if you all went with me to the North Cape

(*To* KANT *while pointing at* ERNST LUDWIG)

He looks a lot like your Friedrich
he basically
has the same facial features
Professor Kant

MRS KANT (*regarding* ERNST LUDWIG). As a child
he fell from a tree
that made him stupid

The Blue Danube *can be heard playing in the large drawing room*

MILLIONAIRESS (*crying out enthusiastically*). My favorite waltz
I love the *Blue Danube*

(ADMIRAL *stands up and asks* MILLIONAIRESS *to dance with him.*
MILLIONAIRESS *exiting arm-in-arm with* ADMIRAL)

My favorite waltz

The Blue Danube *grows louder*

KANT (*turns to* ERNST LUDWIG, *whispers to him*). Do you hear anything
is he still sleeping

(ERNST LUDWIG *peeks under the cover of the cage and shakes his head*)

(*To* CARDINAL) Friedrich evinces no interest whatsoever
in merrymaking

(STEWARD *opens the fifth bottle and pours*)

Under the influence of these tablets
he sleeps for two hours
But I simply cannot
place Friedrich at the mercy of this whole situation
I dreaded this journey
everywhere I go people say
There's Professor Kant
who has never left Königsberg
Mankind has gone mad
Insecurity has increased

(MRS KANT *whispers something in* STEWARD'*s ear*)

Mankind dreads nothing more
than itself
Security is always
only ever a lethal security
Only now am I finally comprehending
what I've been aiming for
glaucoma has
opened my eyes
Mankind has committed treason

(*To* CARDINAL) I've been interested in
equilibristics all life
My talent was once a completely different talent
I was enormously talented as an equilibrist
Truth is in equilibrium
In Chicago you say
a professorship in equilibristics
That is an enormity
All my life I've been interested
in the method of equilibrium
All my life I have suffered from
a weakness of equilibrium you know
shipwreck people
equilibrists
writers of comedies
Before the darkness sets in completely
a couple of punitive illuminations for the crowd
witches' curses
executions of the intellect
My method is the total method you know
The fear of losing my eyesight
has opened my eyes
It's nothing but a race with waning eyesight
I loathe America
I find everything American abhorrent
In truth all the American universities have invited me

but I've accepted none of these invitations
My wife found out
that there are doctors in America
who specialize in glaucoma
glaucoma specialists you know
Glaucoma is still completely unexplained
Glaucoma research is still groping about completely in
the dark
Nothing is known about glaucoma
But it surely has something to do with the destruction of the soul
Basically it's my wife alone
who has brought me onto this ship
in truth she's dragged me onto it dragged me dragged me dragged me
I never would have voluntarily boarded this ship
I dreaded boarding it from the very beginning
On the high seas
what a lethal concept gentlemen
what an enormity

(*The* Blue Danube *grows louder*)

When I compose a lecture
it is always a lecture on death
on illness progressing to death you know
on this process
that from here to infinity will remain unexplained
Health is an act of hubris gentlemen
Health is an act of fornication
The integral is hell

(*A ship's officer approaches with a telegram.* STEWARD *takes the telegram from him.* MRS KANT *beckons* STEWARD *over, takes the telegram from him and reads it silently, then announces*)

Immanuel a telegram

KANT (*inquiringly*). A telegram

MRS KANT. A telegram
from Columbia University

KANT. Really

MRS KANT. Shall I read it out

KANT. From Columbia University
 I can hardly
 see anything at all any more
 I didn't see anybody
 delivering a telegram at all

MRS KANT (*holds the telegram up in the air*). Here is the telegram
 here it is

KANT. A telegram from Columbia University

MRS KANT (*to everybody else*). May I read it to you
 (*Reads the telegram aloud*) We welcome Kant
 to America
 The event of the twentieth century

Applause all around

KANT. I am bringing America reason
 America is giving me eyesight

Applause all around once again

MRS KANT. Columbus discovered America
 America has discovered Kant

CAPTAIN. We must celebrate this
 this bestows greatness on our Chinese lantern party

 (*Raises his glass*)

 To Kant

CARDINAL. And to America

ALL (*rising and exclaiming in only vaguely approximate unison*). To Kant
 and to America
 to America and to Kant

KANT. I thank you for your attention
 If intension
 is like a line

then force
is like a square

(*Everybody sits back down*)

The integral is the hell
in which we all perish do you understand

(STEWARD *opens the sixth bottle and pours*)

Regardless of
whom we're dealing with
it is a lethal process
But history is a feast for the eyes
A feast for the eyes

(*Stands up and for a moment remains completely motionless*)

A feast for the eyes gentlemen

(*Sits back down*)

My wife
is the victim of this lethal science
and Friedrich

(*Turns towards and points at* FRIEDRICH)

its executor
Millions of asses' ears
in my writings
Millions of asses' ears gentlemen
from time to time I think
I am mad
An environmental punishment naturally
An excess
a total lack of kindness
My lectures always end with the sentence
I thank you for your attention
Friedrich has a command of this sentence that is second to none
I thank you for your attention

(*To* CARDINAL) The Church is the beneficiary of my achievements
The Church is the murder of nature

The Church is where
nothing but artificiality reigns supreme
It is an enormous libel suit
I am making this journey
to find my eyesight again
for by now I am almost completely blind
When there is virtually nothing but shadows
reason has no foundation whatsoever
I thank you for your attention

FRIEDRICH. I thank you for your attention
I thank you for your attention

KANT (*turns towards* FRIEDRICH). Do you hear
how he imitates me
he has been noting down everything
Psittacus erithacus
the genius of numbers and numerals
the feathered conscience of my cognitions
the only person
whom I have ever possessed in his entirety

(*Orders*)

Ernst Ludwig
bring him here
He belongs here with me
He has woken up and belongs here with me
Friedrich belongs here with me

(MRS KANT *whispers something in* STEWARD'*s ear.* CARDINAL *whispers something in* MRS KANT'*s ear.* ART COLLECTOR *whispers something in* MRS KANT'*s ear*)

(*To* ART COLLECTOR *while* ERNST LUDWIG *is carrying* FRIEDRICH *to the table*) Art collector

(STEWARD *opens the seventh bottle*)

You are an art collector right
listen

(*Takes the cage from* ERNST LUDWIG *and holds the cage including* FRIEDRICH *up in the air*)

Here my dear Mr Art Collector
I offer you the greatest work of art in the world

(*Lowers the cage*)

my Friedrich

FRIEDRICH. Friedrich Friedrich Friedrich

ERNST LUDWIG *takes the cage including* FRIEDRICH *from* KANT

KANT (*exhausted*). The greatest work of art in the world
Friedrich
my Friedrich

(MRS KANT *stands up and with the help* STEWARD *makes enough room on the table for the cage to be placed on it.* ERNST LUDWIG *places the cage including* FRIEDRICH *on the table*)

(*To* ART COLLECTOR) Here take
what you have been searching for all your life
My Friedrich

(*Tears down the cover of the cage with lightning speed*)

FRIEDRICH. Friedrich Friedrich Friedrich

MRS KANT *whispers something in the* STEWARD'*s ear and slips him a banknote of large denomination*

KANT (*to* CAPTAIN). My captain
my Friedrich

(*Licks his right index finger and holds it up in the air*)

Wind west-northwest
full speed ahead

STEWARD (*springs to attention, saluting*). Wind west-northwest
full speed ahead Professor

ADMIRAL *and* MILLIONAIRESS *return from the large drawing room, in which a waltz is being loudly played.* ADMIRAL *goes to the table and sits down*

MILLIONAIRESS (*now almost completely drunk, walks up to* KANT *and spreads her arms*). Ladies' choice Professor Kant
Ladies' choice

FRIEDRICH. Ladies' choice ladies' choice ladies' choice

MILLIONAIRESS. Ladies' choice Professor Kant

(KANT *rises from the table.* MILLIONAIRESS *takes him in her arms*)

Ladies' choice Professor Kant
come along

MRS KANT. Go on then
Go on

CARDINAL. Kant's dancing
Kant's dancing

ADMIRAL. This is quite incomprehensible

CARDINAL. Kant's dancing

MILLIONAIRESS *leads* KANT *into the large drawing room. Everybody gazes after the two of them*

FRIEDRICH (*screeching loudly*). Kant's dancing Kant's dancing Kant's dancing

DISEMBARKATION

CAPTAIN, STEWARD, STEWARD's *assistant, ship's officers, and sailors are lined up on board to take leave of the passengers*

The steam-whistles sound

On shore are people awaiting passengers; among the expectants are doctors and orderlies from a New York mental hospital

CARDINAL *appears first and is taken leave of by* CAPTAIN. *Sailors carrying* CARDINAL's *luggage follow him down the gangway and ashore*

The steam-whistles sound twice

CARDINAL *is followed by Sunshine the* ART COLLECTOR *and other passengers*

The steam-whistles sound three times

The next to leave is MILLIONAIRESS *with her entourage*

Then KANT *with* MRS KANT, *followed by* ERNST LUDWIG *with* FRIEDRICH *in his cage, as the steam-whistles sound three times.* STEWARD *and some sailors carry* KANT's *luggage*

MRS KANT (*stopping halfway down the gangway and pointing at the shore with her outstretched right arm*). Look
   the delegation from Columbia University

A brass band on shore strikes up. STEWARD *walks down to* MRS KANT *and helps her keep her balance*

KANT. Really
   a delegation from Columbia University

KANT *and his entourage disembark*

ONE OF THE TWO DOCTORS (*walks up to* KANT). Professor Kant

KANT (*surveying his surroundings with head held high, says proudly and distinctly*). You recognized me

The steam-whistles sound three times. DOCTOR *takes* KANT *by the arm and leads him offstage. The orderlies follow.*

THE END

THE GOAL ATTAINED

Les misères de la vie humaine ont fondé tout cela;
Comme ils ont vu cela, ils ont pris le divertissement.
—Pascal

Dramatis Personae

THE MOTHER

THE DAUGHTER

A PLAYWRIGHT

A MAID

In Holland

PART ONE

In town
Early morning
Large first-floor room with an adjoining kitchen
Two doors, two windows, a sofa
Several suitcases, some of them already packed and shut and others still open;
a large oblong traveling trunk
The MOTHER *is sitting in a wing chair and examining an itemized bill*
The DAUGHTER *is making tea in the kitchen*

MOTHER (*wearing a pince-nez and a long, warm raincoat*). It was my idea
   it was my wish
   it was my idea
   Why have we ever gone there
   Now we're getting our comeuppance
   for purchasing season tickets
   We shouldn't have waited so long
   Why ever did I invite him
   A terrible mistake
   Save Yourself If You Can is not a bad title
   A talent I said
   You are a great talent
   even at the time I wasn't all that convinced of it
   Successes are really only a matter of chance
   Any old thing can cause a success
   nobody can tell
   even when all the conditions are right
   nobody can tell

It even could have been a complete flop
From the start I thought it would come to nothing
That gnawing feeling that stubborn nagging feeling
Are these really human beings I asked myself
Then they suddenly applauded like savages
I don't begrudge him that naturally
At first I thought it would come to nothing
wallowing in squalor
throwing people's own muck in their faces
from up on stage
More and more muck on the stage
until the whole stage is full of muck
then the curtain goes down
when the stage is full of muck
What else is it but muck
Yes naturally they have talent
the young people
and the old artists the theatrical hacks
Don't you think
it's trashy to show people
nothing but their own muck

(*Shouting into the kitchen*)

Make it strong
I want to take my tea strong
Do you hear he's demanding eighty thousand
They're all megalomaniacs
a completely megalomaniacal bunch
The whole bunch of them have gotten carried away
with themselves

(*Setting aside the bill*)

I shouldn't have had the vault renovated
I should have left it as it is
The toppled obelisk was really quite a curiosity
eighty thousand just for raising the toppled obelisk
and a bit of concrete
A playwright

what exactly is that
people enjoy a bit of success and start taking advantage of everything
Published thoughts
all of them reams of clichés and aggregated trash
They fancy they're changing the world
He maintains he's an anarchist
that a playwright is an anarchist
An entire hour about actors
and yet he didn't give a single thought to me the whole time
to the fact that I'm old and hard of hearing

(DAUGHTER *comes into the room with the tea*)

and that basically nothing interests me any more
not thespianism at any rate
not the theater at any rate

(DAUGHTER *lays out the tea things*)

The stonecutters are insolent
all craftsmen are insolent
They now outstrip the intellectuals
completely
The triumph of the craftsmen my child
the workers are triumphant
but our kind haven't yet grasped this fact
for forty or fifty years now
the workers have been triumphant
they call all the shots
they dictate they make the rules
they're polishing us off

(DAUGHTER *is about to pour some tea.* MOTHER *stops her*)

It's not time yet
You don't know a blessed thing about tea
you don't know a blessed thing about world history either my child
You've got to let the tea steep
I've been trying to teach you that
for twenty years
Your father wanted an obelisk

he picked it out himself
even back then that was ludicrous
Times have changed from top to bottom
everything's done a complete about-face
everything's been turned upside-down
with an expert hand my child with an expert hand
Now pour the tea

(DAUGHTER *pours the tea*)

Now we're getting our comeuppance
for the fact that I didn't cancel our season tickets
it's all just a matter of habit by now
of course we stopped liking the theater a long time ago
we only pretend to like it
we hate it
because it's become a matter of habit for us
But we even hate Shakespeare
and we hate ourselves
when we go to the theater
Even before the start of the play
we have seen through it

(*Begins examining the bill again*)

I haven't been very quick to pay
it took two years
for the obelisk to be raised
more than two years had passed by the time everything was finished
I haven't paid them anything in two years
Pay everybody back tit for tat child
One mustn't deal with people so straightforwardly
They threaten me with a lawsuit
they threaten me with a second lawsuit
then I pay
and naturally I deduct twenty percent
even then it's still always much too expensive
Of course people are impressed with themselves
if they've even managed
to hammer in a nail

Dilettantism reigns supreme everywhere
but it's especially repellent in craftsmen

(*Drinks*)

If we're lucky
it won't rain
on the other hand I quite like traveling on rainy days
It will rain
I know why I never have anything done here
everything would have to be changed
but I won't let a craftsman in my house
nothing is ever going to be changed here again
Sure if the lights fall down someday
but otherwise nothing
The whole thing is already crumbling to bits
whenever you're walking I'm thinking
the house is about to collapse
you've picked up such an awkwardly loud gait
on the other hand that's just the way you are
I say please don't walk so loudly
but it doesn't change a thing about your gait
We should have sold the foundry while there was still time
and moved to the seaside
nobody not a human being in the world could have stopped us
but we missed the right moment
after that nobody would buy a foundry any more
at least not such an outdated foundry
we had a great offer my child
eighteen million
but I thought that wasn't enough
If we miss the right moment
it never comes again
I thought I could drive the price up sky high
then suddenly it was all over
I thought the same way about the twenty-five million
I gambled away

(*Drinks*)

Some people drink tea
others coffee
they can be divided into those two categories
You're a coffee-drinker
He no longer dared
to touch me
his mere presence disgusted me
I was very resolute
by the time we got back from Rome
he'd stopped touching me
You were already twenty-two
good Lord I thought
what kind of child is this
unattractive somewhat mentally backward
but loveable
You were always more of a daddy's girl
It could have been anybody else
Well it ended up being your father
the foundry played a big part
I wasn't sure
whether I was marrying the man or the foundry
I never really knew
whether it was the foundry or the man
to whom the foundry belonged
and the house at the seaside
I found that enormously charming my child
a man who was by no means hideous
with a house at the seaside
I had always wanted that
a house at the seaside that belonged to me
On the one hand there was the foundry
and house at the seaside
and the security that emanated from that entire constellation my child
I can't say
I had no other choice
no I can't say that
He had turned up

and he told me about his foundry
and that he was all alone
that his parents had lost their lives
the two of them at the same instant
I was moved when he said
they had died instantaneously
between Florence and Bologna
I'd been moved by that my child
and the fact that he had a house at the seaside
Perhaps I'd never been moved so much by any other story
we hear something moving
from a man who because he's telling us something moving
becomes moving in his own right and we marry him
I didn't want to have anything to do with the man himself at all
The foundry and the house at the seaside
and then on top of all that a child
your brother the poor thing
two-and-a-half-years old and he was gone

(*Drinks*)

He had a face that looked ancient
I didn't want to have anything to do with him I found him too hideous
can you picture it to yourself
he had come out looking just like an old man
it happens in one out of every three million births
ancient-looking skin
every part of him was crippled
This is my punishment I thought
now you have been punished
I thought continually about nothing
but how I could throw him away
at one point I got the idea
of incinerating him in the furnace
but what next
I wrapped him back up and sang him a song
I made myself sentimental
and in doing that I made myself much trashier

I kept persuading myself to keep the child
and in secret I wished for his death
incessantly
I didn't dare show my child to the world
everybody wanted to see him
but I didn't show him to anybody
and I kept saying the right time would come someday
I had miscalculated my child
The foundry and the house at the seaside
and the child
I had miscalculated
Then I traveled to the seaside and thought things would get better
    there
but things couldn't have been any worse there
I wanted to pull the blanket over his face
and smother him
but I didn't dare
I thought that if I did that I would have ruined myself
on account of a person who wasn't a person at all
an unprepossessing little beast
I hated Richard
Your father was the most unfortunate person
imaginable
he kept coming out from town and asking
how is our child doing
I hated it when he asked that
I thought the child was all your doing you scoundrel
and now you can't stop asking me
what mischief this cripple is making
I couldn't help wondering what's going to happen
when the cripple is fifteen or twenty
or twenty-five
But he never made it that far
I had yearned for his death so ardently
that he died
how ever much I retched

whenever I pulled back the little curtain
he was still in his wicker pram
but then all of a sudden he was dead
suddenly he had a beautiful face
ancient but beautiful
because I so ardently dreamed of his death
Richard do you understand
your father the Wagner fan
just when I was on the point of showing my child to the world
these were my very words to myself
he was dead
I kept telling people
that I had never seen such a beautiful child
that I had waited so long to show him to everybody
so as not to detract from his beauty
that I had wanted to keep their grubby gazes away from my beautiful
    child
yes I said just when I was on the point of showing him to you
he was dead all of a sudden
it was raining cats and dogs
crazy isn't it
those people couldn't have any idea
what was lying in the coffin
something horrifying
something ancient
a white coffin
and so many fresh flowers
Our Richard
I had that phrase chiseled in stone

(*Drinks*)

Suddenly I became anxious
All my moments were anxious
And I loathed your father
I got him out of the way
I barricaded the door of our bedroom

(*Points at the door*)

For weeks on end years on end
I stared at that door
and dreaded
that he would emerge from behind the blockaded door
he knocked but I didn't open it
he pounded on the door
but I didn't open it
he was already half-dead with pounding when he stopped
then I took my pills
First thing in the morning he was gone
the foundry needed him
I went to Katwijk
I stayed there a whole year
Low and high tide
High and low tide

(*Drinks*)

then I returned
and then you came along
We never escape my child

(*Drinks*)

Pack only the bare necessities
I always tell myself
only the barest necessities
and then we end up with a ton of luggage again

(DAUGHTER *rises and resumes packing*)

I would have helped you
even with my aches
but you refused to let me
They always start in my heels
and then spread up my back

(DAUGHTER *opens the large traveling trunk*)

That trunk has a long history
it was my only contribution to our marriage
that trunk
And do you know what was in the trunk

Have I ever told you
Haven't I ever told you

DAUGHTER. No Mother

MOTHER. An old horse blanket
  of my grandfather's
  nothing else
  that was it
  Your great-grandparents had pretty much nothing
  he was a circus clown a circus clown
  his wife was completely deaf utterly deaf

(*Drinks and sets aside her cup*)

  It didn't taste right
  when you make tea it never tastes right
  brewing tea is a science
  naturally the water matters
  but it's an art
  I want cognac now
  the cognac my child

(DAUGHTER *fetches her cognac*)

  Completely deaf do you understand
  and he was illiterate
  genuinely illiterate
  they brought five children into the world
  poor people have the most children
  two survived
  one of them was my mother
  your grandmother

(DAUGHTER *pours* MOTHER *a glass of cognac*)

She cast me off somewhere in Holland
  at in inn
  she went into the inn
  to the lavatory
  and cut me loose
  and came back out with me
  went to the house of a girlfriend

who took her in for a week
then she went back to work
Only one of us is allowed to drink
only I am allowed to drink

(*Drinks*)

To come all of a sudden from nothing do you understand
to a house like this
a foundry
a house at the seaside
not to mention everything else
But naturally it didn't happen overnight
This hideous individual showed up
with his hideous voice
and told me about his foundry
back then your father had this habit
of saying the first word
of every sentence twice
it was unbearable my child
I was horrified by this man
by the way he'd sat there
and talked about his foundry
And then he had said
when I've had enough of the foundry
I travel to the seaside
I have a lovely house there in Katwijk
naturally I'd had no idea of such a place

(*Drinks*)

I had of course had never yet seen the sea
I had always wanted to see the sea
anybody who hasn't seen the sea yet
isn't a human being yet I always thought
and I still think that today
So I pack my things
and head for Katwijk at the seaside
a big house and high and low tides
which I had never seen high and low tides

he demonstrated them to me
he bent down all the way to the ground
and demonstrated to me the high and low tides using both his hands
I had taken him for a lunatic
A lunatic I thought
But then it had become apparent
that everything he was saying was true
everything about the foundry was true
and so was everything about the house at the seaside
and even everything about the high and low tides
and everything about the money at the bank
I asked my friend
would you do this
even though you couldn't stand the man
the way he talked about the high and low tides and demonstrated
     them
the way he was always talking about his foundry and describing it
and talking about his house at the sea
that his grandfather had bought
he exudes such a horrible stench I said
from his mouth
and I don't care for his fingers
or his hands overall
his face is hideous
but the way he talks about the high and low tides
would you do this

(*Drinks*)

then she just said yes
And what a Yes it was
I can still hear that Yes with crystal clarity
I've had it in my ears for forty-five years
I can't do an impression of it
I should be able to do an impression of it
I can't do an impression of that Yes
Yes she said nothing else
she heard me out and said yes

And then I did it
do you understand
I loathed everything about that man
I even loathed the way he walked
I hated his gait
and the way he sat down
and the way he stood up
and the way he folded his hands
and the way his nostrils flared wide open
when he said low tide
and flared just as much when he said high tide

(*Drinks*)

This friend you understand
the one I asked
to take me in with you
she had never seen the man and she said Yes

(DAUGHTER *puts a beige dress into the trunk*)

I already had the trunk
when you came into the world
I took it with me everywhere
Of course I hadn't gotten around much yet back then
and I still hadn't seen the sea
But I thought the foundry was interesting
just like the fact that my husband said all's well that ends well
he said it all the time
even when there was no reason for it
All's well that ends well

(*Drinks*)

That was a habit of his
He blew his nose too loudly
All's well that ends well
at every opportunity
On the other hand he had very good manners
as befitted a member of the upper gentry
and yet they weren't quite the best manners
in fact he cut a bit of a ridiculous figure

whenever he exerted himself
for example as he was opening a champagne bottle
that was always very amusing
he didn't realize this
and I was always asking him to do it
your father was clumsy
a thoroughly clumsy individual
I was fascinated
by the way he said foundry
he said the word foundry
as though it were a real treat for him
When you say the word foundry
you remind me a bit of him
just a bit

(*Drinks*)

just a bit
He was in the habit
of sleeping with the windows shut
I couldn't stand that
I kept opening the windows
but then he would catch cold
so I simply moved out
At first we shared a bedroom
but that didn't last long
It was stupid of me
to keep lecturing him
on how unhealthy it was
to sleep with the windows shut
I should have said it two or three times
but I kept saying it over and over again
over and over again
and plenty of other things over and over again
all sorts of things that got on his nerves
I preached and he listened
but he didn't understand a single word I was saying
All's well that ends well
Whenever he came in for breakfast

he'd say All's well that ends well
and when he came home from the foundry he'd say
All's well that ends well
We'd be walking along the seashore my child
and suddenly he would stop and say
All's well that ends well
One fine day he decided he wanted a dog
I didn't want to deny him his wish
but it was a silly idea
he started saying All's well that ends well to the animal
I couldn't take it any more
I poisoned the animal
You can't possibly still remember that
it was too long ago
sure you were already around
but you were so little that
you can't possibly still remember the dog
I wouldn't let any dog any animal anywhere near you
When just the two of us were in the park with you
and there was any reason whatsoever for doing so
he'd suddenly say All's well that ends well
he used to say it to your brother too
All's well that ends well
I'd give him books to read
but he never read them
I'd ask him to summarize the books for me
but in doing this I simply tormented him
I'm going to the foundry he'd say
and he'd invariably add All's well that ends well
He loved cufflinks
he had large gold cufflinks that he'd inherited from his father
but I couldn't abide cufflinks of any sort
he also always insisted on putting on a very specific type of sandal at
   the seashore
I loathed those sandals
because they exposed his hideous toes to view

he just couldn't comprehend the fact that he didn't have the right feet
    for sandals
He didn't care for literature of any sort
I of course had always read constantly
because I'd never had anything else
but he loathed literature
and the theater
The only exception was Hans Andersen
he would sit there at that window

(*Points at the window*)

right there do you see it
and read the story of the Little Match Girl
hundreds of times
I let him do that
It would have been wrong of me not to
I was filled with contempt for him as he sat there reading
and my contempt was unfathomably deep do you understand

(*Drinks, then*)

You must pack the coats separately
from the dresses you know that of course
and put the heavy things at the bottom
and the light things on top
If I didn't suffer from these pains
I'd help you

(*Tries to stand up and immediately sits back down*)

It's the humidity in this house

DAUGHTER. It's also humid at the seaside

MOTHER. Yes but not in an unhealthy way
    it's not unhealthy at the seaside
    it's humid at the seaside
    but not in an unhealthy way
    but here it's humid
    and it makes you ill
    everything here makes a person ill

we must make sure
we get away from here
it's more than high time
When at one point I asked your father why
he'd gone into the inn
where he made my acquaintance
he said that he didn't know
that he'd gone into it purely by chance
Then I explained to him
that there were no such things as chance events
I couldn't stand it when he said
that he'd made my acquaintance
purely by chance
It wasn't by chance at all I said
it was calculated
naturally he didn't understand this
When I saw the foundry for the first time
I was appalled
what business did I have being the wife of the owner of a foundry
I'd buried my face in my hands

(*Drinks*)

but suddenly I'd discovered something to take pleasure in there
namely in all the noise
and in the people in the midst of this noise
and in the stench
all that smelting and sizzling do you understand
They had taken advantage of him
your father was stupid
he should have dealt with those people completely differently
he had a manager
who'd been bilking him for years
who'd set aside millions for himself
but I put an end to the whole thing
I cleared away all those people
I fired half the employees
I would have let it come to a trial

but it didn't get anywhere near to coming to a trial
You are the dupe
you are the moron
I said
You're being diddled taken for a ride
A newcomer
has always got an incorruptible view of things
When he came home he was exhausted
All's well that ends well

(*Drinks*)

I put ornamental plants
all around all the common areas
all of a sudden everything looked completely different
inviting do you understand
The trade union had him in their pocket
But then *I* came
and took over everything
as was only proper
We're the dummies I said
not them
We're the ones who are being diddled
not them
There were some protests
but they died out on their own
The employees and I understood each other
Ever increasing demands
and he kept meeting them
it had to stop
You decide what has to happen at the foundry
not *them* I said
it's *your* foundry
not *theirs*
it's *your* life
Our existence
not *theirs*
I had a good hand

We had to fire half of them
in order to convalesce
His illness had flared up
You were seventeen years old then
We were in Katwijk
when his illness flared up
You still had a year of high school to go
I thought then
before anybody had begun thinking it was serious
this is the end for him
It took its time my child
at first it progressed imperceptibly for years imperceptibly
until it finally flared up
Have I told you
how I said to the doctor he's going to die now isn't he
and the doctor answered
Yes he's going to die
It was so obvious
It didn't really upset me very much
I was so busy with the foundry
Then I let him into my room a couple of times
but nothing changed
he made me as sick as ever
When he went out
when nothing had changed and he'd be going out
he would turn round at the door

(*Points*)

there at that door
in that clean nightshirt that he loved so much
and say All's well that ends well
it made sick but I said good night
I knew he'd be dead soon
he didn't know it
he was so naïve my child
he couldn't see anything coming his way
he didn't see the revolution coming
and he didn't see his death coming

but I saw both
the revolution and death
his death
All's well that ends well it sounded so helpless
and yet squalid
I couldn't allow myself to fall for it
I said good night and loathed him
He always insisted on wearing those same ankle-length nightshirts
with the green border of roses on the collar
How I loathed those nightshirts

(*Drinks*)

But I couldn't bring myself to take
a couple of trifles like that away from him
He climbed freezing into my bed
but couldn't manage to get warm
From Saturday to Sunday he would beg
but then I wouldn't let him in

(DAUGHTER *folds a black dress and makes as if to put it into the trunk*)

My mourning dress
I've been dragging it around for twenty years
and in those twenty years at the seaside
I haven't put it on a single time
Let me see it isn't it already in tatters

(DAUGHTER *brings her the dress and holds it up to the light and* MOTHER
examines it)

It had its appointed day
But to put it on a second time
would have been mendacious
But pack it all the same
who knows
I may suddenly get the urge to put it on

(DAUGHTER *takes the dress back to the trunk and packs it*)

Every year these exact same garments
And I haven't bought any new ones in years
because I've got you

with your talent as a seamstress
Most of them have gone out of fashion
Bring along your blue suit

DAUGHTER. Yes Mother

MOTHER. I love it
when you're walking along the shore with me in Katwijk
and you're wearing that blue suit
I love it
And the black shoes I inherited from Mother

DAUGHTER. Yes Mother

MOTHER. You should buy new shoelaces
the old ones are already frayed at the ends
Buy some new shoelaces in Katwijk

DAUGHTER. I'm really looking forward to Katwijk

MOTHER. Yes so am I
it's the same every year
I have only one goal the entire year
Katwijk

DAUGHTER (*points to a gray dress*). Shall I iron it first
(*Holds it up high*)

MOTHER. No
no don't

(DAUGHTER *puts the dress in the trunk*)

Earlier in the day I'll wear my sundress
and in the afternoon I'll have my pleated skirt
which you've already ironed nicely
If I didn't have you
And naturally we'll take the side trip to Amsterdam
obviously
Perhaps this year our virtuoso violinist is already there
Why do these people always have colds
But you'll have your playwright of course
It was my idea

it was my desire
We go weak for a moment
and commit a blunder

DAUGHTER. Why a blunder

MOTHER. To think that I was the one who invited the playwright to
Katwijk
you wanted it
you wanted him to travel to Katwijk with us
I didn't want it
how can I want it
no I don't care for these young people
and I certainly don't care for these intellectuals
these people with their intellectual ambitions
I've never cared for these people
who only ever throw everything into confusion
and turn everything upside-down
It was a mistake to invite him to come with us

DAUGHTER. But he'll only be staying for a day or two

MOTHER. Sure just a day or two easier said than done

DAUGHTER. He was so delighted
he admires you Mother

MOTHER. It was a mistake to invite him
But in the heat of the moment I got this feeling
a peculiar feeling
of loyalty to you do you understand

DAUGHTER. Such a great success Mother

MOTHER. But that doesn't prove anything
the people were in the right mood and they caused a success
but it could have gone the other way and then there wouldn't be any
success
nothing was definite until the very end
nothing absolutely nothing
then there was silence
and the people applauded

DAUGHTER. And how loudly they applauded Mother

MOTHER. I can't comprehend
   why they applauded
   when it was obviously a play
   in which they were all pilloried
   and in the basest manner
   with wit as well to be sure
   but with a malicious wit
   with meanspiritedness even
   with absolute meanspiritedness
   And then they applauded all of a sudden

DAUGHTER. It was a proper a really huge success

MOTHER. *One* success what does that mean
   then the people pour out into the street
   and the whole thing is forgotten
   that means nothing a success on one evening
   As if it amounted to a lifetime achievement

DAUGHTER. Who cares about lifetime achievements Mother
   The people clapped they liked it
   They liked the actors
   They like the whole thing

MOTHER. They liked the actors
   the actors were magnificent
   but the play

DAUGHTER. I think it's quite an extraordinary play

MOTHER. As if you understood even the slightest thing
   about literary drama
   the people understand nothing
   and clap themselves to death
   because they simply feel like clapping
   but they clap at even the most nonsensical things
   They even clap at their own funerals
   they applaud every slap in the face
   that they receive

they're slapped in the face from up onstage
and they applaud this
There is no greater perversity
than the perversity of theater audiences
It was a senseless idea
for us to meet up
with your playwright afterwards
An autograph
What a perverse idea
What have we got to show for it now
Now we've broken with our habit
who knows

DAUGHTER. He agreed immediately

MOTHER. I didn't say
we're going to the seaside come along
of course I didn't want that at all
I said we're going to the seaside
and then he said he'd also
like to go to the seaside
Have you been to Katwijk then I said
and he said no
he hadn't been to Katwijk
then you talked about how lovely Katwijk is

DAUGHTER. It's true Katwijk is lovely

MOTHER. Then I said
she's right Katwijk is lovely

DAUGHTER. Katwijk is quite lovely I said
because we have a whole house to ourselves there
and you can walk alone along the shore for hours on end

MOTHER. And then I said
have you ever been at the seaside at all
and then he said naturally
a playwright
must be familiar with the sea

must be familiar with the high and low tides
a playwright must be more familiar with the sea than with anything
      else
if he's familiar with the sea
he'll also be familiar with the laws of his art
I found everything that he said
very perplexing and pretentious
Suddenly I said to him several times
a playwright
it had struck me as absurd but I said it
A playwright
must always be familiar with the sea and himself
while he is writing
while he is propelling his work of art forward
with the high and low tides

DAUGHTER. High and low tides he said
he kept saying high and low tides

MOTHER. It was fairly preposterous what he was saying
he was agitated
understandably
the people exalted him to the skies
But they could just as easily have annihilated him
with a single blow
that evening
they opted for applause
not for annihilation
But it is a theater
in which both things are possible at any time
applause
or annihilation
and even at the end
applause
or annihilation
I reckon our literary dramatist
had a lot more luck than brains
We see something that we can't excuse

that we loathe
and then applaud
I didn't applaud at first
but then I did applaud after all
I couldn't do otherwise
But then once we'd left the theater
I felt ashamed
I applauded a shameless spectacle
And then that arrogant face of his

DAUGHTER. He isn't in the least bit arrogant

MOTHER. A playwright
is inherently arrogant
megalomaniacal
they're applauded and they're megalomaniacal
or they leave the theater through the back door
with their head retracted

DAUGHTER. Little by little
it leads to catastrophe

MOTHER. Yes
and it's constantly threatening to capsize
When one gives free rein
to actors who have developed such perfection
with such devotion to a work of art
and all the while I'm unsure
whether it really is a work of art or not
They abandon themselves to the audience
with this unparalleled shamelessness
At the end they're all just standing there exhausted
and nobody knows what just happened any more
and they're overwhelmed with applause
Your father couldn't be taken to a theater
under any circumstances
He had his foundry
You got your love of the theater from me

DAUGHTER. Yes Mother

MOTHER. But my passion has diminished a bit

(*Drains her glass and pours another drink*)

I've become rather skeptical indeed about
what comes down from the stage
I didn't use to be
now I ask myself
whether this is still profitable
whether I shouldn't cancel our season tickets
it's nothing but repetition
we've already seen everything
seen everything and heard everything
that comes down from the apron
Good Lord what else does it show you
but that everybody gets sick and dies
violently or otherwise
that they've got to give up the ghost
to be stabbed or not stabbed
poisoned or not poisoned
or they quite simply pass out
which makes for a spooky effect
And we've already seen our fill
of costumes haven't we

(*Drinks*)

DAUGHTER. No no there's always something new every time
it's always entirely new
if we have the will for it
if we really want to see something new

MOTHER. If we really want to see something new
Well who says
that I want to see anything new
Perhaps I never want to see anything new again

(*Drinks*)

Because I've had enough

DAUGHTER. He's offered
to carry our bags downstairs

MOTHER. Has he now

DAUGHTER. Yes he's offered to
A couple of days at the seashore
that will surely do him good
Since we have so much room in our house

MOTHER. Sure
And where will he be accommodated

DAUGHTER. In the room next to yours I guess

MOTHER. That's impossible

DAUGHTER. It would be the simplest thing

MOTHER. No no it's impossible
he'll sleep upstairs in the attic
or downstairs

DAUGHTER. Upstairs or downstairs it really makes no difference

MOTHER. It makes no difference
yes naturally it makes no difference
He'll only be bringing one small bag
for two days

DAUGHTER. He's going to tutor me on the art of drama
He's going to read me *The Broken Jug*

MOTHER. The play by Kleist

DAUGHTER. Yes he promised me to do that

MOTHER. You're going to listen to him
you're going to sit right in front of him and listen to him

DAUGHTER. Yes Mother

MOTHER. And he is going to read you Kleist's comedy
perhaps even outdoors on the open sea
and in a loud voice and you're also going to listen to what he's reading
And then

DAUGHTER. These are going to be a lovely couple of days
Everything's going to be so much more fun

MOTHER. More fun
   that's what you call it

DAUGHTER. But maybe he won't be in the mood for Kleist
   and he'll read me something of his own
   something new he's written

MOTHER. Oh Good Lord you imagine it in such detail
   as if you already knew exactly
   what's going to happen there
   what's going to be there
   (*Drinks*)

DAUGHTER. I don't know
   what's going to be there

MOTHER. I can only imagine

DAUGHTER. Maybe he'll sleep late too
   and stay in bed with the windows open
   to let in the sea air
   it's a necessity for him
   A whole year with the play
   with the comedy as he calls it

MOTHER. The sea air there will certainly do him good
   I often ask myself why a person makes something
   that's basically nothing
   What is it that he makes
   Of course I also ask myself what it is
   that I am making
   And you
   and everybody else
   It's nothing absolutely nothing
   and everybody is utterly consumed with this futility
   that is tailor-made for them and they wear themselves out
   annihilate themselves
   and they do it with such consistency
   What good does it do me to say
   I am a playwright

or
I am the owner of a foundry
or
I am the widow of an owner of a foundry
or does it do you to say
I am the daughter of a widow of an owner of a foundry
What is all this
that's what I ask myself
Or a certain person to assert that he's the pope
and that humankind can't do without him
that's what I ask myself
these are all nothing but tailor-made exercises in futility
and all of them put together are human society
It all fails to convince me
it's always failed to convince me
But why amid so much sheer futility
shouldn't there also be playwrights

(*Drinks*)

Do you think of him as honest
I mean in what he writes
what he's trying to say
after all every playwright
is trying to make a statement
isn't he

DAUGHTER. He is honest Mother

MOTHER. But what he's doing is pointless
    Naturally because everything is honest
    even mendacity is honest
    we say we're honest and yet even then we're lying
    we lie and yet even then we're telling the truth
    perhaps that's the way it is
    Whenever I talk like this I build up quite a head of steam
    but it's pointless
    We go to the theater and see a play
    we step out of the theater and tell ourselves it's pointless

and we don't go to the theater
and don't see any plays and tell ourselves it's pointless
And if he reads *The Broken Jug* to you
it will also be pointless or won't it

DAUGHTER. The *Broken Jug* is his favorite play

MOTHER. Naturally *The Broken Jug* is his favorite play
    but your favorite dramatist is your playwright am I right

DAUGHTER. But you yourself used to like *The Broken Jug*

MOTHER. Yes twenty years ago
    even fifteen years ago
    back then I liked everything by Shakespeare
    but I also liked operettas
    Wasn't that nice
    the way we kept going to operettas
    less to the actual theater

DAUGHTER. I don't know

MOTHER. That was much nicer
    honestly

DAUGHTER. We've moved on

MOTHER. We've moved on from operettas
    and not from operettas to opera
    but rather from operettas directly to the actual theater
    that really is quite remarkable

DAUGHTER. That really is better
    from operettas to plays
    and not just to opera

MOTHER. You say that as if you understood something about it
    It sounds really fine
    it's extraordinary
    extraordinary
    but it's still tasteless
    it's really tasteless my child
    this is all owing to the influence

of your playwright
Even when you say
the upper classes should be abolished
and indeed radically abolished
that isn't coming from you at all
that is your playwright talking
who whips up the downtrodden masses as you say
Say it go on say it my child
the worst sort of drivel go on say it

(*Drinks*)

Rouse humanity to action
that sounds hilarious when you say it
when you say promulgate the truth
It's like when your father said all's well that ends well
it's the playwright talking
it's the anarchist talking
it's the road map talking
But does your playwright really know his way along the road
is there a single human being who knows the way
it's all tasteless all deception
all self-deception

(*Drinks*)

It was a terrible misfortune my child
that you ever stumbled upon literature
If only we'd never set foot in a theater
now we're paying the price
for our for assiduous pursuit of culture

(*Smites her forehead*)

it really is insane
what you're up to now is downright crazy

(*Suddenly in a different tone of voice*)

do you still hear from Johannes every now and then

(DAUGHTER *shakes her head in the negative*)

These people don't accomplish anything either

they make a splendid entrance
embark on careers
tackle everything with youthful gusto
uproarious applause wherever you look
and all of a sudden there's silence
they've turned into nothing
And Raimund
have you heard anything from Raimund

DAUGHTER (*folds a green sundress and places it in the trunk*). Nothing

MOTHER. He wrote to you didn't he
How were things in Paris anyway

DAUGHTER. He didn't write to me

MOTHER. I know for a fact that he wrote to you
Raimund wrote to you

DAUGHTER. He didn't write to me

MOTHER. Everybody pulls away from you
because you've always taken the wrong path
these wrong paths are the problem
To think of all the things I tried
but you were too stupid for my attempts
my simpleton of a child
who never could comprehend anything
I liked Raimund
he was always tight-lipped at the right moment
then talkative again
and elegant he was always elegant
and when you conversed with him
you didn't need to feel embarrassed
the only thing that always bothered me was the way he said *supper*
there was something perverse about it
but otherwise
I was also fond of his parents
You should have made an effort
but you've never made an effort

And Ludwig went to America
that was no big surprise
the troublemaker the visionary
have you heard anything from him

DAUGHTER. No nothing

MOTHER. New York is hell my child
At first it seems to be an enjoyable city
but it turns out to be hell
You're not the emigrating type
I'm not either
I might have let you roam
if I'd been healthy
but it's better for you that you're here
by my side
protected by me
I often ask myself whether you're worth protecting
I don't know
I protect you
Father didn't believe in you
she's going rotten he kept saying
she'll come to nothing
she's got nothing but drivel in her head
she isn't agile enough
she sees nothing
she's unmusical amusical
and she hasn't got any business sense either
Good Lord how easy it was for him to say all that
We're too hard on other people my child
We see and see nothing
one person becomes something
and we never thought it was possible
and someone else becomes nothing
and we sank all our hopes in him
Everybody has a treacherous development
All's well that ends well
Your father was no seer

the foundry crushed him
sometimes at night he would throw himself against my door
which thank God was locked shut and he'd scream
that he couldn't take it any more
I would said nothing in reply
And wait until he'd calmed down
not a word from me nothing
then he'd go back
he'd whimper at the door
I would hear him but I wouldn't open the door
He'd be sinking ever lower I could hear it
he'd knock a couple of more times
and then fall silent
I'd tiptoe up to the keyhole and see him lying there
but I wouldn't open the door
Everybody must cope with himself my child
Everybody wants to escape from himself
but there's no escape

(DAUGHTER *clears away the tea things*)

Always the same movements
always the same facial expressions
You're not changing
but you're aging like everybody else
but I notice it in you
how quickly you're aging
It's just an observation
escaping and getting old

(*Drinks*)

I only hope he's punctual
your playwright
What's so mysterious
about artists
so special about them
They're different that's true
Actors playwrights
we speak quite differently with them than with our own kind

we listen to them more attentively
we observe them more intently
when we see through them we're disappointed
what we're left with is an upset stomach
and a disturbed mind
We stuff them full of extraordinariness and exceptionalness
and tear it back out of them
until it makes us sick
Sure once upon a time I thought
I was going to marry an artist
not an actor a genuine artist
I didn't have any clear idea of what an artist was
but my husband was going to have to be an artist
I hated businessmen the commercial world
But everything turned out differently
When I'd reached the very end of my rope
this man with a foundry sat down at my table
I had been blubbering earlier
My eyes were still sopping wet
where to next I didn't know
All's well that ends well I can still hear it
the word foundry the word seaside
I was repelled and attracted at the same time
repelled by the man
but attracted by the word foundry
The truth is that I had fallen in love
with the word foundry
I thought I was dealing with a crazy person but no
A complete stranger and your father
He was a lazy individual
I don't know a thing about his character
but he had no other choice
I refused to let him go
I clove tightly to him
I embraced him
he had no way of escaping
All's well that ends well he said to me in the park

when I'd just told him that a child was on the way
you are a dimwit I said
you're a moron you're worthless

(*Exit* DAUGHTER *with the tea things.* MOTHER *shouting at her as she leaves*)

I said you're an idiot
I thought I've married a crazy person
And then this child
He was a huge Richard Wagner fan
Richard he said to the old man in the cradle
He'd thrown up as soon as he saw the child
Whose fault is this he asked me
I'm going to smother it I thought

(*Enter the* DAUGHTER *with several coats*)

The letters he wrote me
were too fatuous
he talked me into traveling with him to Basel
where he had things to do
The people he associated with made me sick
But I didn't run away quite the opposite

(*Drinks*)

we were in Naples in Florence
we were in Russia
I got bored my child
I had quickly gotten used to luxury
to the new clothes to the big rooms
I got settled in Katwijk
I ran up and down the shoreline
I had acquired so many things
I'd never even dreamt of

(DAUGHTER *hangs the coats on a hook in preparation for packing them*)

Astonishingly he couldn't dance
I laboriously taught him
a couple of steps
till he could manage to tango

Your father had never been to an art gallery
I hadn't either
so we went to one and looked at the paintings
but I found it boring
high art bored me
I learned to write
to read and write
because the truth was I couldn't do either
when I met your father
at first he was more than my match in all things intellectual
but all of a sudden I had overshot him
at first he didn't notice this
that was my trump card
He fell into my traps more and more often
I could already write letters
I corrected business letters
I quickly learned how I had to dress

(*Addressing* DAUGHTER *point-blank*) At first I had just one dress
and now I have so many dresses
that it almost drives me crazy
It was bound to get out of hand
one pair of shoes
and now
always more and more
but then we quickly lose our appetite for it
A surplus turns into a surfeit
The fact that his parents weren't alive any more
was an asset
naturally the story of their misfortune
didn't move me
he always told it the same way
and waited for a sign that I was moved
but I was never moved
It's good that they're not around any more I kept thinking
We couldn't have gotten married if they were
Richard that horrifying face of his
as if he were already eighty years old on his first day

there was no explanation for it
It was impossible to stop him
from going to the cemetery every Saturday
one fine day I told him
that I would leave him
if he kept visiting the cemetery
you're driving yourself crazy with your cemetery visits I said
all week every week I heard nothing from him but
on Saturday I'm going to see my parents
by which he meant going to the cemetery
that had to stop
But I know that he secretly called on them
The moment Richard was buried
he stopped going there
that happens in one out of every three or four million births
a newborn looking like an old man
Children are a curse in the best of cases
be glad you don't have any children
You were a hideous child
with good-natured eyes but really hideous
it took a long time for a human being
to become visible in that hideous flesh
you smiled that's
what reconciled me to you
but everybody was appalled I know they were
they wouldn't admit it to me
but I saw that they were appalled
You should have been a son
We'll stop by Amsterdam and buy ourselves headscarves right
Ah when we're finally in Katwijk
Of course I don't know a single thing about our playwright
is he from the country or from the city
I know absolutely nothing
I don't know this man from Adam and I say
do come with us to the seaside at Katwijk

DAUGHTER. He's a city person

MOTHER. From Amsterdam

DAUGHTER. No from Rotterdam

MOTHER. Of humble origins no doubt

DAUGHTER. His father worked on a fishing cutter

MOTHER. How does one come to be a playwright
a stupid question
it's like asking
how does one come to be old
Well of course he must be musical as well

DAUGHTER. Indeed he is
he used to play the violin

MOTHER. Used to play the violin
everybody used to play the violin
Rotterdam's not a bad place to begin
I know a few people who are from Rotterdam
and who have amounted to something

DAUGHTER. He left Rotterdam very early on

MOTHER. What did he study at university anyway

DAUGHTER. I don't know

MOTHER. Theater
one can study theater
the art of drama I don't know

DAUGHTER. He lived for a long time on a stipend
but I don't know what kind of stipend

MOTHER. A drama stipend probably
but what is that

(*Drinks*)

Probably one goes to a famous writer
and asks him
to teach one how to write a play

Drivel
One goes to a theater and sees how a play is performed
Drivel
No one knows how to become a playwright
They say his plays have been staged and have been successful
but how did that happen
He could certainly tell me that
explain it to me
There are these plays
that smash everything to pieces
that belittle everything to pieces
A man enters the stage and with the first words he says
he has pronounced his own death sentence
And the woman he's speaking to
he's tearing to pieces along with himself
it's all so ruthless
everybody enters and is sentenced to death
and he even calls his play *Save Yourself If You Can*
because it's clear that nobody can save himself
it's ridiculous to think about saving yourself
everybody is destroyed at the denouement
everybody is running himself into the ground
as they all set about trying to save themselves
they talk and they run into the ground
they sit around and run themselves into the ground
there is no exit
Do you believe that life is like in that play
Save Yourself If You Can that's cynical

(*Puts down her glass, stands up and goes to the trunk and peers into it*)

This was always the coat trunk

(*Takes out a coat and folds it and places it back in the trunk*)

At the seaside all the wrinkles just drop right out

(*Helps* DAUGHTER *pack*)

I always wanted
to go to Peking I don't know why

I had a soft spot for the Chinese
now it's too late
now I've even lost all desire to go there
just a couple of years ago we still could have gone there
not any longer
All my life I dreamt about meeting new people on a ship
about a proper adventure on the high seas
I used to think about a captain
a world-traveler
who knew the world
but in the end I never met one
If the foundry had never existed
and your father made that impossible for ever
How quickly we adjust
assimilate to use that lovely word

(*Lifts a winter coat up high*)

Still quite a beautiful piece of clothing isn't it
So much naphthalene
I really can't stand it

DAUGHTER. Sit down Mother
I can do all this by myself

(MOTHER *goes to the chair and sits down.* DAUGHTER *looks at her watch*)

Will we be ready when he gets here

MOTHER. I have always loathed packing
but also unpacking
of course everything we pack
we have to unpack again

(*Drinks and raises her voice*)

Take a sip
one sip for you come on

(DAUGHTER *goes up to her and takes a sip from her glass*)

What don't I owe you everything my child
And now
do you intend to leave me

No
you won't leave me
you simply can't
you simply can't survive without me
you'd perish without me
if you go away you'll perish
But you are completely free naturally
You can do whatever you want
I've always told you that
free free my child
Now just keep packing
so that you'll be ready when our friend gets here
our dramatic genius our successful writer
who wrote the drama *Save Yourself If You Can*

(DAUGHTER *goes to the trunk and packs the coats*)

Once we're in Katwijk and listening to the *Boléro*
with the windows open what do you think
will you be thrilled by that

DAUGHTER. Yes Mother

MOTHER. When we're sitting side by side
and playing the *Boléro*
as we've always done
or I'm reading something to you
or you're reading something to me
when we draw lots you to me or me to you
It's really quite nice when I'm listening to you
as you read to me
or as I read to you
and you're listening to me
So many books in Katwijk
Or does all that not thrill you

DAUGHTER. Yes Mother

MOTHER. I don't know if it thrills me
I had such a great hankering for Katwijk

and now all of a sudden
the thought of going there makes me sick
I loathe this trip
that empty landscape
that horrifying house

(*Drinks*)

But it's simply a habit
We can't break it
We've been leaving town on this date
for thirty-three years
But for the past twenty years we've been making the trip alone
just the two of us

DAUGHTER. Twenty years are enough
And after all he's only staying for two days

MOTHER. Who knows
He may develop a taste for the place and stay longer
or you may develop a taste for his being there
It was a mistake on my part
I was overhasty
I should have said young man your play is an extraordinary play
and we were really impressed by it
and then we should have left
We should have got his autograph from him
and then vanished straight away
Because I had a weak moment
I said do come with us to Katwijk
Now after this success
you can treat yourself to a couple of days at the seaside
You weren't opposed to the idea

DAUGHTER. I wasn't opposed to the idea

MOTHER. I needn't have invited him

DAUGHTER. But it was quite a good idea
to invite him to Katwijk

MOTHER. That's easy for you to say
  It was not a good idea
  We've got to keep doing something to spite ourselves
  suddenly
  we don't know why
  We'll go with him to the market
  We'll listen to fine music with him
  we'll dine in a fine restaurant with him
  How old is he

DAUGHTER. I don't know

MOTHER. Just over thirty
  am I right

DAUGHTER. Yes perhaps

MOTHER. He didn't take a bow at the end of the performance
  but it's traditional for the author to bow
  at the end of a performance
  He simply has to make an appearance then
  it's something he simply owes the audience
  he faces the audience and takes a bow

DAUGHTER. That's not his style

MOTHER. Not his style
  It's his style to slip outside
  through the back door
  Through the rear entrance
  as if he had a guilty conscience
  Probably our playwright actually does have a guilty conscience
  It's that kind of play
  it's logical for him to have a guilty conscience
  he's got to have one
  he has no other choice
  so he's got to withdraw through the rear exit
  and naturally he doesn't take a bow
  That wouldn't be logical
  and strictly speaking it would be in poor taste

(*Drinks*)

And does he even earn any money
I mean has he got any

DAUGHTER. I believe so yes

MOTHER. Where does he live anyway
Where does he live

DAUGHTER. In Rotterdam

MOTHER. In Rotterdam that doesn't tell you anything
Who knows what kind of life he leads

DAUGHTER. I think everything he does
is quite normal

MOTHER. How can you be sure of that
these people are dangerous
young and dangerous
they sound you out
they sidle up to you
and then they detonate something

DAUGHTER. What

MOTHER. Something or other
It's always spooky being in the company of such people
You embrace them with open arms
and they murder you

DAUGHTER. You make everything so dramatic mother

MOTHER. Perhaps
Perhaps we ourselves
are dramatic material for him
we're a treasure chest
literally a treasure chest for a dramatist
for a dramatist like him
who hauls out everything
from the deepest depths

DAUGHTER. Perhaps

MOTHER. Perhaps you say
He's tasted blood

he's seen us for just a couple of minutes
and has tasted blood
Katwijk what a lode of material for him
for starters there's your father and all the others
how and from what we got to be what we are
He'll come to Katwijk and beat some capital out of us
He takes what people give him
have you seen his eyes
spooky aren't they

DAUGHTER. Do you think so

MOTHER. I do think so
I do
By the way he said
I'd be glad to be your guest
his very words were glad to be your guest
which of course means
we'll have to pay for his train ticket

DAUGHTER. Yes that's what it means

MOTHER. Isn't it unusual
to buy a man one hardly knows
a train ticket to Katwijk

DAUGHTER. But he's actually quite well-known
he's a celebrity

MOTHER. Perhaps he is a celebrity he could be
But I cannot buy him a train ticket to Katwijk

DAUGHTER. Naturally we'll pay for the ticket Mother

MOTHER. I have no intention of doing that
on the other hand
how will I come off looking
if I don't pay for his ticket
if I don't
given that I have after all invited him to Katwijk
Do come with us to Katwijk

was what I said
I didn't say
come see us in Katwijk
so probably I'm obligated to pay for his ticket to Katwijk

DAUGHTER. He'll be a great help to us
You know how much trouble we always have
getting our luggage to Katwijk

MOTHER. If he's strong and nimble

DAUGHTER. He is nimble

MOTHER. But he isn't strong

DAUGHTER. He's nimble
and he's strong

MOTHER. A playwright isn't supposed to be strong

DAUGHTER. Oh but Mother

MOTHER. How can you know that

DAUGHTER. He's strong

MOTHER. These people are megalomaniacal
but they aren't strong
from the fact that he writes strong dialogue it obviously doesn't follow
that he's strong
And who knows perhaps he's lazy
Writers are lazy people
perhaps playwrights are even lazier
But perhaps we'll find him not only dangerous
but also entertaining
that certainly wouldn't be a liability
But once you've seen his play
you've got to be apprehensive about this person
Now we've invited him

DAUGHTER. You've invited him

MOTHER. I've invited him along
I said

come with us to Katwijk
He accepted the invitation immediately
which really astonished me
I didn't think he would accept it

DAUGHTER. He immediately said yes

MOTHER. Even though he had no idea where Katwijk is

DAUGHTER. I think that's sweet
the fact that he accepted without knowing where Katwijk is

MOTHER. People like him are dangerous
people who make up their minds to do something
without hesitating for an instant
these people frighten me
We should learn more about him
about his parents and so forth
Does he have siblings

DAUGHTER. Perhaps

MOTHER. We're taking into our house a person
we know nothing about
apart from this play of his that we've seen
this play with the peculiar title *Save Yourself If You Can*
he's a cynic
But he's still quite young
but that's what makes him dangerous
Are you writing another play yet I asked him
and he said nothing in reply
It would have been so easy to say something
at least yes or no
but no he said nothing whatsoever
He found the question tiresome

(*Examining the bill*)

Raising of an obelisk
Masonry work et cetera
Eighty thousand

(*Sets the bill aside again*)

All year long I think of nothing but the moment
when we can get away from here
but once we've attained our goal
everything is topsy-turvy

(*To* DAUGHTER *point-blank*) Come pour me some more

I need it
I can't put up with this without it

(DAUGHTER *goes up to her and pours her some more cognac*)

To think that you can tolerate it
without touching a drop
You are my pure child
I am your impure mother
your horrible mother isn't that so

(DAUGHTER *returns to the trunk*)

The mother who keeps her child clasped to her bosom
and never lets go of her
until she suffocates
Am I not right

DAUGHTER. You're only torturing yourself

MOTHER. My favorite preoccupation
    is self-torture
    as I torture you
    as I have been butchering you all these decades
    I've also been butchering myself
    with love do you understand
    we are chained to each other in love
    in true motherly love

(*Drinks*)

A mother doesn't want to give away her child
she chains it to herself
and never lets go of it
and if it tears itself away
it's punished with death
as soon as it's torn itself away it's executed

You understand me don't you
You are intended for me
I brought you into the world *for myself*
You are not Richard
the child that got away
You are here for me
for me and me alone
Don't you ever doubt
that you belong to me and to me alone
you belong to me down to every last hair on your head

(*Exit* DAUGHTER *and reenter* DAUGHTER *with one arm laden with skirts that she then sets down on the windowsill*)

I loathe the stench of naphthalene

(*Looks around the room*)

All year long this room stinks of it
Because we never let any air in
But then when we're at the seaside everything is open
Day and night everything is open
and the sea air floods all the rooms
Every time we leave on a trip
I'm condemned to inactivity
then I can't cope any more
then I'm reliant on your help
One fine day the foundry will be eaten all up what then
Then we'll move for good to Katwijk
and give up everything here
and using the money we'll get for this house
we'll live in Katwijk
I of course won't be alive much longer
And for you I'm sure we'll find some solution
But don't ever think about escaping
You've tried it so many times already
but you've never succeeded
I'll never set you free
I brought you into the world for me
for me alone

as long as I'm here you'll belong to me
You enjoy every liberty you know that
but you're duty-bound to me through the end of my life
You can treat yourself to anything
I've never yet denied you any wish
at least not any reasonable wish
but I won't let you go
not now that you've grown completely accustomed to me
We've gotten used to each other so nicely
Ah my dear child
you mustn't make me feel sad

(*Beckons her over*)

Come here
come here right now
I want you to come here

(DAUGHTER *goes to her.* MOTHER *takes her by the hand*)

Even if you've had a rough life
perhaps it's really the only possibility
Kneel down before me
Please kneel down
the way you used to
You were just a little girl
Back then I forced you to kneel down
Now I ask you to

(DAUGHTER *kneels down before her.* MOTHER *kisses her on her forehead*)

We ourselves are to blame for everything
We had no other choice
We are facing the consequences
I've always loved you like this
with you in front of me on your knees
With this regal bearing on my side
And you waiting for me to give you permission to rise
From one second to the next
My little girl
my little girl from Katwijk

come rise
Enough rise

(DAUGHTER *rises*)

I can't stand it when you kneel down before me
But I can't do a thing about it
I want to see it

(DAUGHTER *returns to her work*)

You've never done anything
without my permission
You never would have done anything except at my command isn't that
    right
There's no need for you to answer
He was always saying that you were *his* creature
but you are *my* creature
you came out of me
you've derived yourself from me
I should have kept going to the foundry
but I lost all inclination to go there
It would have been as horrible in its own way
if your father hadn't died
then neither of us would have had to be involved in it at all
What would have become of him
an unfortunate development
He would have ended up with foundry-work on the brain
and never would have taken an interest in literature
and never wanted to hear a note of music
and his brain would have gotten more and more tired
Can you imagine him still being alive
and us having to put up with him
He was getting more and more like an animal
Back then he would lie on the sofa for hours on end
and stare at the ceiling
I've completely lost control of myself he would say
I am all torn up inside
then he would say All's well that ends well
that would calm him down

(*Points at the sofa*)

He lay there and told me I had to read the story of the Little Match
    Girl to him
and I refused
if I'd known that he had only two days left to live
but I didn't know that
I knew he was going to die
but I didn't know he'd die within two days
At the end he didn't ask to see you
He didn't even ask where is our child
I told him you had gone to Katwijk
but that was apparently of no interest to him
although he did quite often cry out for Richard

(*In a whisper*)

For our old man
Early in the morning he wanted to go out
but of course he couldn't walk at all any more
I told him no not today no
I'm sorry
but when I saw him lying there
with his mouth open completely emaciated
he looked as he'd looked at the inn
like the man who told me about his foundry for the first time
I sat there and observed him and loathed him
soon I won't have to see this face any more
this dimwitted expression any more I thought

(*Removes a ring from one of her fingers*)

Come here
You shall have it
You know it's my most valuable piece of jewelry
So come over here
You always hesitate
You needn't hesitate
Perhaps our playwright will fancy it
Come here

(DAUGHTER *goes up to her.* MOTHER *putting the ring on her*)

Your father bought it for me in Amsterdam
I saw it in a jeweler's window as we were passing by
he didn't hesitate at all

(*Takes* DAUGHTER *by the hand*)

How lovely the ring is
I was planning
to give it to you in Katwijk
why not now
We'll have a lovely summer in Katwijk
we've always had lovely summers there
even the rainy summers in Katwijk have been lovely
It's really nice that we're together
that we're alone
without any interlopers
Nobody can be allowed to pull us apart do you understand

(DAUGHTER *returns to the trunk*)

When we form a picture of a person
and we think we're picturing him as he is
we've pictured him all wrong
he's not the way we've pictured him
We tell a story
and it's a completely different story
We go see a person
and he's a completely different person
We're horrified by what we trusted in
In principle I have nothing against other people
if they leave us alone
Where would you be better off
You think about your missed opportunities
everybody has always missed every opportunity
I think we ought to be content
and we are after all by ourselves in Katwijk
Perhaps the violin virtuoso will be there
and his friend the magician

It really was a lot of fun watching the two of them
But we mustn't let them get too close
People fraternize with each other and annihilate each other
Artists are the most dangerous types of all
But is a playwright really an artist
You can observe him
it will quickly become clear that he isn't right for you

DAUGHTER. Maybe for you

MOTHER (*aghast and bursting into laughter*). For me

DAUGHTER. Yes for you
   Maybe he's right for you

MOTHER. Wherever did you get that idea
   It would be absurd a frivolous absurdity

DAUGHTER. He immediately accepted *your* invitation
   I didn't invite him
   I didn't think he would come with us

MOTHER. You never would have dared to invite him would you
   not without my permission
   I said come with us to Katwijk

DAUGHTER. He can read you something
   and you can listen to him
   while I take a walk

MOTHER. Your taking a walk
   while he reads me something
   Do you think I have any interest in that

DAUGHTER. You'll really enjoy it
   And you'll have what you've been looking for for so long
   variety
   and what's more thanks to a dramatic artist
   who's very good-looking

MOTHER. Do you think he's good-looking
   Perhaps you're right

DAUGHTER. It doesn't much matter to me that he's a playwright

MOTHER. You say that with such an insinuating air

DAUGHTER. I'll be happy
if he provides you with some conversation
Most of the time we're bored stiff in Katwijk

MOTHER. Is that true
Do you see it that way
I have never been bored in Katwijk
Here I'm bored
Here where there are supposedly so many opportunities for
conversation
No as long as I'm satisfied with myself

DAUGHTER (*exclamatorily*). Satisfied with yourself

MOTHER. *You* can't imagine that
You can't imagine it
You need a good thrashing

DAUGHTER. Maybe you're right

MOTHER. I'm right about this
But I don't need it
I converse best with myself in solitude
Other people only disturb me
I don't care for interlopers
because they disrupt my conversation

DAUGHTER. Your conversation with yourself
For thirty years forty years you've been engaged in nothing else

MOTHER. I was alone with your father as well
I was totally oriented towards myself
He meant nothing to me I can say that for sure
I couldn't converse with him about anything
he went out of his way to be boring
All his employees were boring
For years I tried conversing with him
and eventually I gave up

But unlike him I never allowed myself to be annihilated by the
    foundry
I had no interest in that
I always conversed best with myself in solitude
People don't understand this
because they always need to be in a group in order to have a
    conversation
I'm a group on my own that's what I am
I'm so many people at once in Katwijk my child

DAUGHTER *(folding a blouse and laying it in the trunk)*. Because you don't
    need me at all in Katwijk

MOTHER. I need you that is clear
    I have always needed you
    but that is something different

DAUGHTER. What

MOTHER. I've grown lethally accustomed to you yes lethally

DAUGHTER. I wait on you
    I'm here for you

MOTHER. Yes my child you've gradually learned
    to read my every wish in my eyes
    or in a subtle hand gesture
    You've learned a great deal along these lines
    And so all your wishes will be fulfilled

DAUGHTER *(bursting into laughter)*. All my wishes

MOTHER. I know your laugh
    it doesn't affect me any more

DAUGHTER. Of course it doesn't

MOTHER. You always laugh the same laugh
    and yet it's always with a different nuance

DAUGHTER. Yes

MOTHER. What if he writes a play
    in which this laugh plays a role

I could imagine him doing that
and he calls his play *The Laugh*
Incredible
And nothing but this laugh is heard over and over again
But *Save Yourself If You Can* is also a lovely title
I like his cynicism

DAUGHTER. You're always the same

MOTHER. People everywhere are always the same
    they try as hard as they can
    to get away from themselves
    to become another person
    in vain
    they put on the face of another person
    but it melts away
    You've never tried to be anybody else
    You wouldn't dream of it
    you're more and more yourself
    it is a process of calcification isn't it
    Your nature is self-calcifying
    that was already evident when you were still quite a small child
    I thought she'll always be herself
    but more and more calcified more dogged
    you never wanted to come out of your shell
    you only ever wanted to go deeper and deeper into it
    Now you're completely trapped inside yourself
    You never give a thought to escaping
    isn't that right
    In Katwijk I'll go straight to the seamstress
    the skirts need to be altered
    the linen needs to be mended
    in the country they still alter things still mend things
    I'd have to go to Katwijk for that reason alone

(DAUGHTER *goes to the kitchen and drinks a glass of water*)

Bring me a glass of water too

(DAUGHTER *returns with a glass of water.* MOTHER *after taking a sip*)

At first we wanted to change everything in Katwijk
now I'm glad
that nothing has happened in Katwijk
Even if everything has gone to pieces by now
the whole thing is in a desolate state

(*Hands* DAUGHTER *the glass*)

But that's the charm
never knowing
whether the rain will seep in
whether or not the whole thing will collapse right over your head
I can love a house like that
I wonder whether he'll like Katwijk
From the way he writes I think I can tell
he'll like Katwijk
But if he likes Katwijk

(DAUGHTER *takes the glass into the kitchen*)

You've only seen him two times
once on your own
and yesterday after the performance

(*Exclamatorily*)

How did things go when you spoke with him on your own

(DAUGHTER *returns, goes to the trunk*)

Did you get the feeling
he was a sincere person
An artist never gives you that feeling

DAUGHTER. It was really quite a brief chat

MOTHER. Was he dismissive

DAUGHTER. No not dismissive

MOTHER. How did it go
Even if it was just a brief chat
you can still say how it went
Did he ask any questions
or did he just talk about himself

DAUGHTER. I don't remember

MOTHER. These people only ever talk about themselves
    I got quite a shock once in Katwijk
    suddenly this man was standing in my room
    A stranger I thought
    but it was your father
    It's quite spooky in Katwijk sometimes
    Are you ever afraid in Katwijk

DAUGHTER. No

MOTHER. That's where we're different
    I'm afraid
    you aren't afraid
    it should be quite the other way round
    Have you ever given any thought to that

DAUGHTER. To what

MOTHER. To the fact that *you* should be afraid in Katwijk
    not me

DAUGHTER. Not me

MOTHER. No you
    not me
    it doesn't make any sense

DAUGHTER. What

MOTHER. That you aren't afraid in Katwijk
    that I am afraid

DAUGHTER. I've never been afraid in Katwijk
    because you're with me when we're in Katwijk

MOTHER. Because I'm with you
    Then for a while you're quite happy
    you have a good complexion
    when we've just gotten back from Katwijik
    Now you're already quite gray-faced
    it can't just be age

the whole atmosphere here
I don't look so good either

The doorbell rings

DAUGHTER. He's here

MOTHER (*after checking her watch*). Fairly punctual fairly

(*Exit* DAUGHTER)

(*Talking to herself*) We'll lodge him in the attic
all the way upstairs
naturally all the way upstairs

(*Enter* DAUGHTER *with* PLAYWRIGHT)

We're almost ready
almost finished packing
We'll be ready in a trice
Please do have a seat

(*She points at a chair, he sits down.* DAUGHTER *puts a waistcoat into the trunk*)

You don't have the best complexion either sir
Everybody's gray here
it's high time we were in Katwijk
It's been thirty years
more like forty years
since my husband was still alive
we haven't changed our rhythm of departure

(*To* DAUGHTER) isn't that right my child

(*To* PLAYWRIGHT) She doesn't remember exactly any more
In any case it's unimportant
The important thing is for us to get to Katwijk in good shape
For forty years we've been taking the same train
By the way how do you like traveling by train

PLAYWRIGHT. I enjoy it very much

MOTHER. I'm a passionate train-traveler
First class naturally

and naturally a window-seat
but one facing the back of the train
on account of the draft
There's no lovelier place in the world
for train travel than here in Holland
don't you agree

PLAYWRIGHT. Yes it's lovely
riding through Holland in a train

MOTHER. My daughter and I
we have quite a specific rhythm
in Katwijk
You are the first person in many years
who has interrupted this rhythm
We've always been quite alone in Katwijk
Are you familiar with Katwijk

PLAYWRIGHT. Unfortunately I'm not

MOTHER. Well you'll soon see what kind of place Katwijk is
It's been in the family for quite a long time
and oddly enough it hasn't changed at all
in all these decades although of course in these same decades
the world as a whole has changed a great deal
My daughter was quite enthused by your play
Don't you feel yourself highly threatened
in enjoying such a huge success
isn't it a threat to your work
aren't you horrified by the reaction
I think a playwright wants to have a success
but once he's actually had one
and it's such a violent success
he's actually horrified isn't that right

PLAYWRIGHT. Yes

MOTHER. I can well imagine
that it's very dangerous
to enjoy such a success
a resounding success as they say

thanks to such an unpredictable audience
thanks to such a genuinely unpredictable set of critics
A playwright
a person who is after all unsociable by nature
suddenly bombarded with applause
Even that's a kind of lack of consideration
No doubt you celebrated all night long

PLAYWRIGHT. No I didn't
I ran away
at first I thought I was going to celebrate
because the actors were celebrating
they were all celebrating
but then I ran away
I wandered around the city half the night
I hadn't the slightest idea
of what had happened

MOTHER. Were you really expecting your success

PLAYWRIGHT. I was hoping

MOTHER. What were you hoping

PLAYWRIGHT. That things would go well

MOTHER. And in fact they went excellently
You can't ask for anything more
now they can call you a successful playwright
perhaps someday even a celebrated successful playwright
Don't let yourself be bothered by too much applause
just calmly revel in it
In Katwijk you'll have enough time to reflect on
what should happen next
There you'll sit on the terrace
and first of all just let everything pass by
And then everything will be clear again
So much applause is completely overwhelming isn't it
Everything is applauded
and destroyed
And then a great deal of time is needed to put everything back in order

DAUGHTER. In the theater I remained standing and applauding
  to the end

MOTHER. I kept saying let's go why don't we go
  enough is enough
  it's all exaggerated I said
  but you refused to listen to me

DAUGHTER. The people wouldn't leave the theater
  they stood in the lobby and talked
  I think they'd all been taken aback

MOTHER. Yes that's nice

  (*With* PLAYWRIGHT's *help*, DAUGHTER *closes up the trunk*)

My daughter is highly receptive
to literary drama
It was always her wish
to perform on the operatic stage
for years she took singing lessons
but it didn't work out

  (DAUGHTER *and* PLAYWRIGHT *press the trunk firmly shut and lock it*)

One has to deal with the fact
that one isn't getting anywhere
Yes that's the way it is sir

  (*To* DAUGHTER) You can call the maid
if everything's ready

  (*To* PLAYWRIGHT *as he takes up his bags*) The theater is one of the
    possible ways
of putting up with it isn't it

  (*Exit* DAUGHTER)

  (*To* PLAYWRIGHT *while looking out the window*) Whenever we go to
    Katwijk
the weather turns nasty

PART TWO

At the seaside
The evening of the same day
A large ground-floor room with a terrace
MOTHER *and* DAUGHTER, *still in their travel clothes,*
are unpacking the trunk

PLAYWRIGHT (*sitting in a chair with an unupholstered seat*). I could have
    taken that path
  but I took the other one
  they said it'll lead to a dead end
  you'll be a failure
  A course of study in architecture madam
  plotted in advance by my father
  Blueprints made of pure imagination
  Imaginary cathedrals
  It seemed as though I were listening
  but I was following the other path
  from the outside it looked as though I were following the path that
      had been plotted for me
  but I was doggedly following the other one
  which I had to follow
  Even though I couldn't have had a clue
  about what a writer was
  even though I had no idea
  of what literary drama was

MOTHER. So you dared
  to go against the grain

PLAYWRIGHT. I did dare to do that
  and I thought against the grain
  I thought against the grain about everything
  Being against the grain held my interest

MOTHER. And did you confide your thoughts to your mother

PLAYWRIGHT. No naturally not even to my mother
  I couldn't allow myself to confide in anybody
  I had to go it alone
  alone with the utmost decisiveness and in the utmost secrecy

MOTHER. To set out on your adventure

PLAYWRIGHT. To set out into the darkness
  I oriented myself towards the darkness

MOTHER. So you made yourself comfortable
  in the darkness

PLAYWRIGHT. If you insist on putting it so grotesquely
  yes
  They told me I had to brush my coat clean
  but I didn't brush it at all

MOTHER. You had always thought along those lines
  and double-crossed your family
  who always meant you well

PLAYWRIGHT. They meant well
  But I also always meant well
  but in a different way

MOTHER. In a different way in what sense

PLAYWRIGHT. I wasn't *quite* as well-meaning as they were

MOTHER. That strengthened you
  You overtaxed yourself against the grain
  You offended everybody
  You destroyed everything
  in order to get your own way
  you had no need to show any consideration

you annihilated everything around you
in order to be able to breathe more deeply isn't that right

PLAYWRIGHT. I felt a sense of solidarity with myself
and with nobody else
I saved myself from the others

MOTHER. You saved yourself at the expense of your family
What sort of people were your parents

PLAYWRIGHT. Everything disturbed me everything irritated me

MOTHER. Everything irritated you

PLAYWRIGHT. They'd slip a jacket onto me and say
this is the jacket you'll be wearing for the rest of your life
and I'd slip back out of the jacket

MOTHER. And they'd slip the jacket back onto you

PLAYWRIGHT. Yes

MOTHER. And you'd slip back out of the jacket

PLAYWRIGHT. They'd slip it onto me
and I'd slip out of it
time and again they slipped it onto me
and I slipped out of it

MOTHER. Until they were exhausted

PLAYWRIGHT. Yes

MOTHER. And then you had a clear path

PLAYWRIGHT. I went away and made myself self-sufficient

MOTHER. Away to where

PLAYWRIGHT. I wanted to see Paris and went to Paris
But in Paris things weren't so easy either

MOTHER. Why not

PLAYWRIGHT. I didn't know a word of French
and couldn't understand anybody

MOTHER. Were you good at picking up languages

PLAYWRIGHT. I picked up French
  in six or eight weeks
  because I was hearing nothing but French
  and I wanted nothing more
  than to speak French
  But once I could speak French
  far from perfectly of course
  I realized
  that Paris wasn't for me
  it was crushing me
  I left Paris before it completely crushed me

MOTHER. And where did you go next

PLAYWRIGHT. To England
  because I already knew English
  and it didn't present any difficulties to me

MOTHER. And how did you support yourself

PLAYWRIGHT. I worked at the port
  Ports are the same everywhere

MOTHER. Because of course you're from Rotterdam
  People from Rotterdam feel better in England
  than in France
  this is always being proved afresh
  You go from Rotterdam to Paris and fail

PLAYWRIGHT. But that experience was necessary to my work
  A writer who has failed in Paris
  has a certain advantage

MOTHER. That's interesting

PLAYWRIGHT. We make an attempt
  to change society
  but naturally it doesn't succeed

MOTHER (*inquiringly*). No

PLAYWRIGHT. Yes we can clearly see
  where all these attempts have led
  namely back to the starting point
  everything ever thought is always
  thrown back to its starting point
  Naturally this is already a step forward

MOTHER. Do you want to change society

PLAYWRIGHT. Society can't be changed

MOTHER. You see

PLAYWRIGHT. But we keep making the attempt

MOTHER. Yes

PLAYWRIGHT. The attempt is what matters

MOTHER. Very interesting
  You write even though you know
  that you can't change society by writing

PLAYWRIGHT. Yes
  No writer has ever
  changed society

MOTHER. It's been proved

PLAYWRIGHT. It's been proved
  We only have evidence for the failure
  of writers
  All writers are failures
  there have only ever been failed writers

MOTHER. What about Shakespeare

PLAYWRIGHT. Even Shakespeare
  I said all didn't I
  they all start from the same point
  namely the thought that they're bound to fail
  if they're worth anything
  Only the dimwitted ones the substandard ones
  have never once had this thought

The thought that one is bound to fail
is the essential thought

MOTHER (*to* DAUGHTER). This is all quite absurd
don't you think
Everything is above-board and everything fails
because it must fail

PLAYWRIGHT. We must come to this realization
that we fail
whether we acknowledge it or not

MOTHER. I don't pay it any mind
as long as it's interesting enough
A writer learns from himself you say
by studying his position

PLAYWRIGHT. By studying himself

MOTHER. My daughter thinks it was quite natural
for me to invite you to Katwijk
I still can't fathom it
After all we don't know you from Adam

PLAYWRIGHT. So it's an adventure

MOTHER. To think that I'm capable
of inviting a person
whom I've seen just one single time
and then only very briefly

DAUGHTER. You saw him two times

MOTHER. I saw him two times
but each time was very brief
For me this invitation
has something revolutionary about it
Probably I thought
this exhausted individual must be helped
we're going to Katwijk
he's got to come with us
that was the idea

DAUGHTER (*to* PLAYWRIGHT). I think you couldn't have asked for better
actors
I can't imagine
that there are any others
who could do your play justice

PLAYWRIGHT. If we're very lucky
and happen upon the best of the best
but we're not always so lucky
then the whole thing is stillborn
even before the curtain rises

MOTHER. You have been that lucky sir
The way that old king
said the word *moralist*
The way he said it

DAUGHTER. And the way the farm girl curtsied
she didn't do anything else
but that curtsy

MOTHER. These horrible silent roles
these characters who are perpetually silent
there actually are such people in real life as well
One person talks and the other holds his tongue
he might have a lot to say
but he isn't allowed to say it
he's got to tough out this onerous ordeal
we offload everything onto the shoulders of the tongue-holder

PLAYWRIGHT. Everything

MOTHER. You also slip a ghastly jacket
onto your characters
All your characters
And they can't slip out of their jackets
like you
who slipped out your jacket
You thrust ghastly jackets
onto all your characters

PLAYWRIGHT. There certainly are jackets
  ghastly jackets
  that I thrust onto my characters
  but of course they slip right into them voluntarily
  they are actors after all

MOTHER. Do you think so

PLAYWRIGHT. An actor wants nothing more
  than a ghastly jacket
  the ghastlier the jacket
  the writer has given him is
  the better
  The ghastliest jacket
  for the greatest actor

MOTHER. As if you were trying
  to make all these people crazy
  as if you had a craving
  to drive them mad

PLAYWRIGHT. Oh no
  it's not like that
  at the last minute all these characters slip out of
  their jacket
  they tear off their jacket
  before they suffocate
  there hasn't yet been an actor
  who's suffocated in the jacket
  a writer has slipped onto him
  the jacket's not lethal
  it's not a lethal jacket madam

MOTHER. How lovely that you're here
  I thought you might have a cup of tea with us

  (*Sits down at the table*)

  Please do sit down
  make yourself comfortable

  (*Looks at the sea*)

You've really have expressed that in the most wonderful way
how a playwright
makes the high and low tides his own

(*Enter a maid, who serves tea*)

Naturally we live in a completely different world
my daughter and I
Our mechanism is completely different
One might argue that it is monotonous
but it's actually that way only on the surface

(*To* DAUGHTER) Come on and sit down with us
A hot cup of tea
at the cold seaside

(*Looks out at the sea*)

It's always raining when we get here
it rains for a couple of days
I get used to the rain
and then I actually start getting annoyed
when the sun comes out

(DAUGHTER *sits down at the table with them*)

I was surprised
that you look so young
a bit exhausted but still quite young

(*Exit the maid*)

I used to enjoy classic plays exclusively
then I suddenly made this habit
into an accusation
on the other hand

DAUGHTER. Someday our writer
    will be a classic

MOTHER. Good Lord this child

(*To* PLAYWRIGHT) you see now you're blushing
The road to becoming a classic is an awfully long one
on the other hand

one is either a literary classic from the outset
or one isn't
This fresh air from outdoors
this is the essence of Katwijk
You will see that it will do you good
You will in any event profit from it
You will leave Katwijk
with a good idea of it
I'm quite certain of that

DAUGHTER. Perhaps it's too peaceful for him here
nothing happens
nothing for days on end
nothing for weeks on end

MOTHER. Perhaps that's just the point
When everything is peaceful on the surface
as peaceful as it is here in Katwijk
then the scene taking place in our minds
is bound to be quite dramatic

(*To* PLAYWRIGHT) have I hit on something
I think I've really hit on something with this remark

(PLAYWRIGHT *looks out at the sea*)

Peace and quiet make a person crazier than anything else
You're searching for good fortune I think
Where is it your good fortune

(*Drinks*)

My husband used to stand out there for hours on end
leaning against the lamppost
and gazing out at the sea
When I asked him what have you seen
because I loathed him when he stood there leaning against the
    lamppost
I kept asking him what in the world do you see
time and again I asked him what in the world do you see
I wanted to torment him
he wanted peace and quiet
I didn't want it

so I tortured him
I kept asking him from over his shoulder
just like now I would sit here and stare at his back and ask
now what do you see
what do you see tell me what you see
Of course you don't see anything I would say
he wouldn't budge
you don't see anything and you're staring out at the sea
Now what do you see out there
I knew he wasn't going to answer me
He would turn around and walk right past me
without saying a word
he never answered
Everybody sees something different when he gazes out there
everybody sees what he wants to see

(*To* PLAYWRIGHT) Even you whom we know nothing about
But we're also not going to ask you

PLAYWRIGHT. Go ahead and ask me

MOTHER. There are some people we interrogate
and drive to distraction
and others to whom we don't pose a single question

PLAYWRIGHT. A couple of years ago
I wouldn't have let myself be interrogated
Now I don't mind it at all

MOTHER. A couple of years ago

DAUGHTER *opens the trunk and takes out the coat on top*

PLAYWRIGHT. Back then I shunned questions

MOTHER. Back then you ran away from questions

PLAYWRIGHT. When a person is a nobody

MOTHER. But every person

PLAYWRIGHT. Yes but there are people
who mustn't be questioned
at least not until a certain definite point in their lives

MOTHER. Not until they've become somebody
    then they dare to answer questions
    But of course you have become somebody
    that's what all the newspapers say
    And Lord knows
    what will be written about your premiere tomorrow
    You have nothing to worry about

PLAYWRIGHT. Who knows

MOTHER. I have a feeling
    you're enjoying a success
    it'll last a good while

PLAYWRIGHT. Then all of a sudden
    it'll end

MOTHER. Maybe
    it's clear that you're enjoying a success now
    and you ought to exploit this success

PLAYWRIGHT. But the way I am

MOTHER. What

PLAYWRIGHT. Unlike you I can't say exploit

MOTHER. Ah yes because you're with us in Katwijk
    and letting yourself go just a little
    and dining well with us
    and walking along the shore

PLAYWRIGHT. I should do that
    (*Turning to* DAUGHTER) Will you come with me

DAUGHTER. I'd be delighted to

PLAYWRIGHT. It's so easily proposed
    and just as easily accepted
    A walk along the shore and back

MOTHER. There's nothing lovelier
    If I were in better shape

DAUGHTER. Mother

MOTHER. I couldn't even if I wanted to

PLAYWRIGHT. On the spur of the moment
   without giving a thought to the future

MOTHER. That is your curse
   the fact that you're constantly thinking about the future
   or about the past
   that's just as bad
   You should think about the present

(*Pensively*)

   Every time we sit here the first night
   we're disappointed
   it's cold and sinister
   don't you think so too
   we talk ourselves into believing it's nice here
   to think of all the things we talk ourselves into believing
   That the air is better here
   that we come up with different ideas
   that

DAUGHTER. All year long Mother has only one goal
   to go to Katwijk
   and then it gives her the chills I've never known her to be any different

PLAYWRIGHT. But we aren't always disappointed like that
   when we arrive somewhere

MOTHER. I remembered the house being much bigger
   And the people friendlier
   the way they always rushed to greet us
   today it was quite different
   Yes disappointment is the right word

PLAYWRIGHT. You must get some rest madam
   Tomorrow things will look quite different

MOTHER. By then you'll have had a good night's sleep
   and taken a morning run
   (*Turns to* DAUGHTER) with you perhaps
   we must make use of these days

we always think there are an infinite number of them
when there are all too few of them left

PLAYWRIGHT (*glancing around the room*). A beautiful house masterly
architecture

MOTHER. Studying architecture
that of course was something else you could have done

PLAYWRIGHT. Undoubtedly
in a certain way it's a bit similar
to the art of drama

MOTHER. Perhaps you'd be a well-known architect by now

PLAYWRIGHT. No that I can't imagine
from the start I couldn't imagine it
I didn't want it
I dreaded building contractors
you have to deal a lot with the government
which is depressing
little by little it destroys your soul

MOTHER. You only need a sheet of paper and something to write with
nothing else
You build your plays yourself
and nobody else stands in your way

PLAYWRIGHT. Right so it's the only possibility

DAUGHTER (*pulling a coat out of the trunk*). Making art on your own as
you do

PLAYWRIGHT (*exclamatorily*). Art art
on my own
what is more terrifying than being alone
with oneself

MOTHER. But you did after all say
that the best company is one's own
that the best conversations are with oneself
that the best impetus is oneself

PLAYWRIGHT. I did say that
  but in practice

MOTHER. Ultimately everybody is alone
  people may join forces as they see fit
  they remain alone

PLAYWRIGHT. But a writer is alone in quite a particular way

MOTHER. He wants to be

PLAYWRIGHT. Yes he wants to be
  he curses it and he craves it

DAUGHTER. I'd always wanted
  to meet a writer

MOTHER. A playwright
  a celebrated one naturally
  success is the attraction

PLAYWRIGHT (*looking out at the sea*). Or a painter
  but everything has already been painted
  everything has already been written
  everything has already been full stop
  We repeat what has already been
  in our own way
  we slip on the jacket that is our subject
  and step out into the street in it
  in doing this we put something new on display
  Look at that peculiar jacket they say
  look at those outrageous trousers
  in doing this we're no different from other people
  from anybody who has ever lived

MOTHER. Every time before we come here I think
  the house really isn't that cold
  and the house turns out to be terribly cold

  (*Wraps herself up in a blanket*)

  Won't you take a blanket
  I used to ask my husband that

won't you take a blanket
he'd refuse because I'd asked him
he was ill then
immobile for three weeks
he didn't budge from the spot
brimming over with pain
he loathed Katwijk
he flourished once we were back in town

(*Enter the maid with* PLAYWRIGHT's *bag*)

(*To* PLAYWRIGHT) Your bag

(*To* MAID) Where was the bag anyway

MAID. In the garage

MOTHER. In the garage
that's really quite odd

(*Exit* MAID)

how in the world did that bag end up in the garage

(PLAYWRIGHT *makes as if to take his bag and leave*)

No don't
You stay put
You can't leave us on our own now
You'll have plenty of time to unpack
once we have unpacked

(*To* DAUGHTER) shall I help you my child

DAUGHTER. No no mother

MOTHER. No no mother
my good child

PLAYWRIGHT. It's like in the old novels
where people always traveled with so much luggage

MOTHER. Yes like in the old novels
like in Tolstoy like in Dostoyevsky
oh how I love those writers
just imagine
I read *War and Peace* here in Katwijk

while sitting on this terrace
in a single day and a single night
consecutively
We used to travel with only three trunks
now we have five
and lots of bags
instead of less luggage we have more
instead of less clothing we have more

PLAYWRIGHT. That flies in the face of the global trend

MOTHER. That was nicely put

(*To* DAUGHTER) He utters one sentence and everything lights up
it makes everything so simple
You know on account of the variableness of the weather
one day it rains and it's cold
the next day terrible heat prevails here
and we mustn't forget when we're going back
it's already almost winter
we must have something for every occasion
For you it's a bit different
You're traveling with one bag
for a day or two

PLAYWRIGHT. For a day or two

DAUGHTER. Or three or four

MOTHER. We'll just have to see
how long we can put up with one another

(*To* PLAYWRIGHT *point-blank*) If it gives you pleasure
as it may very well chance to do
and if this pleasure
can be communicated to us

PLAYWRIGHT. Yes

DAUGHTER. Perhaps we could go to Amsterdam together

(*To* PLAYWRIGHT *point-blank*) Perhaps you'll still be here then
next week

MOTHER. Playwrights never have that much leisure or that much time
It's hardly a well-thought-out idea

PLAYWRIGHT. Right

MOTHER. You are of course no mere copycat artist
your creativity doesn't afford you any time or leisure
That's what drives them all to ruin
I thought that when we got here I'd put on
my summer dress
and here I am wearing my winter coat
and I don't plan on taking it off ever again
What a good thing that we donned our winter coats
when it comes to clothes
one can't allow oneself to be dictated to by the calendar
They say we're headed for another ice age
what do you think of that hypothesis

PLAYWRIGHT. I don't know

MOTHER. There are so many signs of it
science is also saying it
Summers used to be quite different
I never used to wear a winter coat in summer
The Gulf Stream has already almost ceased to have any effect

(*To* DAUGHTER) come here my child
come here

(DAUGHTER *goes up to* MOTHER, *who takes her hand and kisses it*)

I promised my husband
when he was on his deathbed you know
that I would always be there for my daughter
My child has nothing to worry about

(*She lets go of* DAUGHTER'*s hand*)

Tell me
was your mother a cheerful person
you don't have to answer

(DAUGHTER *goes back to the trunk and then opens both French windows
giving on to the terrace even wider*)

I could imagine
that your mother was a cheerful person
There's so much wit in your play
What an inspired phrase *Save Yourself If You Can*
What a magnificent title
It's reminiscent of Shakespeare
How long does it take you to write a play
Perhaps I'm being indiscreet
Writers loathe nothing more than when people interrogate them about
    writing
No I won't interrogate you
Of course we know a ton of things already don't we
Can you support yourself with it or not
that's a stupid question isn't it
like when you ask a singer why do you sing
It's a lucky thing that nothing ever came
of my daughter's career
just imagine by now she'd be a soubrette
Nothing came of it
but it's been twenty years
since she's given any thought to anything like a singing career
That was when her vocal cords gave out
which was a stroke of good luck for me
otherwise I might very well have ended up all alone here
so now I have my child
who looks after me and vice versa
I have chained my daughter to me you know
and vice versa
and we will drag these chains around
for ever for all time
We are my husband's handiwork

(*Suddenly*)

Do you know what a foundry is
Naturally you don't
I didn't know either
Many years ago I met
a man

who said he had a foundry
I thought that was really funny
and that in addition to the foundry
he had a house at the seaside
ah you know people stumble by chance
into the most peculiar situations as I said
And their entire life changes
Tell me why did you immediately agree

PLAYWRIGHT. Agree to what

MOTHER. To travel with us to Katwijk

PLAYWRIGHT. Agreed
I immediately agreed
I don't know perhaps

MOTHER. Don't say it
there are too many possible reasons
for your having agreed
If you're forced to reflect on it you'll see
it wasn't something you did for no reason at all

PLAYWRIGHT. Right perhaps it wasn't

MOTHER. Perhaps you were quite simply fed up
with the city like us
and wanted to go to the seaside
that's understandable
You were lured by the easygoingness
the fresh air
The possibility of an adventure

PLAYWRIGHT. Yes

MOTHER. When we reflect too much
we end up walking in place
but when we surrender ourselves to contingency

PLAYWRIGHT. Spontaneously instantaneously

MOTHER. When we don't ask why and wherefore

(*Looks up at the ceiling*)

we get lots of good ideas upstairs

(PLAYWRIGHT *makes as if to stand up.* MOTHER *holds him back*)

Please stay put
until your room is ready
We've always kept everything very simple here
We've always kept everything very simple in town as well
We've never changed anything
not in Katwijk and not in town
Because we've never been followers of fashion
Believe me
we're happy that you're here

(*To* DAUGHTER) Aren't we my child

DAUGHTER. Yes very much so
I am and so is Mother

MOTHER. Both of us are

(*To* DAUGHTER *point-blank*) You should only unpack the most
important things

The maids will unpack the shoes
(*To* PLAYWRIGHT) But one mustn't leave everything to the help
not the fine fabrics
That of course is why we prefer to do our packing ourselves
and our unpacking ourselves
I don't trust anybody around my clothes

(*To* DAUGHTER) You needn't unpack everything
if you're not in the mood

(*To* PLAYWRIGHT) It's all so expensive and so poorly made
All my things are decades old
We have so much with us
and yet we always put the same things on
but on the other hand we can't just come here with a single change of
clothes
Suddenly
three years ago there was a ball
we attended it

Officers captains the so-called High Seas Ball
Have you ever been to a ball of any sort anywhere

PLAYWRIGHT. No never

MOTHER. That's what I thought
And yet in your drama you describe a ball
and outstandingly well at that
how very odd
so one needn't have been to a ball
in order to be able to describe a ball outstandingly well
one needn't be acquainted with what one describes

PLAYWRIGHT. Of course I've never been in a penitentiary either

MOTHER. And the way you describe it
nearly takes my breath away
You have a good sense of empathy
and style sir
But I don't understand a thing about it
I don't understand a single thing about literature
but my awareness of that has never bothered me
instead of learning how to understand literature I learned
how to add and subtract
But that was an absolutely vital necessity
From a certain point in your life onwards you said
is it permissible to ask certain people questions

PLAYWRIGHT. I didn't put it that way I said
they'll talk if they're forced to

MOTHER. Because they're well-protected enough

PLAYWRIGHT. Perhaps

MOTHER. But we're only alive when we're asking
we only exist when we're asking
even though we know
that we'll get no answers
we never get any answers
that we can bring ourselves to accept is that right

PLAYWRIGHT. That's possibly right

MOTHER. At the end of life we realize
    that all our life we've just been asking questions
    but haven't received a single answer

PLAYWRIGHT. Yes it's depressing madam

MOTHER. But we keep fabricating illusions for ourselves
    we can't believe that everything is so hopeless
    that it's all so evil
    We keep presuming that it's not all that evil
    even though it's pure evil
    Do you think that's the reason everybody has died so far
    because everything is so evil
    because nature is so evil

PLAYWRIGHT. I say as much in my new play
    that people die because everything is so evil

MOTHER (*to* DAUGHTER). Did you hear that
    those are my very thoughts
    perhaps that's why your play fascinated me so much
    because you expressed my own thoughts in it
    everything in the play could have come from me
    even the idea could have come from me
    each of your characters talks the way I talk
    on the other hand it's certainly true that all the characters
    talk like you
    each of your characters thinks like you and talks like you
    In a very precise sense
    they all speak with one voice
    and each of them speaks like all the rest
    in this way the whole thing attains a kind of universal quality

PLAYWRIGHT. That's exactly right

MOTHER. We think this is typical of this person
    and at the same time it's *us*
    Us as well
    but this is verging on spiritualism

I think you'll get along very well
with my daughter
She thinks what you think
but she has no opportunity
to express it publicly
Perhaps you'll give her that opportunity
She'll say it because she thinks it
and you'll publish it

(*She and* PLAYWRIGHT *laugh*)

We've had a piano in the next room
for three years
Can you play the piano

PLAYWRIGHT. I can't play the piano

MOTHER. Almost everybody can play the piano
in my day it was taken for granted
we weren't even four or five years old
and we had to learn the piano

(*To* DAUGHTER) Would it be possible
for you to play us something
Perhaps it'll relax you
You don't have to unpack everything today of course

(DAUGHTER *hangs up a coat*)

Any old etude any old anything

(*To* PLAYWRIGHT) But you do love music

PLAYWRIGHT. Oh yes

MOTHER. But that doesn't provide much encouragement

PLAYWRIGHT. I like listening to music very much

MOTHER. Classical music

PLAYWRIGHT. Yes

MOTHER. She plays Mozart quite beautifully

(*Exit* DAUGHTER)

It's enrapturing hearing it from out there

I love leaning back here and listening

(DAUGHTER'*s piano-playing is heard*)

I think I've annoyed you
I've been posing
meaningless questions
it's difficult to answer
such questions
One fine day we decided
to buy an old piano
we had seen it at the flea market
just imagine
an instrument that was completely out of tune
but the piano tuner said
it was an extraordinarily well-made instrument
Naturally her playing was only amateurish
but we're all amateurish at something
She played this piece
last year
on the evening of our departure
I don't know what it is
do you like it

PLAYWRIGHT. Yes

MOTHER. You say that as if you weren't by any means sure you liked it

PLAYWRIGHT. But I do like it very much

MOTHER. The world is cold
and its devices are gruesome
perhaps this is an apology
for such a faux pas

PLAYWRIGHT. What faux pas

MOTHER. This sentimentality

(*Leans back with her eyes closed*)

that we indulge in
when she sits down at the piano
in a certain way

it's even a perversion
but that's exactly what makes it a sign
of our times
We flee into a secluded house
and listen to tasteless music
to be sure it's Mozart but it's tasteless
we buy an old piano at the flea market
and have it refurbished
We travel with old clothes to an old house
in which any normal person would feel sick
we take all our luggage with us
and also take along a young playwright
how mendacious this all is sir
how mendacious

(*The piano has fallen silent; enter* DAUGHTER. MOTHER *sitting up and looking at the ceiling*)

(*To* PLAYWRIGHT) Once you're upstairs
you'll have an expansive view of the sea
and be completely undisturbed

(*To* DAUGHTER) You haven't practiced in a long time
nobody's played that piano this entire year
it's already out of tune again
it's particularly humid here
A variation wasn't it my child

DAUGHTER. By Beethoven

MOTHER. Beethoven
I basically don't care for Beethoven
Mozart yes but Beethoven no
But out here it sounds fine
A Beethoven variation

PLAYWRIGHT (*to* DAUGHTER). Will you take a walk along the shore with
me sometime

He and MOTHER *look at* DAUGHTER

MOTHER. That's especially nice in the early morning
before six

DAUGHTER. I always enjoy walking along the shore
  with Mother

MOTHER. Will you take a walk along the shore with our playwright

DAUGHTER. Why yes of course
  (*To* PLAYWRIGHT) if you can actually get up so early

MOTHER (*to* PLAYWRIGHT). Early enough to be out by six

PLAYWRIGHT. I get up very early
  I get up at four
  you don't believe me
  but I do get up at four
  my grandfather would actually get up at three

MOTHER. But he wasn't a playwright

PLAYWRIGHT. He was a philosopher madam

MOTHER. The grandfather a philosopher
  the grandson a playwright
  it's quite funny isn't it

  (*As* DAUGHTER *resumes unpacking the trunk*)

  Grandchildren get everything from their grandfathers
  the maternal ones
  did you know that
  Here you can walk alone along the shore for hours on end
  You don't run into any people
  And do you know that winter is the nicest time of year here
  it's cold and you feel quite
  exposed to the elements

  (*Rises and fetches herself a bottle of cognac*)

  I have no willpower whatsoever
  Wouldn't you like a sip yourself

  (*She takes two glasses and pours cognac for herself and* PLAYWRIGHT)

  Yesterday I thought I can't take another drop
  but then I drank an entire bottle
  and early this morning
  And now I'm in the mood again

(*Raises her glass and drinks*; PLAYWRIGHT *also drinks*)

(*To* DAUGHTER) To your health my child

(*To* PLAYWRIGHT) And to your health

(*Rises and goes out to the terrace and* PLAYWRIGHT *follows*)

I asked you
if you would come with us to Katwijk
and it didn't nonplus you for a moment
it nonplussed me more than you
Can you still hear it
Can you still hear it

PLAYWRIGHT. What

MOTHER. The audience clapping the applause
I hear it I hear it
Can't you hear it hear the audience clapping
the applause
You must admit you're happy about it
Even if you say
the applause has destroyed everything for you
you can't get away with saying that
I hear the sea and it's the audience clapping
The roar of the sea is the applause for your play
You've attained your goal sir

(*Takes him by the hand*)

You can hear the ovation can't you

(*Tightens her grip on his hand and leads him back to the table*)

You are the luckiest person in the world
You've just got to comprehend it
You've got to admit it

(*She sits down*; *the* PLAYWRIGHT *remains standing*)

You've got to cope with it
You've got to tough it out
You've got to tough out your triumph
and cope with it

Save Yourself If You Can

(*To* DAUGHTER) Magnificent isn't it
it's quite in my vein of thought
Save Yourself If You Can
and nobody can save himself
nobody has ever saved himself
not a single person out of all those millions and billions
not a single one
and so you call your play *Save Yourself If You Can*
You're a bold individual a brazen one
You've got to know that
you've got to let yourself be told that
and you've got to know that
Now you're here and you have this awareness
You must have this awareness
Say to yourself I have this awareness
force yourself to say it you must force yourself to say it

(*Drinks*)

I don't understand you
You just stand there and say nothing
Come on sit down
Suddenly you're at a loss for words
But that's the way all young people are nowadays
They just stand there and they're at a loss for words
Won't you please sit down

(*The* PLAYWRIGHT *sits down*)

And have a drink with me
take a leaf out of someone else's book
someone else's book someone else's book do you hear me someone
     else's book

(*Drinks and pours* PLAYWRIGHT *more cognac*)

What's the matter with young people nowadays
At twenty they're already thinking about a pension
as if it's something to spend their entire lives working towards
That's what I call a boring youth

they're born and they're bored until they die
and they die the very instant
in which they're born
It's stiff and starchy and speechless
am I right
But that is also your theme isn't it
that is of course something you too have dealt with in *Save Yourself If*
    You Can
the stiffness and speechlessness of youth
who have lost everything even before they exist
I can't believe my eyes when I see today's youth just standing there
instead of waking up and making rubble of everything
that stands in their way
and all of history stands in the way of this generation of youth
and youth has always had the strength
to clear this lazy and spoiled history out of its way
with all its strength with the greatest will to annihilate
every generation of youth
has cleared everything out of its way with the means at its disposal
but this one
never before has there been so spineless a generation of youth
Of course you also say this in your play
You say it in *Save Yourself If You Can*
You say it with your own peculiar cynicism
which is also *my* cynicism
Nothing is being given to this generation of youth even though it's
    being given everything
indeed precisely *because* it's being given everything
and it bides its time it bides its time
instead of taking what's withheld from it
Of course we were quite different in my day
we took the history that stood in our way
and we made it into rubble into rubble
and out of this rubble we made ourselves a new history
But this generation of youth is spineless
and lets itself be crushed by the old history
it silently and idly stands there and contemplates
but it does nothing

You yourself are the best example
You contemplate and do nothing
You see the squalor but you don't attack it
You are the observer of this putrefaction
but you don't clear any of it away

(*Drinks*)

Mark my words youth rightly has the right to annihilate history
to annihilate it in order to make the annihilated bits
into the foundation of a new history
it's duty-bound to do that
But they mustn't just keep waiting till it's too late
and now it already seems to be too late
You say that yourself in your play
that perhaps it's too late
But you just say it
You just say it and you observe how people react to what you're saying
but you do nothing you look on but you do nothing
That is the bane of the playwright's existence

PLAYWRIGHT. But it's still something

MOTHER. It isn't enough sir
    looking on and waiting
    everybody does that
    everybody looks on and waits
    they observe the putrefaction and add to it

PLAYWRIGHT. But someday

MOTHER. Not someday
    right now

(*Drinks*)

Ah yes if I were thirty years younger
if I were only twenty years younger
But what am I talking about that's no excuse
But it is actually something that you say in your play
that the time for it is far more than ripe
But it's not enough for a couple of young people
to bash in a couple of people's heads that's ridiculous

Everything must be wiped away *everything* overnight
it can't just be a lot of shillyshallying as my husband would have said
And just imagine there

(*Points*)

one day he stood there on the terrace
and pondered how to blow the royal palace sky high
He didn't look as though he were thinking anything of the kind
I certainly didn't think he was capable of thinking such a thing
it was a clear summer evening
I was already worrying about the packing
we had to return to town
and he'd been standing on the terrace for a long time
And I spontaneously asked him what in the world have you been
    doing
all this time on the terrace
what have you been thinking about on the terrace
And he said I've been thinking about how I'm going to set about
blowing the royal palace sky high
I had burst into laughter
I used to think he was crazy
but I gradually started thinking he might have meant it in earnest
and today I'm convinced he'd meant it in earnest

(*Drinks*)

Possibly he still had the makings of anarchist

(*Bursts out laughing and the* PLAYWRIGHT *joins in*)

He had an active imagination that husband of mine
The foundry hamstrung him
I didn't let myself be hamstrung by the foundry
I soared thanks to the foundry
but he was hamstrung by the familial foundry
I often thought
it's possible I've stumbled upon an anarchist
he said All's well that ends well to me too often
Why did he keep saying that
He must have had something really dreadful on his mind

on his mind in mind
Don't you sometimes think
of blowing everything sky high
surely that's the most insistent thought in a writer's mind
am I right
the thought of first bringing about a little revolution in his own mind
then a bigger revolution
then an even bigger revolution
and then bringing a revolution from your own mind
into the world as one brings a child into the world
and making everything explode
a playwright really needn't think
about anything else
how am I going to blow the whole world sky high
how am I going to make an end of the whole nightmare
Am I not right

(*To* DAUGHTER) My child gets quite beside herself when I say anything
    like this
but when I *don't* say it
Playwrights don't say it
or they say it and don't do it
Perhaps it isn't even the playwright's job
to blow the world sky high
perhaps the whole thing is an absurd idea
Perhaps I'm still a bit overwrought from the trip
It drives me mad when I consider
that we still have all these things to unpack
and who knows once we've unpacked everything
perhaps we'll head straight back to town
because we can't put up with being here

(*Exclamatorily*)

Basically the very thought that we're here in Katwijk
gives me the chills
But it was my idea
Every summer we travel here on this date

(*As if she feels chilly*)

It's so cold here
but of course we can't turn the heat on in the middle of summer
that would be quite absurd

(*To* PLAYWRIGHT) But don't you fall into the habit
of staying in bed when it rains
that's the most pernicious habit to fall into
When you wake up you must step out of your room
and freshen up and dash out of the house
Whoever stays in bed in the morning my father used to say
soon finds himself staying in bed for good
And I'm right about this
when we stay in bed in the morning
as if we're hamstrung
we get sick of the world
I'm horrified by the mechanism of my own life

(DAUGHTER *tries to push the trunk closer to the window and fails*)

Ah please lend my daughter a hand
the poor girl can't manage it on her own
a real rarity that trunk

(PLAYWRIGHT *jumps up and lends* DAUGHTER *a hand*)

That trunk has quite a peculiar history
basically it's the hub of our existence
That trunk that belonged to a circus clown
you'd never guess that from looking at it
My grandfather was a circus clown you see
he was born in Maastricht
and traveled all over Europe with that trunk
and performed his clown routine
I can show you a picture of him
if you're interested
I have photographs in which he's shown
going through his routine
A real sensation in those days
But he was a drunk
he died at the age of forty-two

at an inn in Kerkrade
hence not far from the town
in which he'd been born
I often tell my daughter
how easily I could have taken the other path
I have taken the other path

(*Drinks*)

Have I told you that I met my husband
at an inn
not far from Apeldoorn
a scattered child
And to think that I was fascinated most of all by the word foundry
I got stuck on the word foundry

(DAUGHTER *and* PLAYWRIGHT *lift a heavy winter coat out of the trunk*)

A foible
We travel to Katwijk in the middle of the summer
and we pack that heavy winter coat
a habit
the habit of my husband her father
on the cold summer evenings
when he went out onto the terrace
he'd wear that coat
a relic of another age
A folly
do please lift it up high high high

(DAUGHTER *and* PLAYWRIGHT *lift the coat up high*)

You can already see right through it
but not because it was worn so often
no
because we keep packing and unpacking it
that wears away at the fabric makes it threadbare

(DAUGHTER *hangs the coat in the window*)

Then we hang it on that hook there
and have no idea what to do with it

DAUGHTER *resumes unpacking*

PLAYWRIGHT. A beautiful garment
  English naturally

MOTHER. Naturally English
  My husband wore English coats exclusively
  back then that was still the height of luxury
  and English shoes naturally
  and the finest English socks
  I was quite dumbfounded when I saw
  the man's lush sartorial luxury

  (PLAYWRIGHT *goes to the table and sits down*)

  You mustn't be surprised
  Here everything has gone crazy
  For example here I always wear do you see it
  a buckle
  to hold my coat shut
  for thirty years and counting I've had this buckle
  in this place
  it's never occurred to me
  to sew on the button that goes here
  Or to sew up that hole there in the curtains do you see it

  (*Points at the hole*)

  that hole has been there twenty-five years and counting
  I know that so exactly
  because my husband made it
  with his umbrella
  He was coming in from the shore
  and his umbrella skewered the curtain
  a funny story isn't it
  This is *our* form of creativity sir
  the fact that we make holes in curtains
  and never close them up
  that we pack and unpack coats

and never put them on
and it's like that with hundreds of other things
stockings socks blouses waistcoats et cetera
In some fashion or other all of this surely
has something to do with my grandfather's traveling trunk
in a mysterious fashion don't you think

There is a knock at the door. Enter MAID

MOTHER (*to* PLAYWRIGHT). Your room is ready

(PLAYWRIGHT *stands up*)

You must be tired
Your premiere just think of it
and your triumph
A one-off triumph
but you yourself can see that

(*Offers* PLAYWRIGHT *her hand, and he kisses it*)

Ah don't kiss my hand
that's simply ludicrous
Where have you seen that
in Austria
Good Lord
and then the trip
and everything else that's come your way

(PLAYWRIGHT *picks up his bag and makes as if to leave*)

And don't be shocked
if you notice
some downright curious objects
in your room
those old clothes and those rifles
and all those hats everywhere
my husband was quite attached to all that stuff

(PLAYWRIGHT *curtly bows to* MOTHER *once again, bows to* DAUGHTER, *and exits*; MAID *follows him.* MOTHER *after a pause, after taking a sip from her glass*)

The question is not at all
whether it was wise to invite him
he's here

(*Suddenly agitated*)

Now I need fresh air

(*Goes up to the French windows giving on to the terrace.* DAUGHTER *brings her the chair that* PLAYWRIGHT *was sitting in.* MOTHER *after seating herself in the chair*)

I'm afraid
he's going to be staying longer than just a couple of days

THE END

SIMPLY COMPLICATED

For Minetti

He was in the right, and so indeed it is.
—*King Richard the Third*

A year in Ludwigshafen
That humbled you
That almost could have cost you your head

Dramatis Personae
HE, *an old actor*
KATHARINA, *a nine-year-old girl*

A run-down room
A chair at stage right, a chair against the wall at stage left
A window at stage left, a door at stage right
A table and chair
A chest
A chamber pot
A bucket
A refrigerator
A tape-recorder on the floor

Scene I

Early morning

HE (*in a shabby black suit and oversize felt slippers with buckles, and with a pair of spectacles hanging from his neck, is kneeling on the floor and nailing in place a piece of skirting board after he has looked around the room several times*). If anybody sees me here
in this posture

(*Contemplates the nail he has just hammered down*)

Complicity
A contempt for craftsmen

(*Looks around the room*)

We have allowed all our talents
to waste away
distinguished for eccentricity
awarded a doctorate in mathematics
A guest of honor on the Isle of Man
Seated beside the viceroy of India

(*Contemplates the nail he has just hammered down*)

One more tap
one tap more

(*Hits the nail. Looks around the room*)

Mice
Who would have imagined that
When we moved in here
there were no mice in the Hanssachsstrasse
The mice are holdovers
Everyone has died off

everyone without exception
first my sisters
then my brother
Initially phobic about hats and other headgear
then headgear
was made an absolute must
Not a medical problem
I said
they didn't believe me
I had always been punctual
A dependability fanatic
Kept every appointment
Made a method of punctuality
Never unpunctual
Either we go to seed
or we're punctual
A chronology of death
first Grandfather
then Grandmother
then Mother
then Father
a sister every year
then my brother
(*Looks around the room*)
Made of dust
I have outrun stupidity
Curricular
Extracurricular horror
But if we hadn't had our seizures

(*Lifts the hammer high into the air and looks around the room*)

My heart made into a den of thieves
Intellectual experience
No temperament for ministration

(*Lets his hand and the hammer fall, exhausted*)

We concoct ourselves our own unhappiness
like an unappetizing soup

and spoon it up
voraciously

(*Glances at the door*)

A matter of taste he said
I got wise to his game
We love our brother to the end of our life
even if at every moment of it we loathe him
must loathe him
must

(*Glances at the window*)

The word capitulation
never spoken
never given up
Up and at 'em

(*Contemplates the nail he has just hammered down*)

In principle
I have always been a gourmet
naturally not
in the usual crude way
An intellectual gourmet
Everyone wasted away
I didn't
Everyone has died off
I haven't
I am a genius
I have always said that to myself
in the face of all assertions to the contrary
We yield to despair quite early on
Exploited despair
made myself into a genius
out of despair
When falsehood holds sway over everything
genius develops unobtrusively
I'm no idiot
I said

I'm refractory
but no idiot

(*Tries to stand up but fails*)

Studied in France at the Sorbonne
at Göttingen
at Cambridge
everything was in vain
A despiser of books
A squanderer of knowledge
A demolisher of character

(*Tries to stand up but remains kneeling and glances at the door*)

The summers
were most propitious
when I let myself go
They were bored to death
while I developed philosophically
I wrote axioms
while they digested their pork
philosophical bust-ups all summer long
(*Looks around the room*)
Always played the role of the killjoy
tried to tell the truth
and went to the street with falsehood
A conspiracy first against my parents
then against the others
a court jester's existence

(*Completely exhausted, he delivers two more blows to the nail he has just hammered down and then glances at the window*)

They all died off
all of them
I didn't
They died
I walked with a brisk step
They loathed me
whenever I bought myself a book

But reading is senselessness
A waste of time
Two whole years
spent only with Shakespeare
locked in my room with Shakespeare
and with Schopenhauer
We can't tolerate anything else
we imprison ourselves with Shakespeare
and with Schopenhauer
we can't even stand music

(*Tries to stand up, but remains kneeling*)

Didn't abandon pleasure naturally
but elasticity
Sang "The Crow"
at the age of eighteen
made a show of myself with Schubert
Italian arias with great pleasure
They naturally didn't think
I'd follow through with anything
They shook their heads
I walked out
and had left them behind me
A tenacity fanatic

(*Stands up and stretches*)

Commonplaceness
has always been abhorrent to me
Always loathed beer-drinkers
Clear-water fanaticism

(*Goes to the window, looks out and turns around and glances at the door*)

Given up my desires
But I haven't
given up myself
We owe nothing to anyone
Everyone owes everything to us
But we owe nothing to anyone

Too lazy
even to cook their own hot soup
too lazy
even to cut themselves a slice of bread
too lazy
even to open *The World as Will and Representation*
We could do everything for ourselves
we don't think about it
You go your way
I said
I'll go my way
you all go your way
while I go my way
The opposite way
that's it
Too lazy
to cook their own chicken soup
We want to go to bed
and are too lazy to do so
We've uncovered ourselves in the night
and we're practically freezing to death
and are too lazy
to pull the covers over ourselves
Loathed my father
Loathed my mother
Loathed the merry-go-round
Loathed sauerkraut
Loathed squeaky doors
Set traps
and waylaid Grandmother
and didn't eat beef
Childhood shoved us off

(*Walks over to the nail he has just hammered down and contemplates it.
Looks around*)

caught by surprise in that laughable state
by surprise by surprise

Ordinarily on Sunday she wore
her blue dress
that I'd bought her in Konstanz
she worried
she might grow out of the dress
she was worried about this at the age of seventy-six
A self-pitying character
At the age of seventy-six she accused me of lying
Always had everything
at my expense
Later in the spring a compulsion to talk incessantly

(*Hammers at the nail he has just hammered down. After a pause*)

Buy mouse poison

(*Stands up and goes to the table and lays the hammer down on it and takes a notepad out of its drawer and writes "Buy mouse poison" on the notepad*)

Buy mouse poison

(*Looks around the room, looks at the notepad*)

A hundred-twenty-three mice
from the third of January to the twenty-fourth of December

(*Goes to the bed, bends down to the chamber pot there, and carries it out of the room while coughing, flushes the toilet offstage, and immediately comes back in with the empty chamber pot*)

Buy mouse poison

(*Places the chamber pot under the bed, walks to the window and looks out*)

Practically nothing to do with it any more
It's no longer of any concern to us
not in the slightest

(*Turns around and glances at the door*)

She slandered me
she simply turned the tables on me
We didn't come into the world
with impunity

(*Leans against the wall and glances at the door*)

A dull-witted thirst for knowledge
Red tape horrible amounts of it in the end

(*Goes to the table, sits down, opens the drawer, takes out a newspaper and a large daguerreotype of Schopenhauer, and sternly contemplates the daguerreotype*)

Seduced into fornication time and again
into intellectual fornication

(*Picks up the hammer and a nail, stands up and hammers the nail into the wall, then hangs the daguerreotype of Schopenhauer. Takes three steps back and contemplates the daguerreotype of Schopenhauer*)

It makes no difference
who we follow
no difference

(*Takes another two steps back*)

If we inherit from our grandfather
nothing but Schopenhauer
we can consider ourselves lucky
no matter what
always loathed
the so-called prima philosophia

(*Turns around and glances at the door and exclaims*)

To paint this place
what a mad idea
Thought about painting this place
it really would be madness
to paint this place

(*Clutches at his head*)

Madness
Madness
Madness

(*Glances at the floor*)

When we aren't even capable
of not needing to be afraid
of having a stroke
even capable of driving in a single nail

(*Shouting*)

Paint the place
paint the place

(*Glances at the window and then at the daguerreotype of Schopenhauer*)

Philosophical fornication
Derisive fortune-telling
World-adulteration
World-swinification
Because we've inherited the daguerreotype
from our grandfather
we hang it on the wall
we keep hanging it on the wall
until we're dependent on it

(*Goes to the table and sits down and looks at the floor*)

A lifelong mishap
A lifelong philosophical mishap
If we still had a manager
we could take him to task
but we haven't got a manager any more
we haven't even got a manager any more
Mr Manager I'd say
liberate me from Schopenhauer
liberate me from Descartes as well
and from Voltaire Mr Manager
I haven't got a manager any more

(*Looks around the room*)

If we're giving names to the mice
we're undoubtedly insane

(*Peers into the corners of the room in succession*)

Admiral Nelson

Admiral Dönitz
Field Marshal Kesselring
or just simply Hans
or Franz Josef
or Minna

(*Stands up and goes to the piece of skirting board he nailed in place earlier and inspects it, then*)

No more mouse hole
No more mouse

(*Looks around the room*)

We can say
that more or less every two days
of our life
we've caught a mouse

(*Stands up*)

From now on we won't be catching them
we'll be poisoning them

(*Goes to the table and sits down and takes a book out of the drawer and reads*)

Very delicate mothers
often have heavyweight babies
that is a fact

(*Slams the books shut and puts it in the drawer and closes the drawer. Glances at the door*)

All night I was thinking
I'd have the place painted
Indeed I've even thought
about painting it myself
Overweening pride
Self-overvaluation
We're already completely exhausted
when we drive a single nail into the skirting board

(*Glances at the daguerreotype of Schopenhauer*)

We have a harder and harder time building momentum
Mr Schopenhauer

(*Opens the drawer and puts the notepad in it and shuts the drawer and opens it back up and takes out the notepad and writes "Buy mouse poison" on it once again in large letters, tears off the sheet with "Buy mouse poison" written on it and stands up and sticks it on a nail in the wall, takes two steps back and reads*)

Buy mouse poison
Of course we must take this to the street
if we want to avoid going to rack and ruin

(*Contemplates his feet*)

We won't be messing around
when we go outside
we won't be messing around
We're saying mouse poison
and we mean mouse poison
I'm saying a packet of mouse poison
and I'm going to pick myself up a packet of mouse poison
We must put a spoke
in the wheel of impatience
a kangaroo-court trial mark my words

(*Glances at the door, then goes to the mirror and gazes into it*)

We don't ask
what is permissible
we strive
for an attractive exterior
every day we recapitulate
our unsoundness of mind as a matter of course
we shan't be understood
we'll let it be
Enlightenment is nonsense

(*Draws quite close to the mirror, nearly touching the mirror with his chin*)

No grace period
All my life I've striven

for the proper tongue-position
How is Amsterdam correctly pronounced
in contrast to Rotterdam
Neman Adige Belt
that was it
Procured merriment
but not too much
Tragedy
but not too much
Philosophy
but not too much
The word metropolitan
spoken three thousand eight hundred times
at the Hotel Krasnapolski
I never paid any attention
to what they were saying
but at the same time I never held back
I'd say I've been to Moscow
I'd say I've been to Helsinki
I'd say I've been to New York
I'd say I've been to São Paulo
I invariably gave short shrift to large parties
I'd say
I don't understand the slightest thing
about surrealism
I'd say Bertrand Russell is a charlatan
I'd say Don't even mention Beethoven
around me
I'd say Bankers are all vultures
I'd say In my youth I played the double bass
not the piano
as a matter of course

(*Sticks his tongue out and draws it back in*)

I'd say Lourdes
cured me
after a certain fashion Fátima probably even cured me more

I talked about Polish seeds
With Cardinal Wischinski
I always thought to myself
If at all possible don't mention Schopenhauer

(*Turns around to face the door*)

A philosophical string-puller

(*Goes to the table, picks up the hammer, kneels before the piece of skirting board that he has just nailed in place, and hits the nail that he has just hammered down. Inspects the skirting board and says very quietly, superdistinctly*)

hidebound
that's the word

(*Stands up and lays the hammer on the table and sits down*)

When we stop answering letters
we stop receiving them
I haven't replied to a single letter
in thirteen years

(*Looks around the room*)

Craziness
to subscribe to the newspaper
to study the help-wanted ads
at the age of eighty-two

(*Picks up the newspaper and flips it open and reads*)

Hotel in Black Forest
seeks middle-aged butler
able-bodied
and with good manners

(*Looks up from the newspaper and glances at the door*)

Scene II

Noon

HE (*sitting at the table in shirtsleeves, with an old blanket wrapped around his shoulders*). Regular work
  they said
  They loathed
  the crossed-grained streak in my thinking
  If I walked quickly
  It was wrong
  If I walked slowly
  it was wrong
  You a cripple an actor
  your father
  you this ne'er-do-well actor
  your mother
  They demanded altruism

  (*Takes a deep breath*)

  In Badgastein the thunder of the waterfall drowned out
  their chatter
  Out of fear
  we land first prize
  out of fear

  (*After a pause*)

  I'll put it on
  I'll put on the crown

  (*Stands up and goes to the chest and opens it. Glances at the door*)

  I last put it on in March

On the twenty-seventh of March
it was raining
first there was rain
then heavy snowfall

(*Bends down and pulls out of the chest a crown and takes the crown to the door and back and looks out of the window and walks back to the door and puts the crown on*)

Possibly mistaken
in this constitution
no scruples whatsoever

(*Presses the crown down on his head*)

Harder

(*Presses the crown more firmly down on his head*)

Harder

(*Presses the crown even more firmly down on his head*)

Even harder

(*Presses the crown even more firmly down on his head*)

First we get excited
then we calm down
No it wasn't by chance
that the idea occurred to me
I said
I was an actor
even before I got the idea
In my mother's belly
I was already Richard the Third

(*Looks around the room*)

No glass cage
Running against it means death

(*Presses the crown firmly down on his head*)

Until my head's bleeding
I'm not really wearing the crown
until my head's bleeding

(Presses the crown as firmly as possible down on his head and presses it even more firmly, while he positions himself in front of the mirror. After a pause)

Always being turned down
with too much white on my face
Played against everyone
Never thrust myself into the foreground
We can't say
that we're satisfied
We set out on a trip
and arrive completely spent
We leave the house
and come back destroyed
We've stopped phoning people as well
we've canceled our telephone service
canceled it
Kept the newspaper subscription
but canceled the telephone service
Too much white on my face
Always being turned down
Everyone's always kept
getting tangled up in contradictions
The art of acting
Terrorism
We've believed nothing
but accepted everything as true
and spat it out
spat it out
spat it out
spat it out

(Spits on the floor. Looks into the mirror again)

Spent weeks
learning
how a king coughs
eight weeks learning how to cough
eight weeks learning

how a king coughs

(*Coughs*)

Learning how to cough
We listened
what we heard
was useless
everything pitched to us
primitive mathematics
high art
all useless
While preparing our supper
we'd be thinking
it's useless
what we've been hearing all day
hearing all our life
nothing but nonsense

(*Makes a grimace at the mirror*)

Kept making a grimace
an impertinent grimace
already the born grimace-maker
as a child

(*Turns round and glances at the window*)

And then all of a sudden the entire grand
classical attitude

(*Looks into the mirror again and sticks his tongue out*)

We exist only
if we are so to speak
the center of the world

(*Goes to the table and sits down while pressing the crown firmly down on his head*)

Fell ill with a single scene
bedridden for years
on account of this single scene
Always put the crown on

without getting any further
Although I didn't know
why everything was crumbling around me
Thought too much about Shakespeare
when I was performing Shakespeare
thought too much about the crown
when I was playing Richard the Third
thought too much about the art of acting
when I was acting
We mustn't think about the art of acting
when we're acting
we mustn't think about Shakespeare
when we're performing Shakespeare
we're wearing the crown
but we mustn't think
we are king
A wretched dog that thinks
it's a wretched dog
Meditated much too much
recapitulated much too much
Traveled around much too much
Believed
I had to get to know the continents
what nonsense
Fell ill for years
with this single scene
And never being able to explain what the art of acting is
people ask
we answer
but know nothing

(*Presses the crown firmly down on his head*)

Under the crown I calm down
I would have acquired the costume as well
if I had expressed a desire for it
I wanted the crown
They thought

I would die at seventy
but I'm eighty-two and counting
they thought
they were celebrating my sixtieth birthday
as my last birthday
but they even had to celebrate my eightieth
I wanted to have the crown
Not the costume
I am myself alone
do you understand
I had expressed a desire for the crown
and I acquired it
Underhandedness
I've always conceded
I'm prone to that
To shiftiness

(*Stands up and goes to the previously nailed-down piece of skirting board. Bends down and inspects the skirting board*)

We've even had our fill
of craftspeople
Especially
of the so-called simple people
we've always loathed the complicated ones
but now we also hate the simple ones
we can't put up with the complicated ones
or the simple ones any more
When we step onto the street
they all make us sick
that is the truth

(*Presses the crown down on his head*)

A truth fanatic
But of course injustice is everywhere
like falsehood

(*Inspects the skirting board*)

To paint the place

what madness
when I'm hardly even still capable
of making myself a cup of tea
For twenty years I've been thinking
I'll paint the place one more time

(*Looks around the room*)

but I'll never paint the place again
I'm satisfied with it
as it is

(*Looks at the ceiling*)

It really makes no difference
if it's painted again
or not
I really can't even tell
if it's been painted or not
any more
Thought about it
for twenty years
After her death I'll paint the place
I thought
Twenty years
Now
that nobody comes here any more
Two days before her death
she was still saying
I'd become spiteful
that all of a sudden I wasn't just odd
that I was also spiteful

(*Glances at the door*)

Our son was to have been named
Sebastian
But I said
Rodrigo is quite a fine name
I begged her
then there was a miscarriage

So many sisters
and only one brother
and all of them degenerates
they grew up indecisively
died suddenly
They left me behind
with this domestic shambles

(*Tries to stand up but fails to do so*)

The catastrophic thing of course was
that I towered over all of them
intellectually speaking
I was ill
I was thoroughly ill
but I towered over all of them
intellectually speaking
we loved ourselves
and loathed ourselves

(*Tries to stand up but fails to do so*)

A wholly contrarian
central nervous system
Domestic disintegration everywhere

(*Stands up*)

A cardinal
they would have liked that
they loathed
the acting profession
but I've also always loathed it

(*Walks to the mirror and peers into it*)

they left me alone
in the Thuringian forest
for three months
they didn't give a thought to me
and I wasn't even eleven years old
We don't forgive them

we're incapable of doing that
our parents are unforgivable
The crime of being born
is unforgivable

(*There is a knock at the door. To himself*)

We can't
escape our fate
inevitably

(*Presses the crown firmly down on his head, turns around, and takes two steps towards the door*)

In relying on myself
I have broken off all
connections

(*In a whisper*)

Richard the Third
inaccessible
completely inaccessible
An unbearable meter
sloppily translated

(*There is a knock at the door*)

We wish to be left alone
and they won't leave us alone
We burn all our bridges behind us
and we're badgered
we wish to enjoy our peace and quiet
and people knock on our door

(*In a whisper*)

To be inaccessible
nobody's partner

(*There is a knock at the door*)

Grew old before their time
they all
died away

overnight

(*After a pause, in a questioning tone*)

Is that you Katharina

KATHARINA. It's me
Katharina

HE. Ah yes my child

(*Walks to the window, looks out and turns back around*)

Wait a second
just a second

(*Presses the crown firmly down on his head*)

I'm just reading a book
Schopenhauer
Schopenhauer

(*Goes to the bed and sits down on it*)

Schopenhauer my child

(*Starts to take the crown off his head, but he does not take it off*)

Wait a second

(*He puts on the jacket*)

I'm just putting on my jacket
I've read Schopenhauer
and I'm putting on my jacket
Why have you come now
we said eleven o'clock
it's half past one now
Ah yes
wait a second

(*Stands up and walks to the door and opens it. Enter* KATHARINA *with a half-full pitcher of milk*)

We think it's the evil spirit my child
and it's the good one
Come in
I'm the old actor

you bring milk to
every Tuesday and Friday
you bring the old actor milk
the old actor
who no longer associates with people
come in my child
People are the problem
it's always people
Come in

(KATHARINA *walks into the room, stopping in the middle of it.* HE *is still standing at the door*)

People are awful my child
and megalomaniacal
The whole of humanity is megalomaniacal
wherever we look
we see only a megalomaniacal humanity
we are in the midst
of a catastrophic process of stultification
The crown right the crown
irritates you
Richard the Third
I played him in Duisburg
and in Bochum
It wasn't a success
I loved the role
but I enjoyed no success with it
For my seventieth birthday
the government of the city of Duisburg presented me with
this crown
which I wore when I played the Richard the Third
this very crown
We enjoy no success
and yet we love the role
In Duisburg my child
I acted on the stage in Duisburg
Richard the Third

that naturally means nothing to you my child
come
give me the pitcher

(*Takes the pitcher of milk from* KATHARINA)

Theater people
only look this dangerous
they actually aren't
Are you afraid of me
In Duisburg I played
Richard the Third
as well as Don Carlos
everything

(*Takes the pitcher of milk to the refrigerator, opens the refrigerator, takes a large bowl out of it, and fills it with milk from the pitcher*)

Every now and then
I get in the mood
to put on the crown

(*Puts the pitcher in the refrigerator and shuts its door*)

Crazy
isn't it
All actors are crazy
all good actors are crazy
the entire theater is crazy
Theater people
crazy people
The theater world
a crazy world
Won't you sit down

(KATHARINA *takes a seat at the table.* HE *sits down in the chair at the window*)

The actor has a crown on his head
but he is no king
the actor wears a coronation robe
but he is no king

the actor speaks in a kingly style
but he is no king
the actor ascends the throne
but he is no king

(*Presses the crown firmly down on his head*)

The actor
who has a crown on his head
is a poor old man
Has your mother given you permission
to let me take you to the opera
as I promised I would

(KATHARINA *shakes her head*)

You see
I told you
she wouldn't let me
take you to the opera
To *The Magic Flute*
That's the most beautiful experience a child can have
going to the opera for the first time
and especially to the see *The Magic Flute*
Perhaps later on
All human beings are destructive human beings
they even ruin
their own child
before he can even properly breathe

(*Presses the crown firmly down on his head*)

For over ten years
since my seventieth birthday
I have put on
this crown in the chest
on the second Tuesday of each month
Do you like the crown

(KATHARINA *nods*)

We're dignified

when we're wearing a crown
But it's really quite foolish
to put on a stage-crown
when one is an old actor
a laughable act
a laughable act
a completely laughable act

(*Addressing* KATHARINA *point-blank*) Did you know
that I've acted in Duisburg
and in Osnabrück
Fools the lot of them
That means nothing to you
The art of acting
is a lethal art
I fear nothing more
Do you understand
I can do
what I want
I'm not afraid of anything any more

(*Laughs*)

Fear is perverse my child
when there's so much stupidity

(*Point-blank to* KATHARINA) Would you like some juice

(KATHARINA *answers in the affirmative.* HE *stands up and goes to the refrigerator and asks*)

Sour-cherry juice

KATHARINA. Yes

HE *opens the refrigerator and takes a bottle of sour-cherry juice out of it and fills a glass with the juice and places the glass on the table*

HE. Wait a second
and don't gulp it down all at once
or you'll catch a cold
People are greedy
and greedily gulp everything down at once

(*Fetches the chair from the window and places it at the table and sits down across from* KATHARINA)

You'll see
everything in the world
is very complicated
It all looks simple
but it's very complicated
everything is complicated

(*Presses the crown firmly down on his head*)

People don't forgive
that is the unfortunate truth
people punish and don't forgive
How was your mathematics class today
was it good

(KATHARINA *nods.* HE *signals to her that she can drink the sour-cherry juice now.* KATHARINA *picks up the glass and drinks*)

Carefully
One sip at a time
Drink slowly
eat slowly
and drink slowly
also read slowly
Today I have kept my head
above water
with Schopenhauer's help
I shan't paint the place
I told you I would paint it
but I'm not going to paint

(*Looks around the room*)

I don't even notice
whether it's been painted or not any more
I don't see the cracks in the wall at all
Are there many cracks

(KATHARINA *looks around the room*)

Probably
there are lots of cracks
It will surely be the death of me
if I repaint the place
Ten years before you were born
my wife died
Have I told you that
her name was Katharina
the same as yours
She was very beautiful
very demanding
and very beautiful

(*Looks at the ceiling*)

Meningitis

(*Presses the crown firmly down on his head*)

The crown on my head
that calms me down
How do I look
with the crown on
now
how do I look with the crown on

(KATHARINA *smiles*)

On the second Tuesday of every month
I indulge myself in this joke
an old man
especially when he is old actor
must surely be allowed to indulge himself in this joke
on the second Tuesday of each month
Actors are like children
that's why you and I get along so well

(*Stands up, goes to the piece of writing paper on the wall on which he has written the words "Buy mouse poison," and points to it*)

Can you read
what's written on that piece of paper

KATHARINA. Yes

HE. What is written there

KATHARINA. Buy mouse poison

HE. Correct
Buy mouse poison

(*Sits back down but stands immediately back up and takes the chair to the window*)

I'm not going to catch mice any more
I'm going to poison them
It disgusts me
to drown them in the bucket
For decades I drowned the mice in the bucket
now I poison them

(*Sits down*)

When my wife was alive
there wasn't a single mouse in the house
No sooner had she died
than the mice appeared
On the ground floor there are rats
It won't be long before the rats are here too
This house is a storehouse
for rats
It all comes down
to which direction we choose
whichever direction we choose
we've made the wrong choice

(*Takes the crown off his head and clasps it firmly to his chest*)

It suddenly makes no sense
to keep the crown on my head
this crown is heavier
than a real one
real crowns worn by real kings
aren't as heavy
I never keep it

on my head
for more than an hour
Apart from you
nobody has yet seen me
with this crown on my head
promise me
you won't tell anybody
you've seen me with this crown
on my head
if you did people would think
I was crazy
An actor can treat himself
to putting a crown on his head
without being crazy

(*Point-blank to* KATHARINA) Come
I shall crown you

(KATHARINA *stands up and goes up to him*)

You must kneel down
you must be kneeling when you're crowned

(KATHARINA *kneels before him.* HE *puts the crown on her head*)

How beautiful you are
with the crown on

(*Thoughtfully*)

But girls like you
have never worn a crown
It's laughable

(*Suddenly shouting*)

Laughable laughable
it's laughable
it's laughable

(*Snatches the crown off her head.* KATHARINA *has leapt to her feet*)

Laughable
laughable
laughable

(*Hurls the crown across the room*)

laughable

(*Collapses in exhaustion, then*)

I'm not crazy
naturally
I'm not crazy
The whole time
I had the crown on
I was completely exhausted
I am completely exhausted
I'm terrified
when you knocked
I thought
you were the people from the insurance company
from the burglary insurance company
I was expecting people
from the burglary insurance company
I'm insured against burglary
isn't that laughable
I'm insured against burglary
I own nothing
but this shabby crown

(*Shouting*)

This wretched habitation
and this worthless crown
and I'm insured against burglary

(*Point-blank to* KATHARINA) Come here
come here please

(KATHARINA *walks to him.* HE *makes as if to touch her face but then
refrains from doing so*)

People haven't understood
that I intend to have
nothing further to do with them
they come when they like
but I've stopped coming to the door for everyone

but you
Are you coming again next Friday

(KATHARINA *nods*)

I'm now going to tell you
a secret
Pay attention

(*Resolutely, with very precise articulation, and yet softly*)

I don't care for milk in the slightest
and so I never drink milk
but I want to see you
every Tuesday and Friday
I want to see you
do you understand that
Not a soul apart from you
still has access to me
not a single one
I have always
loathed milk
As soon as you leave
I always pour the milk
into the sink
milk disgusts me
But don't tell your mother that
You must tell everybody
the celebrated actor in Hanssachsstrasse
loves milk
and he drinks milk
he never eats or drinks anything
but milk

(*Takes her by the hand*)

My dear child
next Friday
bring me mouse poison
so that I can poison all the mice
in this house

(KATHARINA *starts to leave.* HE *holds her back*)

As long as I'm still here
Every day the famous actor in the Hanssachsstrasse drinks milk
he exists only
because he drinks milk
tell everybody that
promise me you will

(*Gives* KATHARINA *the pitcher of milk and she leaves*)

Throughout our existence
we're putting on an act
we're acting on a stage

(*Stands up and takes the bowl out of the refrigerator and empties the milk into the bucket. Listens at the door for some time and exits with the bucket. Flushes the toilet*)

Scene III

Towards evening

HE (*sitting in a shabby old dressing gown at the chair at the window*).
Used to be submissive
attentive
obliging
We rushed headlong
into catastrophe
but we survived
Made mistakes as a matter of course
A year in Ludwigshafen
that humbled you
that almost could have cost you your head

(*Looks around*)

I shan't paint the place
I don't need any renovations
It's enough
if we can sleep well
and aren't in pain
that's enough

(*Clutches at his head with both hands*)

To wear the crown
an cnormity
The spectators were afraid of me
not vice versa
Lifelong intimacy
with me

to the point of megalomania
She'd warble a song
that was enough for her
I married her out of pity
and because I was hoping to sire an heir
hoping

(*Laughs to himself*)

Basically an incapacity for living
Everything will work out
I said to myself
Nothing worked out
Perfected
the art of acting
and fell ill
with this perfection
She had no inkling
that she was bound to die
Perpetual double-dealing
they believe they'll live forever
that is their mistake
they believe they have no failing organs
that is their mistake
Kidney brain liver
everything's eaten away in the end
I exorcized
her urge to travel

(*Stands up and walks to the door and listens*)

I must write to the cemetery's administrative office
Attended no concerts for two years
after her death

(*Glances at the window*)

Victor died
unexpectedly
like her
The wretched thing is

that people have no inkling
that they're bound to die
in the very near future
if they knew
that they're bound to die in the very near future
they would set out one last time for Leipzig
or for the Fichtel Mountains
so they suddenly die
without having been to Leipzig
to the Fichtel Mountains
one last time

(*Ties the belt of the dressing gown more tightly around his waist*)

We don't keep ourselves moving
that's why we get cold

(*Goes to the table and sits down*)

A lifelong flunker

(*Looks at his shoes*)

Eventually we're wearing felt shoes
which we've always loathed
I have always loathed felt

(*Picks up the hammer, stands up and walks to the skirting board, bends over, delivers one vigorous hammer-blow to the nail, looks around the room*)

In this posture

(*Looks around the room*)

A motet
for her funeral
the same motet
for Viktor

(*Tries to stand up but fails*)

The mouse poison under the door
and under the window
Then word will get around

that I am poisoning the mice
They won't see me with traps in the hallway
any more

(*Suddenly cries out*)

Semolina
naturally semolina

(*Stands up and goes to the table, takes the notepad out of the chest and writes the word "semolina" on it*)

Semolina

(*Stands up and sticks the sheet of writing paper onto the nail*)

Woe betide him
who takes proceedings against himself
never take proceedings against yourself

(*In a whisper*)

Never take proceedings against yourself

(*Glances at the door*)

Always despised food I'd cooked myself
The pre-dentures era
and the post-dentures era
When we don't have our own teeth any more
we get a craving to bite into something
Semolina slime

(*Sits down on the chair at the window*)

We loathe Schopenhauer
and exist out of him
we loathe the world
and exist in it
I have always loathed writers
even Goethe
Came into conflict with the courts
A lifelong
fear of prison
Because we believe we are constantly proceeding

incessantly
Committing
In the end we're eating semolina slime
and freezing even when
we're wearing felt shoes
and a heavy winter blanket

(*Stands up and walks to the door and listens*)

Eighteen tenants
which makes things communal
which fosters deceit
and commonness
Only when one of them dies
do we learn his name
I've never gotten involved
in a conversation
with any residents of this building
with the building superintendent yes
but not with the residents as such
Should the building acquire a communal dumpster
they asked me
no no
no no
The janitor
brings me nothing but every possible disease
when I let him come in
I shan't let him into the apartment any more
He has bought himself a house in Kittsee
everybody is buying houses
A horrible house-buying frenzy

(*Listens intently at the door*)

Always lived in your shadow she said
I never forgave her for this insult
A young person believes
he has a future
but nobody has a future

(*Goes to the table, sits down and opens the newspaper. After a pause*)

Civil engineer
wanted
if possible in mid thirties
with experience in Africa
for work in Saudi Arabia

(*Reading. After a pause*)

Bookseller seeks
two bookseller's apprentices
in the city center

(*Lays the newspaper on the table*)

Felled by a stroke
while ironing trousers
a laughable death
a laughable death

(*Stands up and goes to the door and listens*)

Taciturnity
has always gotten on my nerves
I could just as easily
have died in Kenya
all signs were pointing to it
but I didn't die in Kenya
A lifelong dependence on climate
tablet dependency and climate dependency

(*Listens intently at the door*)

We say we don't need people
but it just isn't true
that you don't need people
A lust for life that's what it is
I've always had it
Incessant curiosity

(*Listens more intently at the door*)

Incessant curiosity

(*Goes to the window and looks out*)

An incessant lust for life
even in foul weather

(*Looks down at the street*)

We shan't go down there any more
we'll look down there
but we shan't go down there any more
We have always given people a wide
berth
everybody a wide berth
Now we'll never go down there again

(*Looks at the clock*)

Courted death in Kenya
a laughable death
At the invitation of the big game hunter Thompson
how laughable

(*Looks along the bottom of all four walls*)

Ultimately became famous

(*Pulls down the roller-blind, thereby rendering the room completely dark*)

Panicked fear of greenhouses
of plants in general
Greenhouse-induced panic attacks from childhood
till today

(*Raises the blind, turns on the light and pulls the blind down again*)

Never took a walk
not once in my entire life
lay in bed
with the curtains drawn
on the weekends
Acted at the theater
or lay in bed

(*Goes and winds the clock*)

Paris yes
London no
Sils Maria yes
St Moritz no

(*Glances at the door*)

Ate nothing but low-fat curds for years

(*Walks to the door and listens*)

It all comes down to the intensity
with which we act

(*After a pause*)

Dismissed on account of the triviality of the offence
the case was dismissed on account of the triviality of the offence
they said
Incessantly involved in trials
but never locked up

(*Walks to the refrigerator and takes a sausage out of it*)

The old cheese
or the old sausage

(*Puts the sausage back into the refrigerator and takes a piece of cheese out
of it. Sniffs the cheese*)

The sausage is better

(*Puts the cheese back into the refrigerator and takes the sausage out again,
sniffs the sausage*)

No

(*Puts the sausage back into the refrigerator and takes the cheese out again.
Shuts the refrigerator. Glances at the door*)

The old people's dance
I completely forgot about it
that's why it's so quiet in the house

(*Straightens up and takes the cheese to the table. Spreads a large sheet of
newspaper over the table and sets the cheese on it. Takes out a loaf of bread
from of the table-drawer and cuts himself a thick slice*)

Until two years ago I
still used to go
to the old people's dance

(*Begins eating the cheese and bread. Pours himself a glass of mineral water from a bottle, drinks, and eats*)

Misfortune comes calling
because they've stopped thinking
They've forgotten how to think

(*Glances at the door*)

The old people's dance

(*Glances at the shopping list on the wall*)

Mouse poison
Semolina
A beautiful twenty-schilling piece
for Katharina

(*Sticks several pieces of bread into his mouth and chews*)

He enjoys
worldwide acclaim
they said in the lobby
while I was memorizing my lines
When I recite Prospero's speeches
they listen
they're obviously enraptured by it

(*Stands up and goes to the tape recorder, presses a button, and sits back down*)

Voluntary self-control
without scruples
unscrupulous

(*Now listening to himself speaking from the tape recorder*)

If anybody sees me here
in this posture
Complicity
A contempt for craftsmen

We have let all our talents
waste away
distinguished for eccentricity
awarded a doctorate in mathematics

(*Goes to the tape recorder and stops it. Looks around the room*)

they're obviously enraptured

(*Sits down at the table and continues eating*)

CURTAIN

ELIZABETH II

NO COMEDY

God Save the Queen

Dramatis Personae

HERRENSTEIN, an industrial magnate

RICHARD, his valet

DOCTOR GUGGENHEIM, a neighbor of Herrenstein

MISS ZALLINGER, Herrenstein's housekeeper

VIKTOR, Herrenstein's nephew

COUNT NEUTZ

COUNTESS GUDENUS

THE LADY IN THE RED HAT

OLD LADY NUMBER ONE

OLD LADY NUMBER TWO

HOLZINGER, an executive at Herrenstein's firm

Several chambermaids

At least twenty ladies and gentlemen, all of them, including DOCTOR GUGGENHEIM *and* COUNTESS GUDENUS, *dressed in black*

A grandly elegant drawing room dating from the turn of the century
Sparsely furnished
Upstage and center, a pair of tall double doors leading to a balcony,
Upstage left and right a window
Off right two doors
Off left a window
A grandfather clock
A music box
Three floors up from the Opernring in Vienna
Muted crowd noise coming from the street

Scene I

Half past seven in the morning

RICHARD *is pushing* HERRENSTEIN, *who is dressed in a black suit and sitting in a wheelchair, towards the window at stage left*

HERRENSTEIN (*with prosthetic legs, after a fairly long pause*). I've forgotten my teeth

(*Exit* RICHARD *to fetch the teeth*)

I can't see a thing

(*After trying to turn round*)

These horrible people
This is just what I needed

(*Re-enter* RICHARD *with a tray with* HERRENSTEIN's *dentures on it.* HERRENSTEIN *picks up the dentures and places them in his mouth.* RICHARD *hands him a black cane with a silver handle*)

I see less and less every day

(RICHARD *pushes* HERRENSTEIN *closer to the window.* HERRENSTEIN *stretches forward and falls back exhausted*)

I can hardly breathe
Everything hurts   ·
and everything's disgusting as well
Tell Doctor Friedlander
that he must come today
by tomorrow we won't even be around any more
How many people are coming to this occasion of horror anyway

RICHARD. Twenty or thirty according to your nephew

HERRENSTEIN. What a revolting individual
  I've basically always loathed Viktor
  We wake up
  and see nothing but hideousness
  Feebleness and hideousness

RICHARD. Miss Zallinger is already back from the city

HERRENSTEIN. You always read to me too *loudly* Richard
  Louder I always say
  but that doesn't mean *loud*
  In Badgastein you also read too loudly to me
  To be sure that horrible climate is lethal
  But you did after all advise me against going there
  Doctor Friedländer also advised me against it
  For you Badgastein is *lethal* you said
  Lethal you said verbatim
  but of course for that very reason I was fascinated
  fascinated because you said *lethal*
  Doctor Friedländer also advised me against it
  but precisely because you and Doctor Friedländer
  advised me against it
  I was obsessed with the idea of taking a trip there
  It ended up almost being the death of me
  People with weak hearts catch their death in Badgastein
  but also in Bad Hall
  it's even worse for the likes of me

  (*Signals to* RICHARD *that he would like to be even closer to the window.*
  RICHARD *pushes* HERRENSTEIN *even closer to the window*)

  No sooner are we born
  than we're fleeing from death
  the whole of humankind is merely running away from death

  (*Stretches forward to look through the window*)

  they're fleeing from death humankind that is
  repugnant
  the masses are repugnant
  but woe betide us if we ignore them

they'll trample us underfoot
Do you really believe
that the Altaussee does me good
I've always loathed the Altaussee
those old houses those old people
everything's musty and moldered
everything's dank
when we climb into bed we're climbing into a dank one
I've always felt as if I were being choked at Altaussee
I've never understood at all why there are people
who have voluntarily settled at Altaussee
Writers composers actors
the lot of this riffraff have been buying property there
since before the turn of the century
No sooner do people have money
than they buy themselves those execrable old houses
go around in dirndls and lederhosen
and pal around with butchers and lumberjacks
I don't get any air in the mountains
What do we ever do in Altaussee
we don't get any variety whatsoever there
No I'm not going to Altaussee
just because your aunt lives there

(*Tries to look out the window*)

Everything's cloudy
is it actually cloudy today

RICHARD. It's a sunny day

HERRENSTEIN. I can hardly see anything
    I can hardly hear anything and I can hardly see anything
    but I've gotten used to this condition
    I never see these people

(*Exit* RICHARD)

And all of a sudden they're all coming here
an appalling thought
but I can't refuse

to receive them
then again it is an opportunity
to shake hands with them
and not see them again for years
But of course they've only ever kept a covetous eye on my life's work
even the oldest of them speculate on it incessantly
but I'm not going to bequeath anything to these people
I have of course told you
that I'm not going to bequeath anything to these people

(*Enter* RICHARD *with some newspapers, which he sets down next to*
HERRENSTEIN)

My relatives have always repelled me
more and more with each passing year

(*Signals with a wave that he would like to be away from the window*)

It's become apparent
that all these people are worthless
we follow them and observe them
and discern their worthlessness

(RICHARD *pushes* HERRENSTEIN *into the middle of the room*)

I can't say
that I've ever loved a single one
of my relatives
I have never been able to summon up
even the faintest trace of sympathy for any of my relatives
that is the truth
When we take away their hypocrisy
nothing is left of these people
but their loathsomeness
it makes no difference to me
that I am loathed
I've become accustomed
to the hatred of other people
I didn't sleep a single night in Badgastein
since Badgastein my hearing has been poorer
and my vision has been poorer

but that's entirely my fault

(*Enter* MISS ZALLINGER, *who sets the table for* HERRENSTEIN'*s and* RICHARD'*s breakfast*)

We invest everything we've got
in people
and are subsequently disillusioned
But after all they sleep well
They're healthy
They still have some living to look forward to
They're not encumbered by anything
But let them just wait till they turn sixty
and stop enjoying pain-free nights

(*Looks at the floor, traces circles on it with his cane*)

Their life is fairly well-balanced
Their future is no mystery to them
I see nothing but filth
everything is filthy
But the floor was polished just yesterday

(*Shouting*)

isn't that so Miss Zallinger
the floor was polished just yesterday wasn't it

MISS ZALLINGER. Yes of course Mr Herrenstein

HERRENSTEIN. I see nothing but filth

(*Trains his gaze along the wall*)

I can look wherever I like
I see nothing but filth
It's unbearable to think
that all these people are coming here
today of all days
a shamelessly inquisitive race the Viennese
How many people are coming anyway Miss Zallinger

MISS ZALLINGER. Thirty or forty

HERRENSTEIN. An appalling thought
and this a day before our departure
Thirty or forty
Because I told two or three people
they could come here
and see Elizabeth the Second
thirty or forty are coming
And the occasion
is this ridiculous
But I can't get into these people's bad books
for good
I must talk myself into believing
that I'll enjoy this
I never thought any of these people
would ever come back into my house

(*Looks around the room*)

Everything is getting dirty
Isn't it revolting
today of all days
when we have to go to Heldwein's funeral
the day before we're going to Semmering
I'm still not entirely sure
that I'll go to Semmering
Even when the luggage is all packed
I shan't be sure
that I'm not going somewhere else entirely
perhaps I'll go to the Carpathians
to see my niece
What do you think Richard
wouldn't that be a good idea

RICHARD. Perhaps Mr Herrenstein perhaps

HERRENSTEIN. But everything must be perfectly calm in the
Carpathians
I absolutely must be able to calm down there
but isn't it too mountainous

You can't just keep constantly pushing me back and forth
Of course that's why I agreed to go to Semmering
because we've got that flat level path there
how I loathe that path
nothing but that same path every day
always the same view
but the Semmering air is supposed to be good
for heart trouble
Haven't you thought about the Carphatians

RICHARD. I have thought about the Carpathians Mr Herrenstein
Indeed I've even recommended the Carpathians to you

HERRENSTEIN. Recommended the Carpathians
When did you recommend the Carpathians to me
did you actually mention the Carpathians to me
I'm forgetting more and more things

(RICHARD *starts reading aloud from the newspaper,* HERRENSTEIN *stops him*)

When we've forgotten everything
we have nothing left
then we are dead
we truly exist only
because we haven't forgotten everything yet
Do you know that I've received an invitation to Toronto
this is the first one I've ever received
an invitation to Toronto
These people are unaware
that I'm incapable of walking
otherwise they wouldn't have invited me to Toronto
unless they invited me
precisely because they knew
that I can't walk
Herrenstein the industrial magnate with prosthetic feet
Most likely this invitation is just part of one of those nasty maneuvers
typical of big companies
I haven't taken my aspirin yet

(*Exit* RICHARD *to fetch the pill.* HERRENSTEIN *gazing at the floor*)

I was a wax dummy
alone forever
finally I leapt into the fireplace
What terrible dreams we have
most of them we forget
a wax dummy
that leapt into the fireplace
into the fireplace of a poor family

(*Reenter* RICHARD *with the pill on a tray and a glass of water.*
HERRENSTEIN *takes the pill and drinks a sip of water.* RICHARD *takes
the glass and hands it to* MISS ZALLINGER)

I dreamt
I was a wax dummy
that suddenly leapt into a blazing fireplace
into a poor family's fireplace
isn't it ridiculous
the things we confront ourselves with
Do you ever have such terrible dreams

RICHARD. I can't say that I do Mr Herrenstein

HERRENSTEIN. So you have good dreams

RICHARD. Not terrible ones
    not good ones
    but not terrible ones either

HERRENSTEIN *signals that he wishes to be pushed back to the window.*
RICHARD *pushes him to the window.*

HERRENSTEIN. The solution is
    quite simply to be constantly turning round again all of a sudden
    and to walk farther
    I of all people am saying this
    In Rome I thought
    I could stand up on my own
    I thought I didn't need you
    I tried to stand up

and promptly fell out of bed
it was no accident
it was an act of vengeance against my decision

(RICHARD *starts reading aloud from the newspaper and* HERRENSTEIN
firmly indicates that he must stop)

I was trying to be independent of you for once
but I failed
You know of course that after that I was bedridden
with those horrible back pains for days on end
It makes no sense for a completely immobile cripple
to keep on checking into the Hassler
of all hotels
simply because he's used to it
I've kept checking into the Hassler over and over again
in the final analysis the Hassler is quite simply a loathsome hotel
I haven't the faintest idea why I'm always saying
the Hassler is lovely
I loathe the sight of the Spanish steps
like nothing else
Rome is no longer an option
Lisbon today is like Rome
thirty years ago
we'll go there as soon as possible
I love that town
Hasn't it ever struck you
that nowhere else in the world are there so many cripples roaming
    around
as in Lisbon
on every street corner a face overgrown with cancer
withered noses corroded ears
Diseases enjoy absolute sovereignty in Lisbon
in all likelihood it fascinates me
Do you call it a perversion Richard
I'm attracted to corporeal deformities
to this city's beauty and at the same time
to its mass of corporeal deformities

but naturally there are just as many beautiful people in Lisbon
percentagewise even more of them than in other large European cities
Back when I was a very young man
about fifteen years before my accident
I took two rooms in the Avenida Palace
to get some peace and quiet
an empty room as a buffer so to speak against the nastiness of the rest
    of the world
I can't put up with living wall-to-wall with strangers
the older I get the less I can put up with that

MISS ZALLINGER (*who has finished setting the table by now*). Can I bring
    in the tea now

HERRENSTEIN. Yes of course bring in the tea

    (*Exit* MISS ZALLINGER)

It isn't true
that I no longer have any desire for what the world has to offer
I said that more or less without thinking yesterday
I have a tremendous desire for it Richard

    (*Traces circles on the floor with his cane*)

There are two countries I still want to visit
I want to go to England
and I want to go to Portugal
and naturally to Poland my absolutely favorite country
I was never happier than in Poland
no one understands that
People shake their heads even when they're not shaking them
they shake them interminably whenever I rave about Poland
but of course I went to Poland not long ago
When were we last in Poland anyway

RICHARD. Two years ago

HERRENSTEIN. Two years ago
    it seems like an eternity to me

    (MISS ZALLINGER *brings in the tea*; HERRENSTEIN *is wheeled by*
    RICHARD *to the breakfast table*)

Time and again a higher stage of life
my father always said
what ever did he mean by that
probably he meant by it what I understand it to mean
that people's only misfortune
is to have been born to begin with
we always pose the stupidest questions
of course we ourselves are also stupid
thoroughly stupid
crippled and stupid
everyone is crippled and stupid
physically crippled and stupid
without exception

(RICHARD *sits down across from* HERRENSTEIN; *they eat their breakfast;*
MISS ZALLINGER *stands in place at the door*)

Stupid thoughts are the only ones ever uttered
crippled utterances are the only ones ever uttered
be a thought ever so well thought
it is still a crippled thought
be an utterance ever so well worded
it is still a crippled utterance

(*Ties a napkin around his neck*)

the entire world is riddled with stupidity
the entire world is a crippled world
but naturally there are skillful cripples
skillful cripples

(*Continuing to eat his breakfast with* RICHARD)

Haven't you thought about leading an artist's existence
I once wanted to be an actor
but I failed miserably
I am incapable of memorizing two words in succession
quite apart from the fact that my father would never have allowed
his son to be a practicing Thespian
Thespian became his most disparaging term of abuse
from then onwards he said that word

whenever he was harshly disparaging anybody
Haven't you ever been tempted
to become an artist
that's what people want to be
everyone throngs to the stage
everyone wants to be behind the podium
simply because it is a podium
Thespianizing concertizing scientizing
they all throng to such activities
I imagine you would make a great actor
You are a veritable director's goldmine
a director could work wonders with you
You could play a king or a coal miner
You have all the makings
of a great actor
naturally it's too late now
A career as an actor must be embarked on at a fairly early point in life
not as in ballet when one is four or five years old
but at least by the age of sixteen or seventeen
And yet I have always been revolted by the acting profession
whenever a heap of blockheads come running towards each other on
     the stage
Even your voice is a voice made for acting
Have you really never thought about joining the circus

RICHARD. Never

HERRENSTEIN. As a veritable tot
I got the idea of joining the circus
like my mother
who ran off all the way from Vienna
to Hungary with a gipsy circus
she was four years old at the time
A Crown prosecutor from Budapest
brought her back to Vienna
three months after everybody had given her up for dead
But everybody has a hankering to be on stage
a hankering for debauchery

RICHARD. I've never had such a hankering

HERRENSTEIN. You're a reflective person Richard
   controlled disciplined
   that sets you apart
   you are dependability personified
   You're completely un-Austrian
   on the other hand there's absolutely nothing German about you
   if there were you wouldn't even be here
   you're a singular individual
   your greatest asset is
   that you're not in the least disposed to be a contrarian
   Twenty-five years in Herrenstein's house
   I personally shudder at the very thought of it
   but it doesn't depress you
   You are consistently good-humored
   even in the face of trivial ridiculous occasions like this one
   I am of course also like a father to you
   You are the only person I can put up with
   I can't say why
   that's the case my dear Richard

   (*To* MISS ZALLINGER) Be honest Miss Zallinger
   where would you like to travel to
   to Semmering or to Altaussee

MISS ZALLINGER. To Altaussee Mr Herrenstein

HERRENSTEIN. You're all alike
   in wanting to go to that perverse artists' hole
   where death or at least deathly boredom
   lies in ambush
   I haven't even made up my mind yet
   it ultimately makes no difference
   where I go
   the main thing is to get away from Vienna
   this city is getting more and more unbearable
   I loathe Vienna and I loathe the Viennese
   What's on at the Opera today anyway

RICHARD. *Andrea Chénier*

HERRENSTEIN. That loathsome Giordano
   who's some cousin of mine
   three times removed
   in any case there's a niece of Giordano's
   who's also my niece
   I find it all too complicated
   I don't go to the Opera as readily as I used to
   but I'd sooner go there than to the Burgtheater
   they say there's a new general manager there
   but he is a charlatan just like the rest of them
   the Germans always arrive here like a breath of fresh air
   and before you know it it's the gaping void all over again
   the boring gaping void
   How many general managers of the Burgtheater
   have I already outlived
   and basically nothing has changed
   at that perverse play-annihilating machine
   in no time flat the new faces become the old faces
   and the new spirit becomes the spirit of yesterday
   that house has always been termite-eaten

(*Shouting*)

That's actually the Burgtheater's main attraction
   the fact that it's always been termite-eaten
   and always will be termite-eaten
   Every attempt to clear the Burgtheater of deadwood
   simply leads to an orgy of dry-rot
   I am sick of actors
   I'd much rather listen to the bone-headed vocalists
   in a Mozart opera
   When will they next be putting on *Così fan tutte* anyway

MISS ZALLINGER. Shall I find out

HERRENSTEIN. Yes please find out Miss Zallinger
   the only thing about the opera I ever really liked

(*Exit* MISS ZALLINGER)

was *Così fan tutte*
I don't care who is conducting
that is music you simply cannot ruin
everything else is invariably just atrocious
The nice thing is
that it's only a couple of steps from here to the opera
it would even be too much for me
to have to travel any great distance just to see an opera
I'd never be able to stand that
Basically Richard just pushes me across the street
more or less right across the street
to Mozart and Wagner
But I can't go see *Così fan tutte* every week

(*Reenter* MISS ZALLINGER *with* Die Presse)

When is *Così fan tutte*

MISS ZALLINGER. Today it's *Un ballo in maschera*

HERRENSTEIN. How ghastly
I don't care for Verdi
These Italian tearjerkers
are good for nothing but besmirching one's auditory canal
I only go see Mozart operas
which also bore me
but at the highest level
and Wagner operas
When is *Così fan tutte* going to be on next

MISS ZALLINGER. It isn't even in the program

HERRENSTEIN. That's just like those morons
not putting on
Così fan tutte
the only opera in history worth anything at all
Andrea Chénier
that piece of sentimental heroic kitsch

(*To* RICHARD) But you're no devotee
of Giordano and Company either are you

they positively ooze mendacity
Do you like Giordano or not

RICHARD. Of course not Mr Herrenstein
of course not

HERRENSTEIN. It's unbearable
when you're constantly saying *of course not*
There are days when you say nothing else

(*To* MISS ZALLINGER) Miss Zallinger
do you think Altaussee is good for me
You have no idea
how bad it is for me
In and of itself the Viennese climate is just fine
on the other hand my condition is getting worse with each passing
    day
The air is better in Semmering
in Altaussee I always see the same people
the old countesses who get on my nerves
and their senile husbands and husbanders
In Semmering I never come into contact
with that riffraff
on the other hand isolation is also hell
Do you happen to know who's actually coming here today
I need the Queen of England like a hole in the head
Because I told my nephew
he could come
now forty people are coming
people who have absolutely no excuse for being here

(*Looks around the room*)

the bad air emitted by these people
is death to me
Just today first thing this morning
I had an enormous craving for literature
now it's all completely vanished again
Where did we leave *Elective Affinities* anyway

MISS ZALLINGER. In the dining room

HERRENSTEIN (*to* RICHARD). In the dining room how absurd
    things have come to such a pass
    that you're reading *Elective Affinities* to me in the dining room
    and also still leaving the book there
    leaving it in the dining room
    absurd absurd
    You left it there Richard
    Until half past three in the morning you read me Tolstoy Richard
    a completely failed attempt at distraction
    today would have been a particularly good day for *Elective Affinities*
    I believe by now I've heard you read *Elective Affinities*
    a full dozen times
    This is sheer feeble-mindedness
    but an ideal course of reading
    for the purpose of driving away boredom
    to this day I've always thought of its style
    as neither especially brilliant
    nor decidedly stupid
    a style that's easy on the ears of each and every listener
    and puts each and every one of them to sleep

(*To* RICHARD) *You* of course don't read
    you lucky man
    Goethe hasn't yet spoiled the world for you
    little by little he's put me off the world
    I've definitely made the world a much darker place for myself through
        literature
    and yet not a week goes by
    without your reading a book to me
    reading a book to me book to me book to me
    and each time you do I get bored to death
    but I'm still more at ease with this deadly boredom
    than without it

Exit MISS ZALLINGER

RICHARD. May I draw your attention to the fact
    that Mr Holzinger from the executive team will be arriving shortly

HERRENSTEIN. What he's
coming here today

RICHARD. Yes you ordered him to come here at eleven

HERRENSTEIN. I need this like a hole in the head

RICHARD. But I told you that on Saturday the Queen of England would
be coming
On Saturday I said
the Queen of England will be coming
and so you won't be able to receive a visit from Mr Holzinger

HERRENSTEIN. Did you say that
You said that
You

RICHARD. I said on Saturday the Queen of England is coming
and so Mr Holzinger obviously can't come

HERRENSTEIN. And I didn't listen to you
I actually didn't listen to you
this is a genuine catastrophe

(*Signals to* RICHARD *that he wishes him to wheel him away from the
breakfast table and to the window at stage left and throws his napkin onto
the table*)

I didn't listen
You said that
And I didn't listen

(RICHARD *wheels* HERRENSTEIN *to the window at stage left.*
HERRENSTEIN *looks out the window*).

You say it's completely sunny

RICHARD. A sunny day

HERRENSTEIN. Everything looks foggy to me
I'll never see a sunny day again
and from three in the afternoon onwards I'm also quite hard of hearing
When is the Queen coming anyway

RICHARD. At about noon according to Miss Zallinger

HERRENSTEIN. At about noon
  and at eleven Mr Holzinger is coming
  I can't tell you how much that man disgusts me
  it's the way he speaks
  and what he says
  the clothes he wears
  the way he moves
  the way he keeps saying *abrupt*
  he's constantly saying *abrupt*
  and I can't see any reason for it
  an abrupt closure he says
  an abrupt drop in the interest rate
  People get into the habit of using some ghastly word
  and never shake it as long as they live
  I myself have been saying the word *marvelous* for years
  it's absurd isn't it
  but we naturally end up reflecting our inner world into the outer one
  that's what it is Richard
  Breakfast is simply stagnating in my stomach
  it's been the same thing for years
  but it wouldn't make any sense to change it
  it's the same thing with my dinners
  Eventually everything gets on one's nerves
  and one's nerves fall ill
  But there's nothing remotely alluring about the Queen of England
  about that whole royal bunch
  they all look equally stupid
  but the people are fascinated by them
  I said to my nephew
  all right you can come here
  go ahead and have a look at her
  I have no interest in the Queen of England
  I've never been interested in those kinds of people
  By at around noon when the queen comes
  we'll have completely run out of time
  and I'd wanted to write to Lucius
  about the Filipino shipment first

I can also write to Lucius from Semmering
or from Altaussee
Sixty-eight thousand gun barrels Richard absurd
I'm not going to let myself get worked up about
whether to go
to Altaussee or to Semmering
it obviously makes no difference which direction we travel
How is your aunt doing anyway
does she still get those cramps in her legs

RICHARD. She's receiving treatment from a doctor in Bad Ischl

HERRENSTEIN. From a doctor in Bad Ischl
but the doctors at Bad Ischl are considered
the worst doctors in the world
who kill all their patients on account of some trifling ailment
how old is your aunt anyway

RICHARD. Eighty-seven

HERRENSTEIN. Exactly my age
but if she is active

RICHARD. She was on the Katrin as recently as a year ago

HERRENSTEIN. You don't say
I wouldn't even have been able to do that at the age of twenty
But Bad Ischl is loathsome
the people sit in their houses and freeze
and whenever they leave the house they go
to Zauner's pastry shop
one of the most tasteless pastry shops in the world
the more egregiously tasteless anything in the Salzkammergut is
the more popular it is
People who holiday in the Salzkammergut are the most tasteless of all
    holiday-makers
How does your aunt support herself anyway

RICHARD. She has an annuity

HERRENSTEIN. An annuity
from what

RICHARD. From her husband
who was a tanner

HERRENSTEIN. Tanning tanning
isn't that a dying trade
nothing stinks more gruesomely than a tannery
but without tanners there'd be no lederhosen

RICHARD. She gets two-and-a-half thousand schillings

HERRENSTEIN. That's life for you
that's life
it will always be thus
Have you raised the curtains

RICHARD. Of course Mr Herrenstein

HERRENSTEIN (*stretching forward*). Everything looks foggy to me
And it's completely sunny you say

RICHARD. A completely sunny day Mr Herrenstein

HERRENSTEIN. The proper sort of day for the Queen of England
I don't care for these people
Burberry and Greenfell mannequins
with their stupid smirks
whether they show up with heads of state
or with their dogs
it's always the same
the whole brood is execrable
But you've been to England several times Richard

RICHARD. Seven times

HERRENSTEIN. You're basically well-traveled
possibly better-traveled than me
I haven't been to England seven times
I've only been to England twice
plus two trips to Scotland
the Hebrides are quite fascinating
fascinating rugged cliffs

RICHARD. I've also been to Ireland

HERRENSTEIN. To Northern Ireland

RICHARD. To Northern Ireland and Ireland
   and to Wales

HERRENSTEIN. Anyhow it's easy to see
   that you've been to England and Ireland quite often
   What drew you there so frequently anyway

RICHARD. Friends

HERRENSTEIN. Friends
   I haven't even got any friends in England

   (*Upstage* MISS ZALLINGER *is carrying in a table*)

   At first we want to see everything
   then all of a sudden we don't want to see anything else
   but I've always had a hankering for travel
   even with these difficulties
   An Austrian-wheelchair fate Richard

   (*Looks out the window*)

   Don't offer Mr Holzinger so much as
   a sip of liquor
   these people think
   they've got to drain their glass
   they never leave before they do
   I want this man to clear off back to where he came from right away
   hypocritical creatures the lot of them
   but they're necessary to us
   without them everything would have come to pieces ages ago
   That's the system
   a man who holds everything together
   and a line of such creatures
   who are managed by this man become unscrupulous
   more or less
   but who isn't unscrupulous
   to be sure we don't think about money or property any more
   it's been decades since that was a preoccupation
   our actions are habitual

we've got to keep people on a short leash
and greet them ever-so affably
and tell them they're indispensable
and at the same time keep threatening to sack them

(*Having caught sight of* MISS ZALLINGER's *reflection in the window as she is carrying in the table, exclaims*)

Miss Zallinger
what in the world are you doing
why are you carrying that table in here

(RICHARD *turns the wheelchair and* HERRENSTEIN *slightly*)

What is going on here

MISS ZALLINGER. It's for the buffet Mr Herrenstein

HERRENSTEIN. What buffet

MISS ZALLINGER. For the guests

HERRENSTEIN. That's just terrible
the fact that we're going so far as to prepare a buffet
for these people
I only hope it isn't from Demel

MISS ZALLINGER. We prepared it ourselves Mr Herrenstein

HERRENSTEIN. Even so these people will come here
and devour the whole thing
The fact that I've invited all these people here
is pure madness
Of course *I* didn't invite them
They invited *themselves*
Just my nephew I thought just my nephew
and now forty people are coming
by the end even more than forty will have come

Exit MISS ZALLINGER

RICHARD. Is there even room for forty people here

HERRENSTEIN. I was just wondering the same thing
A person

who lives alone for years
with nobody but you Richard
more or less with nobody but you
Of course Miss Zallinger doesn't count
nobody else at all counts
and suddenly forty people show up
The Viennese are so revoltingly inquisitive
They congregate in the hundreds of thousands
to see a monkey walk down the Mariahilferstrasse
they're completely undiscriminating

(*Enter* MISS ZALLINGER *with a second table which she sets down next to
the first one*)

And all of this
when we'll still have to go to the funeral of Heldwein the late jeweler
this afternoon
we're even game enough to make an appearance at something that
          ridiculous
Köchert Heldwein Fischmeister
they're all dead now
the Viennese jewelers have died out
of course their sons don't count
their sons are worthless
the fact that we actually stoop to associating with jewelers
is an enormity Richard
Basically someone we know has died
every day of this season
and so we have had to keep running to the cemetery
on the other hand I've ascertained
that I look best in my mourning suit
you know Richard
I'm a mourning-suit enthusiast
don't you think it's too much in one day for me
the Queen of England
and all these people
and Heldwein the jeweler on top of that
and Mr Holzinger on top of that

to be sure I could still cancel my meeting with Mr Holzinger
but then I'll have to receive him tomorrow

(*Observing* MISS ZALLINGER)

Why in the world are you dragging that table in here all by yourself
you have assistants don't you
where are the maids

MISS ZALLINGER. The maids only get in my way
this is no trouble for me

HERRENSTEIN. All right but don't you be the one to drag it back out
let the girls do some work
that's what they're here for after all

MISS ZALLINGER. Yes of course Mr Herrenstein

HERRENSTEIN. How many tables do you still have to carry in here
anyway

MISS ZALLINGER. We need five tables for the buffet

HERRENSTEIN (*to* RICHARD). Don't large gatherings of people disgust
you
does it really not bother you
so many people in one place

RICHARD. Of course Mr Herrenstein

HERRENSTEIN. It isn't normal
to be revolted by the masses
people love to flock together
they all strive constantly to be together with each other
I've always wished to be away from everybody
to get away from everybody
that is doubtless my curse

(*To* MISS ZALLINGER) You're wrecking your spinal column Miss
Zallinger
You'll soon see you're wrecking your spinal column
mightn't we hear some music
something classical Richard

Miss Zallinger wouldn't this be a good time
to listen to music

(MISS ZALLINGER *starts the music box. A couple of measures of Mozart.*
HERRENSTEIN *shouting*)

No artificial music
You've got to play it
play something for us why don't you Miss Zallinger
a short little classical piece
You play Chopin so beautifully

(MISS ZALLINGER *stops the music box*)

But it's easily been a year
since you played anything
I don't know why you don't play the piano more often
All of a sudden you gave it up
it's easily been a year
an etude a sonata anything will do
in Semmering we won't even have a piano
Don't act like that Miss Zallinger
when you are after all a trained pianist
and your father was after all a conductor
one doesn't simply renounce
such a highly cultivated talent overnight
now go and play

(MISS ZALLINGER *goes into the music room and leaves the door half open*)

She used to play us something every day
why doesn't she play any more
what a horrible person
And it was always so pleasant whenever she played
wasn't it Richard
Chopin Schumann

(MISS ZALLINGER *begins to play a Chopin sonata*)

I don't care for the piano
it's only fit for people with perverted tastes
even Horowitz is unbearable
but as a stimulant as a stimulant

Breakfast has upset my stomach
Naturally she's completely out of practice
whatever we don't constantly practice doing
breaks down on us
In our parents' time the piano was played every afternoon
for years we had our own hired pianist who would come to the house
just to play then
I never played it
my brother played it
I never did
Miss Zallinger played it for twenty years
It's easily been a year
since she stopped playing

(*In a whisper*)

but her playing is quite ham-fisted
don't you think Richard

RICHARD. It's uninspired Mr Herrenstein

HERRENSTEIN. An abuse of high art
  Not that I consider
  playing the piano a form of high art
  an aural time-killer yes
  but not high art
  there's something truly peacock-esque about the piano

(*Shouting in the direction of the music room*)

That's enough Miss Zallinger
that's enough

(MISS ZALLINGER *slams shut the Bösendorfer and emerges from the music room*)

It's not sounding as good as it used to
Your father was such a distinguished man
isn't he buried in the communal cemetery in Salzburg

MISS ZALLINGER. Yes Mr Herrenstein

HERRENSTEIN. He taught conducting at the Mozarteum

MISS ZALLINGER. Yes Mr Herrenstein

HERRENSTEIN. An excellent man your father
How are your sisters doing anyway

MISS ZALLINGER. My sisters are doing fine

HERRENSTEIN. Good lord not everybody is happily married

(TWO CHAMBERMAIDS *carry in a third table with* MISS ZALLINGER'S *help*)

(*To* MISS ZALLINGER) We're just offering them snacks right

MISS ZALLINGER. Just snacks Mr Herrenstein

HERRENSTEIN. Do I even have to be here
when these people show up
I basically don't have to be here at all
I really am completely superfluous
Don't you also think Richard
that I'm completely superfluous
to this affair
And yet I really do want to see them all
Guggenheim my philosophical neighbor
will surely also come over
I was already playing with Guggenheim in the Ringstrasse when I was
three years old
and also in the city park of course
he never should have come back from England
he was doomed to be disillusioned
the Austrians are a degenerate nation
the Austrians loathe the Jews
and most of all they loathe the Jews who have re-immigrated to Austria
the Austrians have learned nothing
they haven't changed in the slightest
an entire nation that personifies utter moral shabbiness
I'll ask Guggenheim
to visit us in Semmering

RICHARD. Or in Altaussee

HERRENSTEIN. I don't think
  I'll go to that nest of Nazis
  I know full well why I never get any air
  at Altaussee
  it isn't only on account of the mountains
  it's also on account of the Nazis
  who reside there
  the most scenic spots in Austria
  have always attracted the greatest number of Nazis
  Salzburg Gmunden Altaussee
  are nothing but nests of Nazis
  Better to bore myself stiff in Semmering
  in Doctor Guggenheim's company it will be bearable
  Was Heldwein a Catholic?

RICHARD. Yes

HERRENSTEIN. Then of course we'll have to suffer through
  that whole Catholic procedure
  I find nothing more loathsome
  than a Catholic funeral
  Can I still have a glass of water

(RICHARD *fetches a glass of water and gives it to him.* HERRENSTEIN
drains the glass)
  But if we were constantly thinking about all these abominations
  we'd have to stop living in this country altogether
  wherever we look we see
  National Socialist vulgarity and Catholic feeblemindedness
  If the Queen is coming at about noon
  Can't we still make it to
  the Döbling cemetery by three

RICHARD. The funeral isn't till half past three

HERRENSTEIN. The people who go to jewelers' funerals
  are exactly the sorts of people I can't stand
  the whole so-called high-society crowd
  a veritable gaggle of countesses
  Have you brushed down my heavy black overcoat Miss Zallinger

MISS ZALLINGER. Of course Mr Herrenstein

HERRENSTEIN. Of course Mr Herrenstein
 (*To* RICHARD) Are we taking the Renault to the funeral

RICHARD. Of course Mr Herrenstein

HERRENSTEIN. Of course Mr Herrenstein
 Of course Mr Herrenstein
 (*Clutches at his head*)
 Of course Mr Herrenstein
 (*To* MISS ZALLINGER) Is it all cold food
 all cold food

MISS ZALLINGER. Of course it's all cold food
 Mr Herrenstein

HERRENSTEIN. I hardly eat anything at all any more
 I wonder why I am so thin
 and I hardly eat anything at all any more
 I'm suffering from a lack of appetite
 I've never been keen on eating
 I've never aspired to be an eater
 I've always left the eating to other people

 (*To* RICHARD) Your gusto when eating
 is astonishing
 I have only ever seen you eat
 with gusto
 I have always thought it would imbue me likewise
 with an appetite for eating
 but to the contrary
 I've been gradually losing my appetite in your presence
 that isn't an accusation Richard
 But do let me get a proper view of the street

 (RICHARD *pushes* HERRENSTEIN *to the window giving on to the balcony at stage right.* HERRENSTEIN *stretches and looks out the window*)

 I have no idea whatsoever
 why the Ringstrasse is so renowned
 isn't it the most hideous street in the world

nothing but pompous kitsch
the Parliament the Burg the Opera
each a gruesome textbook example of architectural erroneousness
a tasteless architectural hodgepodge
a monstrous confectioner's confection
each one of them more execrable than the next
and yet oddly enough
we adore them as a whole
You say it's a sunny day
in my eyes everything looks cloudy
ever since Doctor Funder died
my visual faculty has been deteriorating
a revolting way of putting it isn't it
An invalid will often wax poetic
he'll unabashedly start spewing kitsch
as if he's stepping into some toothsome garden
The real catastrophe
will be when I can't see anything at all any more
when I can't see anything
or hear anything any more
and I'll be completely dependent on you in my dealings with everyone
and everything Richard

(*Enter* TWO CHAMBERMAIDS *and* MISS ZALLINGER *carrying in a fourth table, setting it down next to the other three, and standing in place.* HERRENSTEIN *suddenly sitting up straight*)

Now I'd like to have my banana

(RICHARD *signals to* MISS ZALLINGER *to go out and fetch a banana; exit* MISS ZALLINGER)

I think that we'll finish *Elective Affinities*
in the Semmering
then what
Schopenhauer perhaps
or Flaubert   .
Nietzsche
Kleist

(*Exeunt the* TWO CHAMBERMAIDS)

I really makes absolutely no difference
what we read
I don't think I'll ready any more Schopenhauer
after all we don't have to keep reading everything over and over
You really do read quite well Richard
as long as I can still hear you
naturally it's uniform monotonous
someday of course I won't be able to hear anything any more
but probably it won't ever even come to that

(*Enter* MISS ZALLINGER *with a banana on a plate;* HERRENSTEIN *takes the banana and bites off a piece of it.* HERRENSTEIN *with his mouth full*)

But it'd be ridiculous to have Schopenhauer read to me
and to wind up as a dead man
whose last moment
was spent listening to one of Schopenhauer's sentences
or to one of Nietzsche's

(*Takes a large bite of the banana*)

or one of Voltaire's sentences
The French were always my favorites
I liked the English least of all
the Russians perhaps

(*Chewing with his mouth full*)

One of Tolstoy's short stories tonight Richard
or Turgenev's

(*Chewing with his mouth still full*)

Turgenev's
Turgenev's

(*Takes an even larger bite of the banana and chews with his mouth still full*)

one of Turgenev's
one of Turgenev's Richard

CURTAIN

Scene II

Half past nine
MISS ZALLINGER *and the maids are setting up the buffet on*
Five side-by-side tables covered with white tablecloths
RICHARD *hands several pills to* HERRENSTEIN, *who grudgingly swallows*
them

RICHARD. The prescription calls for five pills on Tuesday
    Four on Wednesday
    Five on Thursday

HERRENSTEIN (*after having swallowed half a glass of water*). They say
    the Queen of England
    is the richest woman in the world
    but it's also said
    that the Queen of the Netherlands
    is the richest one
    Most likely it's all tabloid twaddle
    I've never confided a single secret to my nephew
    Why have we always been suspicious of our nephew
    and why do we have to mind our Ps and Qs around our nieces
    All our lives we've had a fear of nephews and nieces
    I've had this nephewphobia and nieceaphobia all my life
    Parents invest everything they have in their children
    and thereby ruin them
    This age of ours is a horrible one
    with regard to nieces and nephews

    (*To* MISS ZALLINGER) Put out the Veltliner from the Wachau
    not the other one
    No port

(*More softly, almost as an aside*)

I can always still go to the Carpathians

(*Hands* RICHARD *his glass*)

Now even the water is disgusting
as far back as I can remember
it used to be a great pleasure to drink the Viennese water
The proletariat have ruined everything
even the noble Viennese spring water

(*Directly to* RICHARD) When you take me to the funeral tailgate the
    Heldweins
all the way to the graveside
so that we can get back home right away
I couldn't care less what those people think
Jewelers are members of so many clubs
and societies
that there are bound to be a lot of speeches
it's quite lucky for me
that I can let it all wash over me
while I'm sitting there
If I turn up my collar
I don't need to worry about catching a cold
Most likely these will be the same people
as the ones who came to Köchert's funeral
and to Fischmeister's
I've put millions into these people's coffers
for pretty much no good reason
Noble titles still drive people wild
They've been abolished in Austria
and yet they still drive everybody crazy
what a stupid unteachable nation
The Austrians have the softest of soft spots
for nobles and jokers
whenever some cabaret artist dies
they stream in the tens of thousands to his funeral
Humankind has such wretchedly bad taste
You used to write poems

don't you do that any more
You used to have quite a lyrical streak as they say
but you don't dare
to read any of your own poems to me
but it's all for the best
A writer who reads his own work to other people just makes himself
    look ridiculous
You're too intelligent
to make such a fool of yourself
not everyone is so smart
Of course in Semmering you've got the Threshing-Floor Tavern
you can enjoy yourself there
Of course I won't need you at all times
but I'll need to know
that you're with me during the night
In the twenty-five years
that you've been with me
haven't you ever thought you might want to kill me
to strike me dead
from behind
like this

(*Shows him how to do it*)

it's really quite an obvious thought
I have often thought
perhaps he's going to strike me dead
and yet you haven't done it
never
although you've quite often been in the mood to do it
not the mood
you've perceived the necessity
of killing me
a person like me can sense that very distinctly
I know what you're thinking
when you're standing behind me like that
mostly silent
not saying a word

I'm sure
you won't kill me
I've been sure on that score for a long time

(*To* MISS ZALLINGER) Has the fact that at my house you're Miss
    Zallinger
ever bothered you

MISS ZALLINGER. Of course not Mr Herrenstein

HERRENSTEIN. You've been in my house for forty-two years Miss
    Zallinger

(*To* RICHARD) She broke off her career for my sake

(*To* MISS ZALLINGER) From now on we'll make music every day again
You'll play a different piece each day
so that you can get back into practice
Of course this used to be a perennially musical house
in which patronage held pride of place
The Herrensteins made Hugo Wolf great
and poured scorn upon Brahms
as children we had to go out on to the balcony before breakfast
and say in unison
"Wolf is the greatest of all composers
Brahms is a washout"

(*To* RICHARD) every day Richard every single day
the Ringstrasse waited for us to recite our motto on the balcony
That was our actual morning prayer
"Wolf is the greatest of all composers
Brahms is a washout"

(*Tries to look out onto the balcony*)

Right up to the end of his life
the Herrenstein family
paid Wolf a pension
amounting to something in the neighborhood of a cabinet minster's
    salary
Whenever Brahms was being played at the Musikverein
we would unfurl a black flag

over the balcony here
Even when the Brahms piece in question was merely a bagatelle
we would hoist the black flag
A music-fanatical family so to speak
I personally have never had a desire to be a patron
and music has never interested me as much
as it did my parents
most likely it's a bad thing that
the most celebrated musicians
no longer frequent this place as they used to
Of course I have nothing against art or artists
I just can't put up with them
I'm old and ill
When we get back from Semmering
play us something on the Bösendorfer again Miss Zallinger
It will do us all good

(*Aside*)

What a silly thing
to say

(*To* RICHARD) It always stinks after mealtimes in Altaussee
it's impossible to rid the valley of the stench of kitchens
the kitchen-stench of the entire valley concentrates
on the exact site of our house
the people there cook with old lard
and also only bring stinky fish to their tables

(*Looking at the floor*)

I long for fresh air
But where is fresh air to be found
neither here
nor at Altaussee
In Semmering we are pestered by mice
naturally when the house is continuously unoccupied
it stinks of mouse droppings for days
and if we try to air out the place we catch a cold

(*To* RICHARD) Won't it be better

if I'm not even here
when these people show up
I'll withdraw into my bedroom
I obviously have absolutely no interest in Elizabeth the Second
on the other hand I certainly could
take a look at her
what do *you* think Richard
shall we be present
or shall we be absent
when these people show up
how late is it by now

RICHARD. Ten past ten

HERRENSTEIN. Ten past ten
When Mr Holzinger arrives
tell him I'm not in
don't even let him in here
That's impossible
I have to receive him

(*Listening*)

Has the clock actually stopped

RICHARD (*looking at the clock*). You're right Mr Herrenstein
The clock has stopped

HERRENSTEIN. Well then let's wind it up
lately we have often been forgetting
to wind the clock

(RICHARD *pushes him to the grandfather clock and hands him the winding-key*)

It's this old custom of mine
winding the clock
during my childhood I was already winding the clock

(*Tries to wind the clock but fails.* RICHARD *lifts him up to the clock*)

We mustn't forget
to wind it

(MISS ZALLINGER *and* THE CHAMBERMAIDS *remain standing and look on as* RICHARD *lifts* HERRENSTEIN *up to the clock and as* HERRENSTEIN *laboriously winds it amid much groaning and coughing.* HERRENSTEIN *while winding the clock*)

Each time it's as though
I'm winding myself up

(*Coughs, looks around the room, laughs*)

It's remarkably cloudy today

(RICHARD *helps* HERRENSTEIN *back into the wheelchair and pushes him into the center of the drawing room*)

It amazes me
that you can still put up with me
just as I wind up the clock every day
I wind myself up every day

(MISS ZALLINGER *coughs, and the chambermaids carry in a large wing chair and set it down next to* HERRENSTEIN)

Some of them will sit in the wing chairs
the rest will sit in the ordinary chairs
I could tell you right now
which of them will sit in the one kind of chair
and which in the other kind

(*Coughs*)

Five years ago Dr Friedländer
gave me three years
I'm still here
in that respect I've already lived two years too long
I refuse to die and that is that
To be sure I'm constantly saying I'm dying
but I refuse to die

(*To* RICHARD) Is it possible
for you to put me in the wing chair

(*Stretches his arms and legs out and has himself placed in the wing chair
and lets himself fall back into the chair*)

It's as cold as ice

(*To* MISS ZALLINGER) Did you bring that wing chair down from the
   attic

MISS ZALLINGER. No Mr Herrenstein
from your bedroom

HERRENSTEIN. From my bedroom

(*Looks around*)

Of course my bedroom
is also my death chamber
naturally everything that comes from my bedroom
is cold

(*To* MISS ZALLINGER) But why ever did you take the wing chair
out of my bedroom
that's just crazy

(*Wants* RICHARD *to pull him out of the wing chair and place him back
   in his wheelchair*)

(*To* RICHARD) So go on and help me out of the wing chair
out of this appalling wing chair
out of my death chair
do lift me out of this thing

(*Coughs.* RICHARD *lifts him out of the chair*)

But that really was a crazy idea

(*Coughs*)

carrying my wing chair out of my bedroom
and putting it here
for the use of these people

(*Coughs*)

these people can sit wherever they like
but not in my death chair

(RICHARD *places* HERRENSTEIN *in the wheelchair.* MISS ZALLINGER
and THE CHAMBERMAIDS *carry the wing chair back out of the room*)

An outrage

(*Completely collapses*)

My wing chair
my beloved wing chair at the service of those people
I loathe every single one of those people
and the idea of my wing chair
being abused by those people

(*Looks around the room*)

Do people ever give a thought to anything
when they're doing anything
Have I taken all my pills Richard

RICHARD. Obviously

HERRENSTEIN. The pill before breakfast
and the pill after breakfast
and the pill before lunch
and the pill after lunch
and the pills in the evening
is this a life

RICHARD. It's a necessity

HERRENSTEIN. A necessity
you say when absolutely everything has become superfluous
Wheel me to the window
I want to look out
I want to see something
I'm suffocating here

(RICHARD *pushes* HERRENSTEIN *to the window at stage left*)

I haven't felt as bad as I feel today
in a very long time
the weather is making my head feel weird
Saturdays are always the worst
apart from Sundays
All my life I loathed Sundays
the world looks so artificial on Sunday
more so than on any other day of the week

people are artificial
nature is artificial
everything is artificial on Sunday
Sundays are unnaturalness incarnate

(*Looks out the window*)

Completely sunny you say Richard

RICHARD. A completely sunny day

HERRENSTEIN. The Queen of England
how ghastly
but I don't feel sorry for her
she could abdicate
go away
retire
people make such fools of themselves under the crown
Monarchs have only ever worn fools' crowns
When the so-called Negus
came to Vienna
literally a million Viennese
flocked to the Mariahilferstrasse
Viennese curiosity is of course
the most repellent inquisitiveness in the world
In Semmering I'll
put on my shoes myself
if I have the strength to do so
You mustn't help me do it Richard
You must let me do it alone
You're asking yourself
why does Herrenstein need shoes on his feet
which are after all only prosthetic feet
Just ask yourself that question Richard
Putting shoes on prosthetic feet
is the greatest of pleasures
Nobody enjoys putting his shoes on more than
a man whose feet are both prosthetic

(*Directly to* RICHARD) A drunk made me into a mannequin

a twenty-five-year-old joke of a person
A routine collision
nothing but a routine collision Richard
There's no need for you to rack your brains over it Richard
because I have already racked my own brains over it
Supposing I'd gotten to Altaussee
Supposing I were counting millions of sheep
out of sleeplessness
I'm opting for Semmering

(*Looks out the window*)

It isn't chirping

RICHARD. What did you say Mr Herrenstein

HERRENSTEIN. The bird isn't chirping
    but at this time of morning
    the bird always chirps
    even on Saturdays it's always chirped

RICHARD. Of course Mr Herrenstein

HERRENSTEIN. People have been hounding me with their hatred
    as far back as I can remember
    all sorts of distinguished people
    healthy people
    affluent people rich people
    They invite me to their parties
    but I don't go to their parties
    they're constantly sending invitations
    but I don't respond to them
    On my birthday I want
    all the curtains to remain drawn shut throughout the day
    it will get no response
    Congratulations are jeers of derision
    Not a cloud in the sky you say nothing

RICHARD. It's completely sunny Mr Herrenstein

HERRENSTEIN. We're compelled
    to withdraw into ourselves completely

that's very interesting very interesting

(*Shouting*)

Miss Zallinger.

(MISS ZALLINGER *rushes up to him*)

Do you remember how
for the past thirty years at least
the bird on the other side of that window
has chirped
has the bird chirped or hasn't it
the bird has chirped

MISS ZALLINGER. Of course Mr Herrenstein

HERRENSTEIN. Even on Saturdays
the bird has chirped
You've heard it
just as I've heard it
You are living proof
that even on Saturdays
the bird on the other side of that window has chirped
but now it's stopped chirping
No bird chirps for three decades in a row

(*Exit* MISS ZALLINGER, *walking backwards at first, while* THE
CHAMBERMAIDS *carry in and put down several chairs*)

It should have been obvious beforehand
that everyone
the whole pack
would want to see the Queen of England

(*Coughs*)

What's going on
if the dehydration pills don't help any more

MISS ZALLINGER (*announcing* MR HOLZINGER). Mr Holzinger

HERRENSTEIN. Yes of course
I have after all been expecting him

(*Exit* MISS ZALLINGER; *re-enter* MISS ZALLINGER *with* MR HOLZINGER *who stops at the threshold of the room with a file folder in his hands.* HERRENSTEIN *still looking out the window*)

So come in why don't you
the whole routine is settled
You give me the folder
and I sign
and then you can go back

HOLZINGER *hesitates, then steps into the room and up to* HERRENSTEIN

HERRENSTEIN. Give it to me

(*Takes the folder from Holzinger. To* RICHARD *as he hands him the folder*)

Read it to me

RICHARD (*opens the folder and reads*).
I request your permission to summon Kreiseleder
to appear before the board of directors
no later than on the twenty-third of October

HERRENSTEIN. It's as simple and ordinary as can be

(RICHARD *hands the folder back to* HERRENSTEIN)

Have you got a pen Mr Holzinger
That obnoxious Kreiseleder fellow

(HOLZINGER *takes a pen out of his jacket pocket and hands it to* HERRENSTEIN. HERRENSTEIN *signs a piece of paper inside the folder and shuts the folder*)

That obnoxious Kreiseleder fellow
I thought it was something out of the ordinary Mr Holzinger
it's only to do with Kreiseleder

(*Hands the folder back to* HOLZINGER)

Today isn't like the usual ones Mr Holzinger
today I have no time for you
a crowd of people are coming
all of them want to see the Queen of England
do you see what I mean

every single one of them wants to see the Queen of England
(*Looks* HOLZINGER *in the eye*)
Elizabeth the Second
do you see what I mean Mr Holzinger

HOLZINGER. Obviously Mr Herrenstein abruptly

HERRENSTEIN. The Queen of England
doesn't come to Vienna just every day
probably she'll only come to Vienna just once
in her life

HOLZINGER. Obviously Mr Herrenstein abruptly

HERRENSTEIN. We'll see each other when I get back from Semmering

HOLZINGER. Obviously Mr Herrenstein

HERRENSTEIN. Has your wife recovered her health

HOLZINGER. Obviously Mr Herrenstein abruptly

HERRENSTEIN. An invalid is a curse
a single invalid will wipe out entire families
if he has to

(HOLZINGER *bows, turns around, and exits*; MISS ZALLINGER *follows him*)

I thought it was something important
it was only about Kreiseleder
that obnoxious Kreiseleder fellow
but of course everything is important
Everything is important
we're constantly forgetting Richard
that *everything* is important
there's no such thing as an unimportant thing
don't you agree Richard
that there is no such thing as an unimportant thing
that everything is important
everything boils down to this fact
that everything is just as important as everything else
and no more or less

Enter MISS ZALLINGER *with decanters filled with wine; she puts them down on the buffet; enter behind her* GUGGENHEIM, *holding a Union Jack flag; he sneaks up behind* HERRENSTEIN

HERRENSTEIN. People were all much happier
when they knew
that everything was just as important as everything else
so now they're constantly suffocating in their unhappiness

(RICHARD *has taken two steps backward because he has noticed* GUGGENHEIM. GUGGENHEIM, *now standing behind* HERRENSTEIN, *puts his hands over* HERRENSTEIN's *eyes*)

I know perfectly well
who you are Guggenheim
please sit down
and stop making a fool of yourself
I knew you're first one
You want to see the Queen of England most of all
You with your Union Jack

(GUGGENHEIM *sits down catty-cornered to* HERRENSTEIN. RICHARD *dusts* HERRENSTEIN's *jacket*)

(*To* RICHARD) Oh Richard do please leave us alone for a couple
of minutes
But while you're away sort the mail
and try to find a Baedeker
with a description of Semmering

(*Exit* RICHARD)

You have no idea
what an awful situation
I've gotten myself into
Because I told my nephew
he could come here
and have a good look at Elizabeth the Second
Forty people are going to come
and this only a day
before we leave for Semmering

GUGGENHEIM. But weren't you planning to go to Altaussee

HERRENSTEIN. No
    I'll never go to that nest of Nazis again

GUGGENHEIM. But you have that lovely house there

HERRENSTEIN. That makes no difference to me
    I also have a lovely house in Semmering
    We can't very well travel to every place
    where we have lovely houses
    and who says those houses are all lovely
    most of the time I
    find those houses hideous

GUGGENHEIM. Your house in Altaussee is really lovely

HERRENSTEIN. My dear Guggenheim
    I have always loathed
    houses from the turn of the century
    Verandas wooden balconies
    Mountain views
    what could be more execrable
    I basically feel most comfortable here in my
    Viennese house
    But from time to time I have to get away
    The Viennese are still the most bearable kind of people
    I find country people revolting
    you can't talk to them about anything
    they don't understand a word you say
    they just gape at you
    and think about all the money
    that they can suck out of you

    (*From this point onwards* THE CHAMBERMAIDS *carry in as many regular chairs and armchairs as possible*)

    Every time I've arrived in the country I've thought
    this is just what I needed
    Most of all I miss *you* Guggenheim
    There is so much talk about helping out one's neighbor
    the two of us put it into practice

sometimes you come to see me
sometimes time I come to see you
we've never run out of things to talk about
Just picture it forty people if not more
and these being the very people I loathe and despise the most
people I've wanted to have nothing to do with
for decades
It would be no great loss if I cut all ties with these people Guggenheim
They're all just waiting for me to croak
But of course you know these people aren't going to inherit a thing
I've already made sure they won't

(*Leaning over to* GUGGENHEIM)

You don't know about this yet
But Richard has threatened
to leave me
an attempt at blackmail possibly
probably an attempt at blackmail
he's told me some preposterous long-winded story about America
    California
I've been living under this threat for weeks
it should have been obvious all along
that this liaison was going to fall apart someday
I offered him an enormous raise
oddly enough he wasn't impressed
But without Richard I'll be finished

(*Exit* MISS ZALLINGER, *who has been doing a bit of dusting*)

I believe he has even begun
a new liaison
I'm quite sure of it
I even know who the person is
But of course you know this fellow Doctor Schuppich

GUGGENHEIM. Schuppich

HERRENSTEIN. Exactly that Doctor Schuppich

GUGGENHEIM. But he was in Australia for three years

HERRENSTEIN. Four years
 I once had him under contract
 not unlikeable but dangerous
 Richard takes advantage of every opportunity
 to be alone with Schuppich
 Imagine Richard taking off
 and leaving me stranded
 I've more or less promised him
 half my estate
 he hadn't reacted to this at all
 as if he were turning a deaf ear to everything I was saying about it
 It's all calculation Guggenheim the most cunning calculation

GUGGENHEIM. I can't imagine
 Richard leaving you
 after all he's been with you for over twenty-five years

HERRENSTEIN. That means absolutely nothing
 Whenever we stand in greatest need of a person
 he abandons us
 I can't bear the presence of a stranger
 by my side
 Richard's dependability
 leaves something to be desired
 There isn't a moment of the day when I don't catch him
 getting something wrong
 but I never say anything
 I say absolutely nothing
 he mustn't ever think I'm aware of these slip-ups

GUGGENHEIM. But didn't Schuppich write that book

HERRENSTEIN. Yes
 the one in which I'm spitefully caricatured
 he changes my name
 but it's obviously me
 the book's full of details
 that he could only have picked up from Richard
 At first I was quite eager

to sue the man
then I realized how ridiculous such a lawsuit would be
Passing it over in silence is the only method
I would only have defamed myself
defamed myself more by suing Schuppert
than I'd been defamed by the contents of Schuppert's book
I have no interest in the Queen of England
that's something for the young people
who fatuously live in grand style
and for the city's old-school high-society riffraff

GUGGENHEIM. I of course am excited
    that Elizabeth the Second is coming here
    and that I'll be able to see her
    I was at Oxford for twelve years as you know
    I owe to England nothing more and nothing less than
    my existence

HERRENSTEIN. I hadn't thought about that

    (*In* GUGGENHEIM'*s ear*) Richard wants to go to Altaussee
    because Schuppich has a house there
    The Schuppiches are an old Nazi family
    Schuppisch's father was a lieutenant colonel in the SS
    But I'm going to Semmering
    I loathe Semmering and yet I'm going to go there
    As a child I already loathed the Semmering
    Of course Altaussee is a beautiful locale
    but I'm not going to go to Altaussee
    for all these reasons Guggenheim
    I'm going to the Semmering
    even though I dread the thought of going there
    Nowadays the feral proles
    roam about the Semmering in their braces and baggy trousers
    nowadays every hotel is a workers' holiday camp
    It would suit Richard down to the ground
    to leave me sitting on the terrace at Altaussee
    and go gadding about with Schuppich

What if Richard really leaves
I think he's just threatening me blackmailing me
That preposterous story he told me about America
is completely made up Guggenheim

(MISS ZALLINGER *places a large bunch of flowers on the buffet*)

(*To* GUGGENHEIM) Miss Zallinger is planning to go to Lourdes

(*Calls out*)

When are you leaving for Lourdes Miss Zallinger

MISS ZALLINGER. On the twenty-first

HERRENSTEIN. On the twenty-first of November
not October
because then of course you will be in Semmering
When were you at Fatima

MISS ZALLINGER. Three years ago

HERRENSTEIN. People make a pilgrimage
and are convinced
that it's going to help them

(*To* MISS ZALLINGER) Your grandmother went to Lourdes didn't she

MISS ZALLINGER. Yes Mr Herrenstein

HERRENSTEIN (*to* GUGGENHEIM). As you may not know
Old Man Zallinger was
one of our most distinguished conductors
unfortunately he was constantly ill
he wasn't in the top tier
but he was truly distinguished
He never conducted at the Vienna State Opera
but he did quite often at the Volksoper
and at the Bavarian State Opera in Munich
a great pedagogue for years Guggenheim
His daughters have inherited his talent
Today for the first time in many years Miss Zallinger
has given us a sample of her art
a short piece by Chopin

(*Enter* HERRENSTEIN's NEPHEW, *who halts after taking two steps.* MISS ZALLINGER *signals to him that he should approach* HERRENSTEIN, *and he approaches* HERRENSTEIN, *who refrains from offering him his hand*)

This is just what I needed
forty people coming here
to see Elizabeth the Second
I said *you* could see her
I said nothing more than that
and now forty people are coming
You're putting me in a terrible position
you know full well how ill I am
instead of protecting me from these people
you're delivering me into their hands
I loathe all these people as you know
On top of that we've got to go to Heldwein's funeral today
You'll be going to it as well obviously

THE NEPHEW. Obviously

HERRENSTEIN. Not once this week have you
    checked in on me
    I might have croaked
    I'm sitting here and I have a perfectly healthy nephew
    and I'm going to wrack and ruin
    If I didn't have Guggenheim

    (*To* GUGGENHEIM) There's no relying on Richard either any more

    (*To his* NEPHEW) You used to come every two days
    which was admittedly too often
    but you could visit your ailing uncle
    at least once a week

    (*To* MISS ZALLINGER) Isn't that right Miss Zallinger

    (MISS ZALLINGER *nods*)

One can't simply take
one must also give
but the youth of today give nothing
they only take

they snatch up everything
and give nothing
You're lucky Guggenheim
to have no nieces or nephews
and therefore to have no nephew or niece problems

(*Takes a pill out of his jacket pocket and swallows it*)

We invest everything we've got in young people
and they disdainfully reject it

(*To his* NEPHEW) Why are you still standing
When Richard leaves me I thought
at least I'll have you
You heard what I said

(*Very softly but distinctly*)

Richard intends
to go to America
with this fellow Doctor Schuppich
who he's having an affair with
after that I'll be on my own here

(GUGGENHEIM *has stood up following the entrance of four ladies*)

(*To his* NEPHEW) Richard meets up with this Schuppich fellow
in Altaussee on weekends
I have proof of this
and of course they meet in my house
I'm going to Semmering
I loathe Semmering
but I'm going to Semmering
come hell or high water

(RICHARD *has entered with a Baedeker on Lower Austria and is greeting
the ladies*)

(*To his* NEPHEW) Just think
of what's in store for you
in the end you are the only person
I can still trust
Miss Zallinger is of course

in cahoots with Richard
they make common cause with each other
I've been having the most horrible nights
not sleeping a wink
what with these spasms and self-accusations
Why did your mother have to die so young
everybody dies off
the survivors are spared nothing

(*Greeting the ladies*)

Please do sit down
please take a seat
there are plenty of places to sit

(*Having slumped back into his wheelchair*)

I am in no condition
to make conversation
But of course my nephew is here

(*To his* NEPHEW) Go get started
start looking after the ladies and gentlemen

(*The* NEPHEW *pours the ladies drinks, and they all sit down upstage*)

(*To* RICHARD) Who in the world is that tall woman

RICHARD. Countess Ergens

HERRENSTEIN. Not Countess Gudenus
she looked like Countess Gudenus

RICHARD. Countess Ergens
and the Weisweiler sisters

HERRENSTEIN. I need them like a hole in the head
That Ergens woman
is downright sickening
Hardly anybody alive is stupider
than the Weisweiler sisters

(*Enter four ladies, who are greeted by the* NEPHEW)

Is it really already time for this

RICHARD. It's about half past eleven

HERRENSTEIN. All this time I have had this pain
here

(*Points*)

in my chest
look Richard here

(RICHARD *draws closer*)

Here Richard here
right there
there that's right
right there

(RICHARD *is obliged to touch the spot*)

An ominous spot
Hopefully Friedländer can be gotten hold of
Don't forget
that he's stopping by again
before we leave for Semmering
I haven't made up my mind yet
but I really don't care for Altaussee
I hate Semmering
But I think I'll go to Semmering
we always go to the places
that we loathe
we never get to
where we want to go
Have you heard any more news from America

RICHARD. No new news

HERRENSTEIN. It would be awful for me
if you walked out on me
I'm obviously not long for this world
why don't you just stick it out for this brief period
Consider what America has to offer you
a man in his mid-fifties
at your age a person can't go to America

and start his life over
that whole plan is obviously doomed to failure from the start

(*Attempting to take a look at the new arrivals over his shoulder*)

I can only see silhouettes

(*In a confidential tone*)

you say that's Countess Ergens
the divorcee
she's been even more insufferable
since she published her cookbook
I have never had a worse meal than at the Ergens'

(TWO GENTLEMEN *and* TWO LADIES *have entered and sat down after*
MISS ZALLINGER *has whispered something in their ears*)

What will become of me
if I shake all these people's hands
I'm obviously half dead
I don't need to pretend to be half dead I actually am

(*Beckons* RICHARD *towards him until their faces are almost touching*)

Everyone envies me my life
this wretched existence
What is Countess Ergens wearing anyway

RICHARD. A yellow dress with a black floral pattern

HERRENSTEIN. Yellow with a black floral pattern
Silk

RICHARD. Of course it's silk Mr Herrenstein

HERRENSTEIN. Silk silk
a black floral pattern

RICHARD. And a black hat

HERRENSTEIN. A black hat
Probably because she's also
going to Heldwein's funeral
I think they're all going to it
I think I'll see all these people again

at Heldwein's funeral
They're all bound to keep calmly sitting down wherever they like
until the Queen of England comes
hopefully she'll come soon
of course the punctuality of monarchs is proverbial
proverbial proverbial Richard
The Viennese are a curious people
they're repulsively curious
These people are really making things easy for themselves
first they're coming to my house
to see Elizabeth the Second
and from here they'll go straight to the jeweler's funeral
The jewelers have always been a rich lot
but not as rich as us
this has always embittered these sorts of people
You can do whatever you like at Semmering
you just mustn't leave me on my own
I'm entirely reliant on you
it's not just a decades-old habit

(*Tries to get hold of* RICHARD's *coat. Enter* THREE GENTLEMEN, *who are invited to sit down in three chairs by Miss Zallinger*)

Suddenly they're all showing up
How many are here so far anyway

RICHARD. Ten eleven twelve twenty

HERRENSTEIN. But there are supposed to be forty

(*Tugs at* RICHARD's *coat*)

I have always counted on you more
than on anybody else Richard
If I were healthy
I'd gladly go with you to America
but probably America is just a ruse
that you've foisted on me
a cunningly foisted ruse
You've always deceived me Richard
After all you're an alumnus of my school

(*Suddenly raising his voice to a shout*)

Viktor
Viktor

(*The* NEPHEW *goes up to him*)

(*To his* NEPHEW) Open the window just for a moment

(*The* NEPHEW *goes to the window at stage left*)

Not *that* window
That one *that* one the one on the left

(*The* NEPHEW *opens the window at stage right, and nothing but ordinary
street noise is heard*)

Shut the window again
it's just letting in bad smells

(*The* NEPHEW *closes the window.* HERRENSTEIN *looking at the clock*)

I can't tell what time it is

RICHARD. Twenty past eleven

HERRENSTEIN. Twenty past eleven

(RICHARD *hands him the* Baedeker)

Right about now I'm usually sitting here half-asleep
and you're reading to me

(*To his* NEPHEW) Don't just stand there
look after our guests
After all they're *your* guests
Your guests

(*Aside*)

not mine

(*The* NEPHEW *withdraws*)

I must have been really cross with him
what's the use of that

(*Coughs after much straining*)

In Badgastein I came quite close to dying
I didn't listen to you

Either to Friedländer
or to you

Enter THREE LADIES, *one of whom, who is wearing a red hat, refuses to be kept away from* HERRENSTEIN, *goes to up to him, and stations herself directly in front of him*

THE LADY IN THE RED HAT. My dear Rudolf
how well you look
I heard you'd been in Badgastein
you lucky fellow
have you heard the news
Frundsberg has bought the Aschenhöhe
now we're rid of it

HERRENSTEIN. I've never been to the Aschenhöhe

THE LADY IN THE RED HAT. But of course you have Rudolf
On New Year's Eve of thirty-six
At four in the morning you took flight
because my husband had waved his rifle at you
Everyone was always terribly jealous of you
How well you look Rudolf
don't you think he looks well Richard
Rudolf looks marvelous
You're a veritable apostle of healthy living Rudolf
And is everything else going well

HERRENSTEIN. I've never been to the Aschenhöhe
and your husband never waved his rifle at me
I've never even heard of this Aschenhöhe place

THE LADY IN THE RED HAT. Good Lord Rudolf
you've always been prone to cracking jokes
when is the Queen coming anyway
does anybody know exactly

RICHARD. At about noon

THE LADY IN THE RED HAT. At about noon
why it's at least ten-till-noon now
Good Lord I'm famished

that buffet's looking like just the thing for me
I'm so glad to see you Rudolf

(*Goes to the buffet*)

HERRENSTEIN. Was that Countess Gudenus

RICHARD. Countess Winterhalter

HERRENSTEIN. Countess Winterhalter
I thought she was Countess Gudenus
who always has those gaudy rings on her fingers
Do you think
they'll all leave
when the hullabaloo is over

RICHARD. Yes of course Mr Herrenstein

HERRENSTEIN. Yes of course Mr Herrenstein
These people often get stuck in their seats

(*Opens the* Baedeker, *tries to read it, then shuts it*)

We invite them to spend the morning here
and they lounge about until four in the afternoon
that has always been my experience of them
You don't know how much my thorax is bothering me
Have I taken all my pills
Didn't I mention the bird is chirping
My nephew
Is he dressed decently
as befits my heir apparent

RICHARD. Yes of course Mr Herrenstein

HERRENSTEIN. If I had my druthers I'd leave nothing to anybody
I'd leave a heap of ruins behind if I had my druthers
it makes no difference who we bequeath our estate to
it's always just perfidious nonsense it's ghastly
I've always loathed the Catholic charities

(MISS ZALLINGER *stumbles and drops a large tray of full wine glasses; a general uproar ensues*)

What was that

RICHARD. Nothing nothing at all
  Miss Zallinger just stumbled

HERRENSTEIN. Silly girl
  Her eyesight is even poorer than mine
  She's come a cropper on me too many times already

  (MISS ZALLINGER *has stood back up; the girls are picking up the shards of glass*)

  Miss Zallinger is a Jill of all trades
  apart from the useful ones
  The silly girl never checks in on me
  For all she knows I might even be in the mood
  for a sip of wine

RICHARD. But Doctor Friedländer

HERRENSTEIN. Shut up about Doctor Friedländer
  people like him are nothing but spoilsports
  a sip of wine never hurt anybody
  Now go and get it right away
  white white

  (RICHARD *fetches a glass of white wine, and* HERRENSTEIN *drinks half of it*)

  When push comes to shove we can't
  give up absolutely everything

  (*Two gentlemen have entered and stationed themselves at the buffet*).

RICHARD (*whispering into* HERRENSTEIN'*s ear*). The Bartenstein brothers

HERRENSTEIN. Shameless
  I'll get back at Viktor back for this
  The Bartensteins in my house
  they're presumably exploiting this as an opportunity
  to spy on me and my house
  they're really horrible people the Bartensteins

  (*Half to himself*) Those swine

  (*To* RICHARD) What are the two of them wearing anyway
  are they dressed in black as well

RICHARD. Yes of course Mr Herrenstein

HERRENSTEIN. Which naturally means
   they're also going to Heldwein's funeral
   First they go to Herrenstein's
   to the old swine's house as they put it
   and then the Queen of England will come
   and then they'll trot along behind old Heldwein
   Selling jewelry in Vienna
   has always been lucrative
   that hasn't even changed in the republic
   the proles buy the most jewelry
   lately even the men have been wearing
   gold chains the length of sausage strings around their necks
   When you visit the baths at Krapfenwaldl
   you see the socialist cabinet minister
   diving into the water
   with a ton of gold chains around his neck
   Probably Countess Gudenus will also come
   I'm sure she will
   she won't want to miss this
   Once everybody is here
   I could of course say a few words
   or not
   what do you think Richard
   is it appropriate
   I find nothing more tiresome
   but it probably behooves me
   We'll get a break from all this in Semmering
   Since my return from Badgastein
   I've altogether stopped being able to abide the presence of people
   I can't abide their smell
   Even *Così fan tutte* would have to be more or less
   a performance just for me
   because I can't abide other people's perspiration any more
   But they won't put on *Così fan tutte*
   the new general manager of the opera is a washout
   First he announces they'll be putting on *Die Frau ohne Schatten*

then he postpones the premiere
then he postpones it again
and yet again
and then he cancels *Die Frau ohne Schatten* altogether
Singing yes speaking no
I can't abide spoken drama any more
But you quite like going to the theater don't you

RICHARD. Of course Mr Herrenstein

HERRENSTEIN. The opera is less of a strain on my nerves
I myself have actually written a play
I wrote it at the age of thirteen
The Battle of Ludwig
good Lord it's so easy to write something like that as an adolescent

(*Beckons* RICHARD *towards him until their faces are almost touching*)

What do you think
should I say something to these people
something in connection with Elizabeth the Second
or would that just be bilge

RICHARD. Perhaps you should say a couple of words

HERRENSTEIN. A couple of words
but what sorts of words

RICHARD. Words of salutation

HERRENSTEIN. Words of salutation how frivolous

Three ladies and four gentlemen have entered

RICHARD. A single sentence would suffice
Any old sentence

HERRENSTEIN. You're right
I should just say a single sentence
any old sentence
I've always loathed speeches
Nothing but pure bilge is ever said in them

(COUNT NEUTZ *has entered, and he walks straight to* HERRENSTEIN *and greets him, but* HERRENSTEIN *refrains from offering him his hand*)

I'm not going to shake hands with you
it's possible I have
a contagious illness
Are you Count Croy

(RICHARD *whispers something in* HERRENSTEIN'*s ear*)

You're Count Neutz
I thought so
My nephew tells me
You've sold Kurring is that correct

NEUTZ. Yes Kurring has been sold

HERRENSTEIN. At a loss no doubt
    Do you still own the Trautensee
    I quite often used to fish there
    not a good lake for fishing
    but the surroundings are pleasant

NEUTZ. The Trautensee is still in the family

HERRENSTEIN. What does *still* mean
    Are you planning to sell it

NEUTZ. Certainly not
    not as long as my Aunt Elvire is still alive

HERRENSTEIN. Elvire
    I thought she'd died a long time ago

    (RICHARD *whispers something in* HERRENSTEIN'*s ear*)

    Elvire is the older sister
    the younger Neutz sister is dead

NEUTZ. She is terribly ill indeed

HERRENSTEIN. Like me
    that doesn't mean
    she's going to die soon
    she used to be quite beautiful
    but not my type

    (*Stretching out his hand to him but not offering it to him*)

Please do find yourself a cozy spot
before the queen arrives
We have that Jochinger Veltliner
that you've always enjoyed drinking
give my regards to Berta

(RICHARD *whispers something in his ear*)

Elvire
give my regards to Elvire my dear Neutz

(NEUTZ *joins the others*)

The fact is they really have lost everything
even the Trautensee
out of sheer stupidity

(*Enter three ladies*)

of course it isn't true
that he still owns it
Why do these people lie
I can't comprehend what leads these people
to lie incessantly
Neutz has perniciously bad breath
haven't you noticed
The Neutz sisters were always hideous
interchangeably hideous
a comical pair
they were always running around in powder-blue dirndls

(*Beckons* RICHARD *towards him until their faces are almost touching*)

You must surely know
what's supposed to be said at a moment like this

RICHARD. Just say a single sentence
no matter what it is

(*Looks at the guests as if he is counting them*)

HERRENSTEIN. Why not
when the time comes spin me round quick as a flash
so that I can see all of them
and I'll say my one sentence

we'll get it done that way
Why do we make everything so complicated

(*Beckons* RICHARD *towards him until their faces are almost touching*)

Do you think I can forgo seeing the dentist
my dentures are loose
I won't need any teeth in Semmering
my nephew will drive us there
and pick us back up
Altaussee will lead to nothing Richard
you need to get that out of your head
Dr Schuppich is after all the man
who published that revolting book
in which I'm caricatured
Nothing that Dr Schuppich
has written about me in his book is true
and yet
How long have you known Doctor Schuppich anyway
But of course you've known him for ages
Has Dr Schuppich won you over to America yet
I don't mean to pump you for answers
but I obviously take an interest
in the concerns of the person
who I'm closest to
and that person is nobody but you Richard nobody but you

(*Tugs at* RICHARD's *jacket*)

you do know don't you Richard
You know perfectly well
how I feel about you

(*Tries to look into the drawing room, then turns away from it*)

I see nothing but a grayish-black mumbling mass
Incomprehensible rubbish claptrap
Of course I don't need to tell you

(*Enter three ladies and two gentlemen*)

how very fond of you I am
that's obviously not news to you

but perhaps it needs to be said
at least once
If you leave me you'll kill me
Without you I'm worthless you know that
without you I'm nothing but a cripple
or rather a lifeless cripple
What if I bequeath my house in Atlaussee to you
that would definitely prove it
But you're really not a bad person
In Semmering I'll amend my will
as you see fit Richard as you see fit

(*Everybody has sat down. Herrenstein in a whisper*)

If you stay
you can have everything I own
literally everything

Enter TWO OLD LADIES (*who nonchalantly walk up to* HERRENSTEIN *and
    exclaim in unison*). Rudolph
It's incredible how good you're looking

(*They offer* HERRENSTEIN *their hands, but he refrains from shaking them*)

Viktor invited us
what an enchanting nephew

OLD LADY NUMBER ONE. I was actually supposed
to be in Salzburg at my sister's right now
but I couldn't miss
seeing the Queen of England
no certainly not

OLD LADY NUMBER TWO. A once-in-a-lifetime
opportunity

OLD LADY NUMBER ONE. I'm quite beside myself
how good you're looking
it's plain to see
that Badgastein has done you good Rudolf
good old Badgastein
Miss Zallinger

the same as she ever was
what would the Herrenstein household be
without Miss Zallinger

TWO OLD LADIES (*simultaneously*). How good you're looking
no you really look fantastic

(*They withdraw and join the others*)

HERRENSTEIN. This is sheer torture
I've been out of touch with
these people for years
and now they're all here
To be sure I know why
I cut off
severed
all my ties with this pack
severed all my ties with society
it was just what I needed

(*The guests all burst into peals of uproarious laughter*)

Boneheaded riffraff

CURTAIN

Scene III

After noon

The guests are all laughing as the curtain rises

HERRENSTEIN *is staring at the window and evidently seeing nothing through it*

RICHARD. What a lovely day it is Mr Herrenstein

HERRENSTEIN. Nothing's to my liking any more

   (NEUTZ *standing in contrast to all the other guests, such that they all can hear him*)

   Whereupon the Kaiser simply said
   Now knaack it owaff
   I've heead it up to heeah wid you

   (*The guests all burst into peals of uproarious laughter that are slow to subside*)

   What a fop
   what a nitwit
   He has squandered his entire fortune
   to be sure the Trautensee has belonged
   to the Fürst of Scwhwarzenberg for years
   The Neutzes oughtn't to dare to show their faces in public these days
   what a detestable wiseacre

   (*Beckons* RICHARD *towards him until their faces are almost touching; Meanwhile* NEUTZ *is telling another joke*)

   We'll talk over everything in Semmering

RICHARD. Of course Mr Herrenstein

HERRENSTEIN. I mean the will
  Obviously I can amend it whenever I like
  Obviously my nephew needn't get everything

RICHARD. But you said that

HERRENSTEIN. Every day I say something different
  you're very well aware of that Richard
  that is indeed the terrible truth
  I firmly make up my mind
  and then change it again completely
  it's been this way for years

  (*Looking around*)

  It's time for the Queen to come
  Don't you think
  the rainy season is about to arrive
  since the weather has been nice for so long
  It starts to rain in the middle of October
  and never stops after that
  the rain turns into snow
  and Christmas is the low point

  (*Enter as many new guests as possible from this point onward. All the
  guests burst into loud laughter*)

  This is nauseating me
  And to think it's happening in my house
  I'd completely forgotten about Neutz
  If I'd known he'd come here
  I'd have called the whole thing off
  Isn't Countess Gudenus here

RICHARD. No

HERRENSTEIN. Many women remain beautiful
  no matter how old they get
  Countess Gudenus is a jewelry fanatic
  which is admittedly repulsive
  but she's the only woman
  I can talk to

even about Nietzsche
isn't that so Dr Guggenheim

GUGGENHEIM. Yes Countess Gudenus

HERRENSTEIN. She really would have been a good match for you
Countess Gudenus
She's got a keen intellect
she married into the high nobility
an absurd idea
The Countess has always had her eye on you Guggenheim
You're a widower
and she's a widow
the only person who isn't a windbag

(*Enter* COUNTESS GUDENUS *just as the guests have once again burst into uproarious laughter*)

They're laughing at literally everything
Neutz says

RICHARD. Here she is now

HERRENSTEIN. Countess Gudenus

COUNTESS GUDENUS *goes straight to* HERRENSTEIN, *and* HERRENSTEIN *kisses her hand*

COUNTESS GUDENUS. I couldn't resist
I just had to be here

(GUGGENHEIM *kisses her hand*)

My dear Guggenheim
I have already finished reading your book
the second part was outstanding Guggenheim
An apocalypse it's simply spectacular
from every sentence I can tell
you used to be a professor at Oxford
a magnificent book
No doubt you worked
on it for years
every detail is a delight

After you die the Guggenheim line will be extinct
it's thoroughly philosophical
the whole thing is permeated with the English spirit
What do you think Herrenstein
Is our emigrant friend not an utterly exceptional mind
these minds are dying off
there won't be any left when our Guggenheim dies

(*All the guests in the background burst into laughter*)

Once again Neutz is enjoying his day in the sun

(*To* GUGGENHEIM) Wouldn't you rather have stayed in England

GUGGENHEIM. Oh no I feel quite at home here

COUNTESS GUDENUS. So you say
A dreadful country this Austria
surely you can't much care for it
given that you lived so long in England and in Oxford to boot

GUGGENHEIM. No no my dear Countess
I'm staying here and I'll die here

COUNTESS GUDENUS. Guggenheim is our arch-Austrian
isn't that right Herrenstein

Everyone in the background bursts into laughter

GUGGENHEIM. It's gone through two printings

COUNTESS GUDENUS. That's astonishing
for a work of philosophy
most of them
sell a few hundred copies at most
just think of the *Tractatus Logico-Philosophicus* for example

GUGGENHEIM. Today young people are more actively interested
in philosophy than ever before

HERRENSTEIN. Don't get me started on the youth of today
they're thoroughly sentimental
and anti-intellectual
they run away from thinking whenever they can

COUNTESS GUDENUS. I must say you're right about that Herrenstein
Good Lord my own grandchildren
don't read a single passably written sentence in the entire year
At best they glance at *Die Presse*

HERRENSTEIN. That obnoxious rag

GUGGENHEIM. To which you happen to have a subscription

HERRENSTEIN. Because my family has subscribed to it
for almost a hundred years

GUGGENHEIM. But you actually read *Die Presse* every day

HERRENSTEIN. This is indeed true
it's irritating
that paper is truly awful
and I read it every day
but everybody's paper's like that
for everybody
they're terrible
and yet they're read

COUNTESS GUDENUS. I believe the Queen is running late
my dear Herrenstein

(*She joins the others*)

HERRENSTEIN. There's something about that woman that fascinates me
I don't know what it is
I loathe everything about where she comes from
and yet she fascinates me
admittedly it's just her
everything else from this perverse kitchen repels me

Everyone bursts out laughing

NEUTZ (*very loudly*). Whereupon the Archduke Ferdinand simply said
I'm sorry your Majesty
but I'm wearing nothing but my underpants

Everyone bursts out laughing

HERRENSTEIN (*to* GUGGENHEIM, *who has sat back down next to him*).
Ah Dr Guggenheim

what would I do without *you*
the old guard
have all died out by now
I'd really like to take you with me to Semmering

(*Takes his hand*)

I'm inviting you Guggenheim
I'm inviting you
Pack a few things
And come with me to Semmering
there's obviously nothing keeping you here
in this hellish town
we'll take up a topic of conversation
and chew away at it
while we get nice and toasted
what do you think of that

GUGGENHEIM. Sure if that's what you want

HERRENSTEIN. Of course it's what I want

GUGGENHEIM. All right if it can't be avoided

HERRENSTEIN. Now pull yourself together
    and pack up your minimum necessities
    and ride with us to Semmering tomorrow
    we'll make ourselves as comfortable as possible up there

(*All the guests again burst into uproarious laughter*)

    Viktor will be our driver
    Richard will be our escort

(*To* RICHARD) What time is it anyway

RICHARD. Almost half past twelve

HERRENSTEIN. Almost half past twelve
    In that case the hullaballoo will be over quite soon

    (*To* GUGGENHEIM) Perhaps you could bring along that edition of
        Hegel
    that you so warmly recommended to me
    Semmering is a good spot for Hegel

or for Montaigne
I don't care what book it is
as long as it's something great

(COUNTESS GUDENUS *bursts out laughing by herself*)

(*To* GUGGENHEIM) Young people are absolutely worthless
and yet they grow up
and the world doesn't fall to pieces
it's crazy isn't it

(*To* RICHARD) Listen up Richard
the instant these people are gone
drive me to the Döbling cemetery

(*To* GUGGENHEIM) of course you know
Heldwein the jeweler died
it's funny
just this year the man
had somebody build him a window display
that looked just like a funeral chapel
exactly like a funeral chapel
and when I saw it I said to Richard
what a fine funeral chapel
and now the man is dead
Countess Gudenus got on with him famously
I don't care for jewelers
You're so lucky
You don't have to go to Heldwein's funeral
People like you
hardly ever have to go to the cemetery at all
because you've never been chummy
with any of these execrable people
But the proprietor of the firm of Herrenstein
is required to go to all these funerals
take my word for it they're nothing short of horrifying

(*A steady crescendo of jubilation from the Ringstrasse percolates through
the windows*)

I believe this is it

(*The guests have all leapt up and are all thronging onto the balcony, which* MISS ZALLINGER *has opened; she has opened wide the balcony door and stationed herself beside it. Everybody is thronging onto the balcony. The jubilation rising from the Ringstrasse continues to get louder and louder*)

(*To* RICHARD) How many people do you think that is
anyway
that must surely be more than forty people
it sounds almost like a hundred
more than a hundred

RICHARD. Eighty or ninety

HERRENSTEIN. Unbelievable

MISS ZALLINGER *also steps out onto the balcony*

GUGGENHEIM. I believe
this is the first time Elizabeth the Second
has come to Vienna

HERRENSTEIN. I assure you she's never been here before

RICHARD. Shall I push you onto the balcony Mr Herrenstein

HERRENSTEIN. Whatever you like Richard
the whole thing is of no interest to me
it's just for the scum of the earth

(*Looks at the floor*)

Revolting riffraff
who I've decisively severed all ties with
this is the last time
these people
will ever be in my house
they're the most execrable people in the entire world
they're exactly the kind of people
I most deeply loathe
the riffraff of the healthy
Straight to the Döbling cemetery
the instant they're gone

(*To* GUGGENHEIM) My dear Guggenheim
sleep all this off and ride with me to Semmering
tomorrow
it'll do you good
Fresh air is just what philosophy needs
Nothing is more vital to philosophy than fresh air
fresh air is the thinker's perfect food
my dear Guggenheim
You are the philosopher of my life
the philosopher of my existence Guggenheim
Semmering is a philosophical locale
unlike the Salzkammergut
in which only imbeciles flourish
second and third class people
not first-class people like in Semmering
But you're every bit as familiar with Semmering as I am
Nothing is more fashionable nowadays
than to go to Semmering
which is only meant to be visited by really old people
that's precisely why I go there

GUGGENHEIM. When I was a child
we went to Semmering every year
we'd stay at the Hotel Panhans
is it still there

HERRENSTEIN. Everything is still there Guggenheim
But you won't recognize any of it
Socialism has let everything at Semmering
go to wrack and ruin
But I like the socialism in Semmering
and the socialists in Semmering
a thousand times more than the National Socialism
and the National Socialists in Altaussee
Now get out onto the balcony Guggenheim
and pay your respects to your queen

(*With the Union Jack held high* GUGGENHEIM *joins the others on the balcony; on his way out, he says* God save the Queen. *The jubilation wafting up from the Ringstrasse becomes indistinguishable from the jubilation emanating from the crowd on the balcony.* RICHARD *turns the wheelchair so that* HERRENSTEIN *can look directly at the balcony door*)

Don't you also want to see
Elizabeth the Second

HERRENSTEIN (*firmly*). No

(*The jubilation has reached its climax*)

A repulsive spectacle

(*A sudden din and outcry from everybody standing on the balcony; the balcony breaks off and tumbles down to the street.* HERRENSTEIN *clings to* RICHARD'*s coat.* RICHARD *slowly pushes* HERRENSTEIN *all the way to the threshold of the balcony.* HERRENSTEIN *tries to peer down at the street The dust has settled.* RICHARD *pushes* HERRENSTEIN *a bit farther forward. After a pause*)

They're all dead probably

RICHARD (*after an equally long pause and over the sound of the ambulances and fire engines that are already approaching*). Surely

CURTAIN

The translator wishes to extend his sincerest thanks to flowerville for her invaluable insight and assistance in reviewing the complete preliminary draft of the translation.

PAGE **3** | *blindness armbands*: Yellow armbands with three dots in triangle formation on them, worn by the blind to make them easy to identify by the sighted.

PAGE **5** | **one cautiously pushes the hemispheres . . . with the point of the cerebral scalpel**: Bernhard took this passage, along with all subsequent passages describing dissection, directly from an autopsy handbook that he had requested and obtained from his half-brother Peter Fabjan after the two of them attended a pathology lecture together when Fabjan was in medical school. The handbook instructs the student in the dissection method of the nineteenth-century pathologist Carl von Rokitansky, who is first mentioned on p. 24 (see Thomas Bernhard, *Werke*, VOL. 15 [Manfred Mittermayer and Jean-Marie Winkler eds] [Berlin: Suhrkamp, 2004], p. 466).

PAGE **109** | **Hail Star of the Sea**: The title and first line of a medieval hymn to the Virgin Mary.

PAGE **109** | **Marienlieder**: Johannes Brahms's cycle of settings of German folksongs about the Virgin Mary.

PAGE **122** | **and the doctor tells me I've already got him**: *him*, i.e. cancer, the German word for which is *Krebs*.

PAGE **186** | **Nature . . . imperceptible ones**: Bernhard seems to have taken this passage, along with most of the remainder of Kant's dialogue pertaining to astronomical phenomena, from Kant's *Allgemeine*

Naturgeschichte und Theorie Des Himmels (Universal Natural History and Theory of the Heavens), a work anonymously published in 1755.

PAGE **184** | *which isn't to say . . . in the theater:* From a 1924 essay by Antonin Artaud entitled "L'Évolution du Décor." Bernhard quotes it in German translation.

PAGE **187** | **the philosopher-in-himself / in itself / in-itself:** Apparently a complicated pun on Kantian terminology whose gist is that *Psittacus erithacus* both contains and embodies the essence of a philosopher.

PAGE **196** | **headpiece coins:** *Kopfstücke*, coins of small denomination featuring bust portraits of reigning monarchs. Headpiece coins were current in various states of the pre-Unification German-speaking world.

PAGE **382** | **He was in the right, and so indeed it is:** William Shakespeare, *Richard III* 5.3.275

PAGE **276** | *Les misères . . . pris le divertissement:* "The woes of human life were responsible for all this; having seen this, they took refuge in distraction." Blaise Pascal, *Pensées* 1.10–167.

PAGE **498** | **I've heead it up to heeah wid you:** That is, "Now, knock it off / I've had it up to here with you." Neutz's impression of the Kaiser is in broad Viennese dialect, which I have opted to approximate via a phonetic rendition of a New York City accent.